; showing Durham House where Raleigh lived, the Gatehouse where
he was executed, and Whitehall Palace.

Published in the United States
by DUFOUR EDITIONS, INC.
Chester Springs. Pa. 19425

SIR WALTER RALEIGH

Sir Walter Raleigh

by
NORMAN
LLOYD WILLIAMS

LONDON
EYRE AND SPOTTISWOODE
22 HENRIETTA STREET · WC2

FOR
CHANG MING TSE

First published 1962
© 1962 by Norman Lloyd Williams
Printed in Great Britain
by Butler & Tanner Ltd
Frome & London
Cat. No. 6/2457/1

CONTENTS

[v]

ILLUSTRATIONS

Endpapers

[vi]

PREFACE

This biography presents Raleigh as far as possible by means of his own words and those of his contemporaries. I have attempted to weave into a connected narrative his letters, the surviving anecdotes, official records, eye-witness accounts of his trial and execution, and his own published writings. It is a method which, I hope, brings out the tones and character of his life.

For his first twenty-odd years, which are the least well documented, I have filled in the essential background. At other times the contemporary material, for example on the trial in 1603, is so plentiful that it carries the story without any help beyond being fitted into order.

There is no certainty as to exactly when most of Raleigh's poems were written. My placings are by such documentary evidence as exists, and by style and situation, but these last are matters on which everyone has his own opinion.

In the Bibliography on page 277 there is a short list of 'convenient sources of texts and references'. In the Notes I have given references for the verbatim extracts from sixteenth- and seventeenth-century material and also, unless they can be found easily through the 'convenient sources', for facts stated in the ordinary text.

Spelling is modernised, and so are dates.

N. L. W.

ACKNOWLEDGEMENTS

For permission to quote the following: the poem 'Now we have present made' from *The Queen and the Poet* by Walter Oakeshott, to the author, Messrs Faber & Faber Ltd, Mr Lionel Robinson and Mr Philip Robinson; from *The Other Face* by Philip Caraman, to the author and Messrs Longmans, Green & Co. Ltd; from *Queen Elizabeth and Some Foreigners* by Victor von Klarwill, to the Bodley Head Ltd; from *Thomas Platter's Travels in England, 1599* by Clare Williams, to the author and Messrs Jonathan Cape Ltd; from *Willobie his Avisa* ed. G. B. Harrison, to Mr Harrison and the Bodley Head Ltd; from *The Autobiography of Phineas Pett* ed. W. G. Perrin, to the Navy Records Society.

The following acknowledgements are due for the illustrations: to the National Portrait Gallery for the Nicholas Hilliard miniature of Raleigh and the portrait of Raleigh and Wat; to the Trustees of the British Museum for the John White drawings, the Hulsius engravings, and the map from *Speculum Britanniae*; to the Mansell Collection for the portraits of Lady Raleigh and Queen Elizabeth; to the Marquess of Salisbury for the portrait of Sir Robert Cecil; to the Governors of Alleyn's College of God's Gift for the portrait of Prince Henry; to the Society of Antiquaries for 'The Tower of London' by Hayward and Gascoyne; and to the National Gallery of Ireland for the 1597 portrait of Raleigh.

SIR WALTER RALEIGH

I

John Aubrey (1626–1697):[1]
He spake broad Devonshire to his dying day.

Raleigh was born in 1554,[2] in a thatched farmhouse called 'Hayes',
two and a half miles from the Devon coast at Budleigh Salterton,
half-a-dozen from Exmouth and Exeter.

Devon was known for piratical seamen and rough tin-miners;
ingenious farming and coarse woollens; trackways abominable to
horse and man, and rudeness to visitors.

He was the fifth son of Walter Raleigh, a man in his fifties
married for the third time. Mr Raleigh had sea interests, like other
Devon gentlemen, and while his three grown-up sons occupied
such lands as the family still owned he himself held the 'Hayes' farm
on a lease.

The fields of Devonshire farms looked much as they do today,
separated by banks on which were hedges. From these enclosed
fields Devon fed itself, and fed English, French and Spanish boats
which brought linens, sail-cloth and wine, and took away woollens
and tin. Both the foreign boats and Devon drank Devonshire cider.

Farming prospered; fishing, temporarily hit by the no-fish
Friday of the Reformed Religion, had made up for it with the
profits of pillage, which were patriotic and quick.

2

The Reformed Religion had upset the Devonshire peasants also.
In 1549, five years before Raleigh was born, the distant London
government had introduced the Book of Common Prayer, and

banned practices and prayers without which religion was to them no religion.

There is a story in Holinshed's Chronicles[1] of Walter Raleigh senior riding one day from 'Hayes' to Exeter, and overtaking an old woman who had a rosary in her hands. He told her – disinterestedly, for her own good – that she could be punished under the law, and so could others who did not follow the reformed faith. She hurried to church, where everyone was at service, and told them that Mr Raleigh was going to burn them out of their homes if they did not give up their beads and holy bread and water. 'In all haste like a sort of wasps they fling out of the church.' They overtook him. He had with him some Exmouth seamen by whom he was rescued, but the commotion increased, and he was captured and shut up in a church tower. Indeed the western peasants rose in great numbers against the new religion and had to be slaughtered by the Devon gentry under the command of Lord Grey of Wilton.

By the year of Raleigh's birth, 1554, Mary had succeeded Edward VI. Parliament was hearing Mass again, but objecting strongly to her intended marriage to young Philip of Spain, which might bring the Spanish Inquisition and Spanish domination. A cousin of Raleigh's mother, Sir Peter Carew, tried to make the citizens of Exeter sign a petition against the marriage; and Sir Thomas Wyatt tried to prevent it by leading some thousands of Kentish men on London. But Wyatt's men were hanged, four hundred a day, and to escape arrest Sir Peter Carew fled to France in a boat belonging to Raleigh's father.

The burnings for heresy started – Rogers, Saunders, Hooper; Ridley, Latimer, Cranmer; among the laymen there were few gentry, the majority of the victims being small people – but there were none in the west until, when Raleigh was three, a woman named Alice Prest was tried for heresy and burned at Exeter.

John Foxe (1516–1587):[2]
During the time of her imprisonment . . . there resorted to her a certain worthy gentlewoman, the wife of one Walter Raleigh, a woman of noble wit, and of a good and godly opinion, who coming to the prison and talking with her [Alice Prest] said her creed to the

gentlewoman, and when she came to the article 'he ascended . . .', there she stayed, and bade the gentlewoman to seek his blessed body in heaven, not in earth; and told her plainly that God dwelleth not in temples made with hands; and that sacrament to be nothing else but a remembrance of his blessed passion . . .

So that as soon as [Mistress Raleigh] came home to her husband, she declared to him that in her life she never heard a woman, of such simplicity to see, to talk so godly, so perfectly, so sincerely, and so earnestly. Insomuch that, if God were not with her, she could not speak such things.

'To the which I am not able to answer her,' said she, 'who can read, and she cannot.'

Of his mother only this single story remains; it suggests a flexible sympathy. Of his father the only story is Holinshed's which suggests good intentions and a gift for being misinterpreted.

3

It was chiefly through his mother that the infant Walter was related to Champernownes, Carews, Grenvilles, Tremaynes, Courtenays, St Legers, half the gentry for fifty miles. His uncle, Sir Arthur Champernowne, was Vice-Admiral of the West. Cousins of one degree or another joined Sir Peter Carew across the Channel and were set up by the French Protestants to plunder ships passing between Spain and the now-Spanish Netherlands. Another relative was Kate Ashley, who was attending the Princess Elizabeth in semi-captivity.

His mother's sons by a previous marriage to Otho Gilbert of 'Greenway' on the River Dart, twenty-four miles from 'Hayes', were John, Humphrey and Adrian Gilbert. Humphrey Gilbert became for a while page to the Princess Elizabeth.

In 1558, Elizabeth became queen, inheriting an empty treasury, an exhausted credit, a neglected navy, depots empty of munitions, a Council and clergy who had served Catholic Mary, and Protestant extremists made more obstinate by persecution.

[3]

Four years later Humphrey Gilbert was wounded at the siege of Le Havre, fighting for Queen Elizabeth in France's civil war. Of all that England once possessed in France, nothing remained. Elizabeth had bargained with the Huguenots that she should have Le Havre in exchange for 'volunteers', who would help take it from the French king. But Huguenot joined after all with Catholic to drive out the English, who came home bringing plague.

England was at its smallest since 1066, but at least in the few years since Elizabeth's accession the Crown's credit had improved, munitions had been conjured out of the Netherlands, and in the hope of future self-sufficiency there were English experiments in mixing gunpowder, and in mining copper and lead for brass cannon. Foreign policy had still to be economical, defensive and cunning.

Spain had explored and exploited vast and wealthy territories to the west, in the Americas and across the Pacific in the Philippines. And Portugal had explored east, planting forts and trading stations on the coasts of Africa, India and the East Indies, taking the monopoly of Asian trade from Venice.

England's trade had expanded less majestically; but the sharing out of Church lands at the beginning of the century had led to speculation, and now there was capital prepared to look beyond the wool market in north-western Europe if returns were likely to be high.

In Mary's reign the Muscovy Company had sent ships to Russia, and the Guinea Company to the west coast of Africa, for a few years both making good profits. And in Raleigh's boyhood boats left the River Exe each spring to fish the Newfoundland banks, and returned laden in the autumn.[1] John Hawkins broke into the slave trade, taking from Sierra Leone three hundred negroes, selling them in the Spanish West Indies (although, by Spanish law, goods could be imported into a Spanish colony only from Spanish sources and under quota), and arriving much richer back in Devon. In a second trip he had more fighting to do but came back with 'gold, silver, pearls and other jewels great store'. And the next year Drake stormed Nombre de Dios on the Isthmus of Panama and staggered Devon with his silver and gold. Hawkins's third voyage, more heavily financed, ended with the loss of most of his ships, crews and cargoes, and

[4]

West Africa was then left alone for twenty years. A few thousands of idle money – the Queen's, courtiers', some business men's – equipped privateers to venture out from the Channel into the more profitable Atlantic.

Hawkins had been bootlegging, Drake housebreaking, the privateers robbing on the highway. Humphrey Gilbert, a man always with an idea, aimed higher. He addressed the Queen in a 'Discourse' on the practicability of sailing to China, Japan and the East Indies by the north coast of America, and seizing from Portugal the Far East trade in spices, silks and jewels.

Gilbert was not the first (by about forty years) to think about this North-West Passage, nor was Frobisher who also wanted to attempt it. Nor was it the only short cut to the East – Willoughby and Chancellor had already tried a North-East Passage for the Muscovy Company. But Gilbert's was the first thoroughly argued treatment of the subject in English. However he received no licence and went instead to seek his fortune in Ireland.

Others of the boy Raleigh's relatives – Richard Grenville, Henry Champernowne, Philip Budockshide – were seeking glory and loot fighting the Turk in Hungary, where Spain led Christendom against the infidel.

In the Netherlands Spain was leading Christendom by massacring rebels and heretics. Elizabeth held on to Spanish gold on its way to Alva, and in retaliation Alva seized English goods, and then Elizabeth seized Spanish goods. Sixty times in a year Englishmen pillaged the Spanish coast; in a year Spain burned twenty-six Englishmen as heretics.

This was the world in which Raleigh grew up and, as the fifth son of a gentleman of moderate means, would have to make a living. The sole record of himself as a child is his careful signature at the age of six on a document connected with his father's fish business, leasing tithes of fish and larks at Sidmouth.[1]

Opportunity for fortune-making arose in Ireland. Humphrey Gilbert was in a scheme with his cousins, Warham St Leger, Sir Peter Carew and Richard Grenville. They had bought some land on the south coast, between Cork and Kinsale, from the Earl of Desmond, the overlord – who, by Irish custom, had overlordship rights, not freehold rights, and therefore no right to sell.

First the idea was to plant a small English colony, and develop the fishing. Then it became a scheme to confiscate all the lands of the native Irish in Munster, the whole south-western quarter of Ireland, and to run the province as a private corporation.

Perversely the Irish rebelled. Gilbert, of blustering rages and soft brown beard, choleric complexion and sad face, dark hair and dark pig-eyes, was made colonel of the army in Munster to put them down, and, in the most successful months of his life, he did. As a man of ideas, he fought by principle. He made it a rule that if a castle or fort did not immediately yield, he took it by force and destroyed every man, woman and child. He would lay out the day's heads as an avenue leading up to his tent. He flung himself against the Irish and beat them against odds of twenty and more to one, showed violent personal courage on a big black horse, reduced Munster to peace, desolation and hatred in a few months, was replaced by the less theoretical Sir John Perrot, and knighted.

Raleigh might have sought exercise and profit under his half-brother in Ireland, but there was greater attraction in France's civil war.

Fighting in France was a better apprenticeship to the trade of soldier than fighting the swords and darts of unarmoured Irish kern and the spears of small-horsed Irish horsemen. On the continent, techniques of land-fighting had been studied more thoroughly than in England, and drills had been developed for the more effective use of firearms.

And France had cultural prestige – half the literary output of England was translation or imitation of French literature.

Further, in the French fighting a boy of fourteen could get portable loot and ransom money for prisoners in proportion to his

[6]

exertions, while in Ireland the prizes were lands and castles to which a boy was unlikely to gain title.

It was the Queen's policy to help the Huguenots (with as little expense and publicity as possible) against the French government. On the other side of her Scottish border was the Dowager Queen of France, heir to the throne of England; and Catholic rebellion and Catholic invasion on behalf of Mary, Queen of Scots, were to be Protestant England's greatest worry during the next twenty years. While Pope Pius V released English Catholics from all allegiance to Elizabeth, Elizabeth herself tried to keep France entangled in its own affairs, telling the French king's representatives that if any Englishmen were fighting in France it was none of her business, and swearing that all she desired was his Majesty's friendship and his brother for a husband.

William Camden (1551–1623):[1]
1569 [The Queen] permitted Henry Champernowne . . . to carry into France a troop of a hundred volunteer gentlemen on horseback . . . Amongst these volunteer gentlemen were Philip Budockshide, Francis Berkeley, and Walter Raleigh, a very young man, who now first began to be of any note.

So Raleigh, aged fourteen or just turned fifteen,[2] went to France, armoured, with horse and servant, sword and lance.

Presumably, like other Englishmen of the time, he was impressed by the fine stone buildings but thought them less comfortable than England's timber and occasional brick. Presumably he checked on the truisms that the French were always eating, always talking, dirty, shallow, vain, given to dancing and tennis, slaves of fashion; their horsemen very good, their foot very bad, their marching pace quick, their discipline slack.

Of what he did, or for that matter what the other volunteers did, almost nothing is known, but one or two memories of these years found their way forty years later into his *History of the World*.

Describing the army of Alexander the Great on the march in India:[3]
They were pestered with the spoils of so many cities as the whole

army seemed but the guard of their carriages (not much unlike the warfare of the French).

Discussing Alexander's use of fire to force a difficult passage:[1]
I saw in the third civil war of France certain caves in Languedoc, which had but one entrance, and that very narrow, cut out in the midway of high rocks, which we knew not how to enter by any ladder or engine, till at last by certain bundles of straw let down by an iron chain, and a weighty stone in the midst, those that defended it were so smothered, as they rendered themselves with their plate, money, and other goods therein hidden.

After he had had a year of this religious war there were a couple of years of murderous semi-peace, and then in April 1572 Leicester came to Blois and negotiated a league of friendship between Elizabeth and the French king so that the latter might feel secure enough to fight Spain. In May a group of noblemen, which included Raleigh's uncle Sir Arthur Champernowne, came to Paris for the king's oath of confirmation. The volunteers were no longer required.

Three months later Huguenot nobles were pulled from the Louvre and killed in the courtyard, while Henry III leaned from his bedroom window and shouted 'Kill! Kill!' Te Deums were sung in Rome for the slaughter of more heretics in a night of peace than in the previous twelve years of intermittent war; Philip II – the single instance of his life – smiled; and Elizabeth, after a proper pause, continued her negotiations to marry Henry's brother.

Raleigh had probably left France before the St Bartholomew massacre, since none of his references implies that he was a witness. He may meanwhile have been attracted by the Huguenot port of La Rochelle from which Spanish ships were privateered in the Channel; or have visited Humphrey Gilbert in the Netherlands, where some thousands of English volunteers, intervening in the nascent war of the Dutch against their Spanish rulers, were being commanded by Gilbert with indiscreet and disastrous generalship (there are traditions but no firm evidence that Raleigh at some time fought in the Netherlands).

By the end of the year he was in England, an undergraduate.[2]

Francis Bacon (1561–1626):[1]
There was in Oxford a cowardly fellow that was a very good archer. He was abused grossly by another, and moaned himself to Walter Raleigh, then a scholar, and asked his advice what he should do to repair the wrong had been offered him.

Raleigh answered: 'Why, challenge him at a match of "shooting".'

He was eighteen when he went up to Oriel College. Undergraduates ranged from nine or ten years of age to about twenty-five. They studied Logic, Rhetoric and Philosophy in forms which had begun to seem out of date; took part in disputations as to whether life could be prolonged by medical art, whether women were happier than men; shot with bows and arrows; went to hear the news on Saturday nights at Barnes's bookshop at the west end of St Mary's; and drank, roistered and wenched.

The new geography based on the Spanish and Portuguese voyages and on the maps drawn in recent years by Ortelius and Mercator, of interest to a half-brother of Humphrey Gilbert, was not yet the concern of Oxford. And Sir Henry Savile's lectures on Geometry (to Euclid I 8), of use perhaps to navigators, were a year or two in the future.

Oxford was active in religious contention, which was of more general interest and for which it was better staffed. The more overtly Papist dons had been purged since Elizabeth's accession, but there were still numbers under surveillance for Catholic beliefs and practices, and many more, not wholly committed to Catholicism, who were fellow-travellers. Edmund Campion, in nine years to be hanged, drawn and quartered on Tyburn as a Jesuitical traitor was Proctor. Robert Parsons, later a heavy-footed Jesuit propagandist, was at Balliol. There were Puritans like Dr Humphreys, President of Magdalen, whose loose gown, Elizabeth had said when he bent to kiss her hand, became him better than his narrow notions. And in between were Cooper of Christ Church, who had written a history of the world; Bodley of Merton, Greek scholar, lecturer on natural philosophy, and future library-restorer; and Toby Matthew, bright young Anglican careerist.

Among Raleigh's own friends were a Somerset cousin, Arthur Gorges; a Devonshire cousin, George Carew; Richard Hakluyt, destined to be a parson but interested in geographical discovery; a Champernowne cousin; and, according to the Oriel records, a 'W. Child'.

Aubrey:[1]
Mr Child's father of Worcestershire was his chamber fellow, and lent him a gown, which he could never get, nor satisfaction for it.

6

When he is next heard of he is in London, perhaps supplied by his family, perhaps still possessed of some war-loot.

Register of the Middle Temple:
1575, 27 February. Walter Raleigh, late of Lyons Inn, Gentleman, Son of Walter Raleigh of Budleigh, County Devon, Esquire.

Young gentlemen down from the university frequently attached themselves to an Inn of Chancery, such as Lyons Inn (off Drury Lane), and then to one of the Inns of Court, sometimes to study law (but Raleigh said at his trial that he had never studied it), sometimes as if to a club of approved standing where there were no children as at Oxford and Cambridge. They read, talked, developed gentlemanly skills in music and dancing, sowed a few more oats, and haunted any well-placed relative who might be able to find them a job.

One was scarcely a gentleman if compelled to earn money; but also of slight standing if not active and responsible somewhere within the governmental framework, salaried by perquisites and presents.

One of the lawyers of the Middle Temple at this time was Richard Hakluyt, who gave geographical advice to the Muscovy Company, and was uncle of the Richard Hakluyt who had been with Raleigh at Oxford. The Hakluyt of the Middle Temple had a collection of books and maps, was passionately devoted to the cause of discovery and colonisation, and had already inspired his nephew to dedicate his life to collecting 'The Principal Navigations, Voyages and Discoveries of the English Nation'.

The London to which Raleigh came was a city of 200,000 or more, emerging from a depression into twelve years of boom. It was ten times greater than any other city in England, the most important commercial centre in north-west Europe since Antwerp had been ruined in Philip II's endeavour to govern the Netherlands, strong enough to lend Elizabeth money which earlier she would have borrowed abroad.

The profits of peace and privateering were flowing into new investments and gold chains (the street of goldsmiths was a tourists' wonder) and free spending. The shops were stuffed with goods, among them the products of new English industries – fans, pins, buttons, buckles, glass – and the industries of refugee Flemings, Dutchmen and Huguenots, and spices, drugs and Eastern luxuries brought by the Muscovy Company from Persia via the Volga and the Baltic (this was a dangerous route, and Company agents were active in embezzlement – the trade lasted only a few years).

The streets were so crowded you could scarcely walk. Visitors, especially foreigners, could find themselves yelled at and attacked by hooligan apprentices, hit by the casks on the backs of hectoring water-carriers, barged by the servants which gentlemen liked to have following them in the street, each with a silver coat of arms on the left sleeve. The lower populace were said to beat the world for disrespect, coarseness and sheer savagery of nature.

Londoners dressed in better materials than taste; ate well and drank enormously, beer and ale and eighty kinds of wine. There were more alehouses and taverns to the acre than anywhere else in Europe, patronised by women as well as men, respectable women as well as whores.

Londoners' other entertainments included ball games in the streets; hunting and hawking in the fields and woods outside; bear-baiting, bull-baiting, play-going (all blamed for the decline in archery

[11]

practice at the 164 targets in Finsbury Fields), and strolling in the less-than-ten-years-old Royal Exchange to hear the music (the City waits played for an hour in the late afternoon).

The authorities took misdemeanours seriously but unsuccessfully, hanged three hundred people a year, and brought up a few prostitutes each morning for a public naked beating at Bridewell. The burning of Protestant heretics had been replaced under Elizabeth by the hanging, drawing and quartering of Catholic traitors. The skulls of about thirty noblemen who had been executed in recent reigns were another show-piece, stuck on poles on London Bridge, and indicated with extra flourish if a distant relative were the third from the right.

At London Bridge the river, the main thoroughfare, fell a foot or two, and going down-river in a wherry at high tide you noticed the fall; at low tide you did not go under London Bridge at all. The river wherries had embroidered cushions to sit on and lean against, and hoods for rain and hot sun, but the water could be choppy. They were hired at the stairs which were at the foot of any of the lanes leading down to the Thames. You shouted 'Oars!' until two disgruntled boatmen tied up their boat, declared your destination not on their way home, and stated the fare as if they doubted whether you could afford it.

Aubrey:[1]
I have heard old Major Lock say that Sir W. Raleigh did not care to go on the Thames in a wherry-boat: he would rather go round about over London Bridge.

If nevertheless you rowed up-river you passed on your right the watergates of the noblemen's houses along the Strand, then Whitehall Stairs and the Privy Stairs of the Queen's palace of Whitehall, then Westminster Hall and the wretched lanes around the Abbey, the horse ferry, and the country houses of Chelsea. On your left were the suburb and cathedral of Southwark; Paris Garden with its bear pit; the Queen's barge at its moorings; and Lambeth Palace. Further up-river were the Queen's palaces of Richmond, Hampton and Windsor.

[12]

Down-river were the Tower with its cannon, and Limehouse, and on the right the shipyards and naval stores of Deptford, the Queen's palace of Greenwich, and the shipyards of Woolwich. On the surface were ships wafted up on the tide from France, the Netherlands, Germany, with an occasional Venetian or Portuguese, and English trading ships and the Queen's fighting ships; under the surface, sturgeon and salmon.

And in the air, bells. Church bells were constantly ringing, for a service or a death or the Queen passing through the parish, or because Englishmen in exuberance or drink or for exercise wanted to make a noise.

The church services, of the Anglican religious compromise, were satisfying neither Catholics nor Puritans, but they satisfied many.

As a by-product of reformed religious services, the writing of music to English words instead of Latin was helping to lighten church music; and in turn the music of William Byrd and Thomas Tallis, earning their 7d a day in the Chapel Royal, was helping to make English verse more flexible.

As it needed to be. In 1576 when Raleigh was twenty-two he wrote a poem, and like most poems of the decade it sounded like a man hammering nails. It was written in commendation of 'The Steel Glass', a satire by George Gascoigne, the 'steel glass' being a mirror which showed inner truth, unlike glass mirrors imported from Venice. It is his earliest known composition, sardonic, sceptical, moralising, contemptuous of small minds; and it includes the word 'medicine', which would still be giving him pleasure, forty-two years later on the scaffold.

Raleigh, in commendation of 'The Steel Glass':
> Sweet were the sauce would please each kind of taste;
> The life likewise were pure that never swerved:
> For spiteful tongues in cankered stomachs placed
> Deem worst of things which best (perchance) deserved.
> But what for what? This medicine may suffice
> To scorn the rest, and seek to please the wise.

Though sundry minds in sundry sorts do deem,
Yet worthiest wights yield praise for every pain;
But envious brains do nought, or light, esteem
Such stately steps as they cannot attain:
For whoso reaps renown above the rest,
With heaps of hate shall surely be oppressed.

Wherefore, to write my censure of this book,
This 'Glass of Steel' unpartially doth show
Abuses all to such as in it look,
From prince to poor, from high estate to low.
As for the verse, who list like trade to try,
I fear me much, shall hardly reach so high.

7

Gascoigne had been one of Gilbert's men in the Netherlands, and
in this year of 1576 he published the *Discourse on a North-West
Passage* which Gilbert had written ten years before and to which he
had had no response from the Queen.

The Muscovy Company had by their charter the right to explore the North-West Passage, but content with their Russian and
Persian trade which brought profits, had done nothing about it.
Elizabeth had at last called on them to send an expedition themselves
or license someone else. They gave a licence, but to Martin Frobisher, not Gilbert. Publication of the *Discourse* was a reminder that
Gilbert had been the first Englishman, or one of the first, seriously
to urge the enterprise; and it was good propaganda for the Passage
even if Frobisher had the handling of it.

In June Frobisher sailed from the Thames in two tiny ships,
financed partly by courtiers, partly by merchants. He got as far as
what we call Frobisher Bay on the east side of northern Canada,
thought it was Asia, picked up bodily an Eskimo in his kayak,
reasonably thought him an oriental from the east coast of Russia
(Russia afterwards lodged a formal protest against the abduction

of Russian subjects), and was back in London in October with samples of vegetation and rock, in particular some black stone. Two experts said it contained gold, three others said the gold was marcasite (iron pyrites), but one of the minority extracted a pile of gold dust, and England thought she had found another Peru.

Meanwhile Gilbert had a new project, 'How her Majesty may annoy the King of Spain'. She should seize the Spaniards' Newfoundland fishing fleet, and with five or six thousand men (assembled ostensibly to colonise 'St Lawrence Island, the late discovered countries in the north, or elsewhere') take an island or two in Spain's West Indies as a base from which to plunder.

The plan was considered, but priority given to a plan of Drake's. Drake would pass through the Straits of Magellan (which no Englishman had done) into the Pacific (which he had once seen from the top of a tree on the isthmus of Panama), have a look for the Australian continent believed to exist somewhere to the west, and then sack undefended Chile and Peru. Further north, he would look for a way back to England along the north coast of America, by the North-West Passage in reverse, since the western end of the Passage might be further south and easier to find than the eastern. On the whole the City was against ventures of this sort – the Spaniards would probably take reprisals on English trading vessels and on English goods in Spain – but Elizabeth did not mind other people's risks if the Treasury was likely to gain, and Drake would hit at Spain without, probably, provoking war. She invested in him, and through the summer of 1577 the first semi-official attack on Spain's American empire was being prepared.

Meanwhile Frobisher had sailed again. He was home in September, shot by an arrow in the buttocks, but with many tons of black rock which was removed to safety under armed guard.

And on 13 December Drake sailed off. In the same week Raleigh's name comes to the surface again.

Middlesex County Records:

1577, 19 December. Recognizances, taken before Jasper Fisher Esq., J.P., of Thomas Cobham of Golding Lane, Co. Middlesex, Esq., and John Riggs of Davis Inn, London, gentleman, in the sum of forty pounds each, and of Richard Paunsford, yeoman, servant to Walter Raleigh Esq. of the Court in the sum of one hundred marks [= £66. 13. 4]; for the appearance of the said Richard at the next session of the Peace, Co. Middlesex, to answer to such matters as may be objected against him.

Another servant of Raleigh's, another Paunsford, had been in trouble a few days earlier, when the county records showed that Raleigh was living at Islington. It was a village in the fields a mile north of Aldersgate: the road led past the Charterhouse to the fork of roads at Islington Green, where there were half a dozen or more taverns, and on the road to Islington Church a pump and a pond in the middle of the 120-foot road. It was a place where young men took their girls on Sundays.

By the end of 1577, then, Raleigh had at least two servants who did not lead the quietest of respectable lives, and he was 'of the Court'. He may already have been an Esquire of the Body Extraordinary, as he was certainly three years later.[1] Esquires of the Body were in attendance as required wherever the Queen might be; some accompanied her on progresses, some slept in the Presence Chamber each night. Raleigh was an Extraordinary, that is to say a reserve.

These and the other unimportant young Court gentlemen were a pool from which men could be drawn at any time to swell the Queen's entourage for ceremonial purposes, to attend a visiting potentate, to tilt in the tournaments at Whitehall, to take letters. They spent their own money or their fathers' on keeping up appearances, hoping month-in-month-out, sometimes year-in-year-out, to be selected for some minor civil post or a military or naval captaincy, which carrying some degree of command also carried patronage and the disbursement of funds; and to be selected ultimately, after showing worth, for something loftier.

In the pool were Raleigh's cousin, Arthur Gorges, and John Lyly, who was petitioning in vain to be Master of the Revels, and Ralph Lane who complained that he had served twenty years, spent £1,200, bruised his limbs, and not had a groat for it.

It was a predominantly male Court, where the presence of wives was discouraged, but for flirtation purposes the Queen's gentlewomen and Maids of Honour were available even to gentlemen in the pool. One of these gentlewomen, Elizabeth Knollys, in due course found in her pocket a poem.[1]

Raleigh:

Lady, farewell, whom I in silence serve!
  Would God thou knew'st the depth of my desire!
Then might I hope, though nought I can deserve,
  Some drop of grace would quench my scalding fire.
But as to love unknown I have decreed,
So spare to speak doth often spare to speed.

Yet better 'twere that I in woe should waste
  Than sue for grace and pity in despite,
And though I see in thee such pleasure placed
  That feeds my joy and breeds my chief delight,
Withal I see a chaste consent disdain
Their suits, which seek to win thy will again.

Then farewell hope and help to each man's harm!
  The wind of woe hath torn my tree of trust,
Care quenched the coals, which did my fancy warm,
  And all my help lies buried in the dust.
But yet, amongst these cares, which cross my rest,
This comfort grows: I think I love thee best.

There is here, granted the contemporary conventions of love and verse, sensuality combined with a predisposition to withdraw cerebrating aloud, at any rate where a woman of his own or a higher level was concerned.

While Drake was plundering the Pacific coast of South America, soon to decide that his safest way home was around the world, Frobisher in May 1578 sailed with his third and largest expedition, powerfully financed, to get more black stone and found a mining colony. He founded no colony, but brought home tons of black stone – to find that all he had brought before had been thrown out to make roads. His voyages had cost £20,000.

In June Gilbert received a charter to explore the coast of North America and plant a colony. Eleven ships were prepared, some in the Thames (including one of the Queen's), some in Devon, and the ordnance and company of each were noted for the records.

From a list in the Public Record Office, 18 November 1578:[1]
The *Falcon* . . . the Queen's ship of 100 tons, having in her of cast pieces 15, fowlers 4, double bases, 12.

Captain Walter Raleigh, brother to Sir Humphrey Gilbert, a captain of an ancient by land.

Ferdinando the Portugal his master . . .

The whole number of gentlemen, soldiers and mariners are 70.

Elizabeth, who cherished her property, must have looked well at Raleigh before trusting it to him.

Gilbert met with nothing but trouble. It began with Henry Knollys, the second-in-command, the son of the Treasurer of the Household and cousin of Elizabeth Knollys, capturing a pirate and his two prizes; he let the pirate go and kept the prizes. It finished with Knollys deserting with four ships. Delays spread into months and ate up victuals and money – waiting in Devon for the London ships held up by winds, then setting sail only to be driven back up the Channel; then again, only to be driven back again.

The *Falcon* and the other six ships which remained were got to sea at last in November. There were 365 men in the fleet, including Raleigh's cousin, George Carew, and, as the new second-in-command to Gilbert, Raleigh's full brother (older by two or three years) Carew Raleigh.

There is no certainty as to what they were after. November was too late for the North-West Passage or a colony in Newfoundland, or for the Spanish treasure fleet. Two treasure fleets left America each year, one in spring reaching Spain in about June, the other in late summer arriving at the end of October or the beginning of November. The return route was from Havana through the channel between the Bahamas and Florida, then north with the Gulf Stream to the latitude of Cape Hatteras on the coast of North Carolina, then east to the Azores, then directly or very indirectly to Cadiz.

Gilbert may have intended to sail south to the coast of Africa, then west to the Indies, and perhaps then north to the mainland. It should then have been possible – if they had enough stores to last the winter – to raid the spring treasure fleet on its route north, or some of the towns in the islands. They were equipped for fighting, not planting.

England was officially at peace with Spain. The Spanish ambassador, Bernardino de Mendoza, protested against the expedition, but Elizabeth, after stopping it when it was not ready, let it go. Every ship, for one reason or another, returned to port almost immediately, except one . . .

John Hooker (1526–1601):[1]
. . . wherein his brother, Walter Raleigh, was captain, who being desirous to do somewhat worthy honour, took his course for the West Indies, but for want of victuals and other necessaries (needful in so long a voyage) when he had sailed as far as the islands of Cape de Verde upon the coast of Africa, was enforced to set sail and return for England. In this voyage he passed many dangerous adventures, as well by tempests as fights on the sea; but lastly he arrived at Plymouth in the west country in May next following.

They probably planned to recoup their losses by quick privateering, but the Privy Council urgently ordered the Devon authorities (Sheriff, Vice-Admiral, Justices of the Peace, Commissioners for Piracy) to make Gilbert, Raleigh and their associates stay on land, and to inquire, moreover, into the pirating from Dartmouth harbour of a Spanish boat laden with oranges and lemons.

They had arrived home in the middle of an invasion scare. For years Irish Catholics had sought help from the courts of France, Spain and Rome: if help were forthcoming, Ireland would immediately rise and drive out or exterminate the English heretics. Now James Fitzmaurice, cousin of the Earl of Desmond, had ships in Spain ready to sail, the support of the Pope, and, it was said, arms, men and money. Ireland, the under-developed colony of no importance except when rebelling or invaded, was defended, thriftily, by one disabled ship and a handful of soldiers, with little money, little victual, little powder and shot. It was not the moment to irritate Spain for a few lemons.

Gilbert was directed to stop Fitzmaurice from landing in Ireland, but he missed him. Fitzmaurice's little fleet, after taking a Bristol ship and throwing its crew into the sea, landed a mixed band of six hundred men in the extreme south-west corner of Ireland, and made a fort.

Gilbert with three of his ships cruised for a while off the Irish coast, in the service of the government but finding time to pirate a Portuguese ship and a couple of French. He then retired to England, leaving his ships under the command probably of Sir John Perrot, who succeeded him on sea as he had once succeeded him on land. Gilbert somehow never got them back, except for the 8-ton *Squirrel*.

News of Drake's successful pillaging in America set everyone to talking of new expeditions of a similar kind, but Gilbert, with new passionate obsession, turned his mind to the planting of a genuine colony on the coast of North America, and sent the *Squirrel* to reconnoitre.

Meanwhile Raleigh was getting into trouble.

Acts of the Privy Council, 7 February 1580:
At Whitehall. The Presence: the Lord Chancellor, the Lord Treasurer, the Lord Admiral, the Lord Chamberlain, the Earl of Bedford,
the Earl of Leicester, Sir Henry Sidney, Mr Vice-Chamberlain, Mr
Secretary Wilson . . .
Sir Thomas Perrot, knight, and Walter Raleigh, gentleman, being
called before their Lordships for a fray made betwixt them, were by
their Lordships' order committed prisoners to the Fleet.

Six days later they were called before the Council and released on
their bond to demean themselves quietly.

A month later Raleigh was before them again, for fighting by
the Tennis Court at Whitehall. Again he was committed to prison,
this time to the Marshalsea. In the Marshalsea next day was his
cousin, Arthur Gorges, for 'giving the lie' to a nobleman in the
Presence Chamber.

For a gentleman a few days in prison was simply a stay in third-
class furnished rooms where meals could be sent in; one's friends
could come and go, and so sometimes could oneself, but one had to
observe certain hours and keep on the right side of the landlord.

The Court was rarely free from quarrels and fights. A few months
earlier Philip Sidney had been called a puppy by the brilliant and
unstable Earl of Oxford, who wanted the tennis court Sidney was
using; Sidney 'gave him the lie', to which the only answer could be
a duel. The Queen did not permit a commoner to quarrel with a
nobleman, so Sidney withdrew from Court. Oxford was said to
have plotted afterwards to murder him.

Oxford was married to Burghley's daughter but, early in 1580,
he was paying attention to a new young lady of the bedchamber,
Anne Vavasour. Raleigh showed a protectiveness for her virginity
which echoes his reluctance to lay siege to Elizabeth Knollys, and
he bravely or foolishly put in writing his warning against the
important and wild nobleman.

Raleigh, advice to Anne Vavasour:

> Many desire, but few or none deserve
> To win the fort of thy most constant will:
> Therefore take heed, let fancy never swerve
> But unto him that will defend thee still.
> For this be sure, the fort of fame once won,
> Farewell the rest, thy happy days are done.
>
> Many desire, but few or none deserve
> To pluck the flowers, and let the leaves to fall:
> Therefore take heed, let fancy never swerve
> But unto him that will take leaves and all.
> For this be sure, the flower once plucked away,
> Farewell the rest, thy happy days decay.
>
> Many desire, but few or none deserve
> To cut the corn, not subject to the sickle:
> Therefore take heed, let fancy never swerve
> But constant stand, for sowers' minds are fickle.
> For this be sure, the crop being once obtained,
> Farewell the rest, the soil will be disdained.

Anne Vavasour ignored the warning, had a baby, and was sent for a while to the Tower, as was also Oxford. Like Sidney, Raleigh was said to be on Oxford's murder list.

The two fights in which he had been involved may have been on such matters as these, but more probably on the policies and personalities needed in Ireland. One antagonist had been Sir Thomas Perrot, son of the pungent-mouthed Sir John Perrot who had trodden there on Gilbert's heels and was a possible Lord Deputy to handle the Irish emergency. As also, theoretically, was Humphrey Gilbert.

The arrival of Fitzmaurice in Munster had been followed by the rebellion of most of the province under the Earl of Desmond and his brothers. There were reports of a great fleet and thousands of men ready in the ports of Spain. In England men and ships were mustered, and the Queen at length appointed a Lord Deputy: Lord Grey of Wilton, a Puritan nobleman of some military experience, the patron of Raleigh's dead friend Gascoigne, and son of the Lord Grey who had put down the Devon peasants thirty years before. Among the captains he appointed from the available ex-soldiers in the Court's pool was Raleigh.

Acts of the Privy Council, 11 July 1580:
A letter to the Lord Treasurer that where Walter Raleigh, gentleman, by the appointment of the Lord Grey is to have the charge of one hundred of those men presently levied within the City of London to be transported for her Majesty's service into Ireland, his Lordship is desired to deliver unto the said Walter Raleigh, by way of imprest, one hundred pounds.

In Ireland he is at last seen in action.

I

Acts of the Privy Council, 11 July 1580:
A placard for Walter Raleigh, gentleman, being to repair for her
Majesty's service into Ireland, for one cart, five post horses, and to
be provided of convenient shipping where he shall think meet to
embark.

The City of London was to have the conscripts and their 'furniture' ready for inspection before he took them into his charge, as a
precaution against too many paupers and convicts, and corselets
difficult to breathe in and march in, and unusable muskets and
calivers. He had then to ensure that a proportion of the men and
furniture did not disappear before he reached Ireland.

Six days after he collected the men they reached the Isle of Wight,
via Portsmouth, and they were fifteen days there waiting for a ship.
They probably had arms drill and formation drill ('To the right,
double your ranks!' 'To the left, double your files!'), for both the
pikemen and the shot. The group of pikemen, wearing armour on
their heads and bodies and with 15-foot pikes, formed a mobile
strong-point from which the shot, who were nimbler men, unarmoured except for the head, issued and fired their pieces and to
which they returned. In the middle was the captain's standard in the
charge of an ancient, and protected by a few halberdiers.

Raleigh had a lieutenant, Michael Butler, about four junior
officers, about ninety live men and a few dead. It was so usual
for a captain to have on his roll a few dead men and pocket their pay,
that captains were authorised to have five or six dead men but no
more. His pay as a captain was 4s a day, and if he had five dead men
he received a further 3s 4d.

They were seventeen days on the sea before they reached Cork,
where he was posted. Cork was in the military charge of the

seasoned, downright, but long unpromoted Sir Warham St Leger. He was chief of those cousins who with Gilbert ten years earlier had wanted to run Munster as a private corporation. He probably welcomed Raleigh with whiskey, prophylactic against Ireland's diarrhoeas and colds, and with curses at the Queen's Council for sending out a new Lord Deputy. He had recently been cock-a-hoop because Sir William Pelham, who had been governing Ireland for the last year, had taken up his idea of getting all the Munster lords who were not in active rebellion – both Irish and Anglo-Irish, what was the difference? – to come to Limerick for conference. Once at Limerick they had been locked up. But they would charm themselves out of Grey's hands. Desmond's followers had been reduced by Pelham to a handful, of whom only the Seneschal of Imokilly was of any importance, and Desmond had been ready for terms, but now he had heard a new Lord Deputy, probably more manageable, was on the way.

Cork was the fourth city of Ireland (after Dublin, Waterford and Limerick) and had one long street. It was English-speaking, but with the years the English had gone native to the extent that officers found their beds dirty and lousy, and when their rooms were swept, about once a week, the dust was left in a corner for a month.

There were already 850 troops in Cork to tell Raleigh's band that there was no bread, no beer, no money, and the butter was hairy. And that the natives more than made up for the famous absence of snakes. The Irish wrapped themselves in enormous yellow shirts and did not take them off again until they were worn out. They wore their hair hanging over their eyes so that you could not tell when they were lying. If they had money after selling a cow they spent the lot on a two or three days' drunk. They ate once a day, at night: that awful butter, with oaten bread and sour milk; on feast-days some half-raw meat. They slept, men, women and children, all in a heap, in huts not as good as English pig-sties. The men were large and the women handsome. Not a virgin in the land.

The native wealth was in cattle. Great herds of small cattle, with their cowmen and families, wandered from pasture to pasture, and fed the rebels. The horses were small too, and the natives tied a plough to the tails of half a dozen in spite of disgusted remonstrations from the English.

[26]

The best presents to send home to a patron were hounds, hawks and whiskey.

2

While Raleigh was knocking his men into shape, destroying crops in accordance with Pelham's policy, and doing stray jobs such as sitting on a commission to condemn one of Desmond's brothers, the situation became blacker in all four provinces of Ireland.

In Leinster, which contained Dublin and the 'Pale', the country most settled with English, a nobleman, Baltinglas, had raised the Pope's standard against the heretical, excommunicated, bastard Queen of England. Grey, as soon as he arrived in Dublin, conscientiously went out to fight him, attacked against the advice of officers who knew the enemy and the country, and lost both experienced men and new untrained levies.

In Ulster, Turlough Lynagh O'Neill, who had married a Scots wife and had some thousands of Scots mercenaries, was also on the move. Since he had a taste for liquor, Grey, who was unable to spare men to keep him quiet, sent him a butt or two of sack.

In the west, in Connaught, usually tranquil under a tough campaigner, Sir Nicholas Maltby, there was burning and murdering, and the only loyal lord was hiding in the woods with no one to bring in his harvest.

And from the west coast of Munster word came that forces from Spain had landed, and a fleet from Spain was off-shore. Leaflets were circulating which described great forces from Rome and Spain being sent to save Ireland and England for the Church.

More of the newly levied troops arrived, some at Cork in the charge of Sir William Morgan who had fought in France at the same time as Raleigh. He complained that he had had no ammunition to train his shot, several of the bands had been without officers, and many men had died of the heat in their ill-fitting armour. He wrote immediately to the Privy Council to complain that he wanted to march against the invaders but St Leger would not let him.

[27]

The invaders had landed in the second week of September. In the first week of October the Lord General of Munster, the Earl of Ormond, marched out of Cork with the troops he had gathered there, including Raleigh and his band. No one knew the size of the invasion that had to be met. They marched seventy-odd miles through country devastated not long before by Pelham, skirmished with the invading forces, captured the Papal Nuncio's altar cloth, noted that the invaders numbered only six hundred at present but had arms and gold for the strengthening of Desmond, and, having no artillery to deal with their fort at Smerwick, withdrew to Rathkeale.

The invading force may have been small but the entire country had now risen, including all whom Pelham had forced to promise loyalty.

At Rathkeale Grey arrived from Dublin with more troops, and Ormond handed over his forces and went home. Behind Grey's back, villages were burned within a few miles of Dublin, and his messengers were killed. He left one or two bands to follow on, and hurried with his main forces against Smerwick fort.

Hooker:[1]
Captain Raleigh, notwithstanding that the Lord Deputy had raised his camp at Rathkeale and was gone towards the fort, yet he tarried and stayed behind, minding to practise some exploit. For it was not unknown unto him that it was a manner among the Irish kerns that whensoever any English camp was dislodged and removed they would after their departures come to those camps to take what they there found to be left.

Thus therefore lying and keeping himself very close, he tarried and abode the coming of the said kerns, who suspecting no such trap to be laid for them came after their manners and usage to the said place and there took their pleasure; who when they were in their security the captain and his men came upon them and took them all.

Among them there was one who carried and was laden with withs, which they used instead of halters; and being demanded what he would do with them and why he carried them gave answer that they were to hang up English churls, for so they call Englishmen.

[28]

'Is it so?' quoth the captain. 'Well, they shall now serve for an Irish kern.'

And so commanded him to be hanged up with one of his own withs. The residue he handled according to their deserts.

A kern was an Irish peasant turned fighter, still looking like a peasant, wearing no armour or uniform but armed with a bow and arrow, or some darts, or a sword and a light spear.

Prisoners were commonly killed, by either side, unless there was clear material advantage in mercy. In Grey's recent defeat, for instance, George Carew's brother had got so hot fighting uphill that he sat down, was taken prisoner, had his armour taken off him, and was then, naturally, killed. The execution of only one of the kern was an act of moderation, and a good death speech does not affect the need, if there be one, of an execution.

The exploit in itself was a proper piece of military enterprise, but across the centuries it has an air of 'clever', 'busy', as if this were the air worn by Raleigh himself.

3

With his band he followed Grey to Smerwick, where the invaders had strengthened the little fort which had been made the year before by Fitzmaurice, and was called by them Castel del Oro because it stood by a wrecked shipload of Frobisher's black stone.

From inside their fort, the invaders had written to Philip II for 8,000 foot-soldiers; artillery; 2,000 arquebuses to arm the natives; and victuals, shoes, and money, especially money: 'These fishermen will not serve except for a wage of four gold crowns . . . They wish to be paid in advance.' Just then Philip was not ready for England: he was annexing Portugal, its navy, empire and trade.

Grey could not attack without artillery, which in a country of bogs, woods and no roads was difficult to transport by land. He had to wait for some of the Queen's ships and hope they came before Desmond's forces linked up with the invader.

The ships arrived, and their ordnance was off-loaded and brought into action with great skill and vigour. The Pope's crusaders, if Desmond did not come, no longer had lives.

Hooker:[1]
They desired a parley with the Lord Deputy, who utterly denied it ... Then they requested that they might have liberty to depart with bag and baggage, which also would not be granted. Then they requested that certain particular men among themselves might have their free passage, and certain other conditions; but my Lord refused both this and all other conditions, requiring an absolute yielding or nothing at all.

When they saw that they could not prevail any way, then at length they hanged out a white flag, and with one voice they all cried out: 'Misericordia! Misericordia!' and offered to yield both themselves and their fort without any conditions at all ...

When the captain [of the fort] had yielded himself and the fort appointed to be surrendered, Captain Raleigh, together with Captain Mackworth, who had the ward of that day, entered into the castle and made a great slaughter, many or the most part of them being put to the sword.

The Spanish Ambassador, Mendoza, to Philip II, 11 December 1580:[2]
They slaughtered 507 men who were in it and some pregnant women, besides which they hanged 17 Irish and Englishmen. Only a single one of the Lord Deputy's men was injured. In the fort were found 2,000 corslets, and arquebuses and other weapons, sufficient to arm 4,000 men, besides great stores of victuals and munitions, enough to last for months, in addition to money. The English say that if the fort had held out for four days until Desmond arrived, the Lord Deputy's retreat would have been cut off, and the Queen's ships could not have held their own, to the great peril of the English in Ireland.

The families of one of the English bands fighting at Smerwick had been massacred by the Irish only a few days before and this news may have reached the troops.

No explanation or justification of the massacre is necessary however – total massacre was orthodox military practice. Elizabeth congratulated Grey and complained only that without reference to her he had treated the leaders, some of whom he had spared, better than the rank and file.

4

The bands soon withdrew from the south-west, and Raleigh scoured the country east of Cork, while winter passed miserably. The soldiers sickened through inadequate food and clothes. The Irish peasants became thinner, their harvests destroyed and their cattle continually taken by one side or the other, and more bitter in hatred.

The English officials reflected in their own way the general wretchedness: in Dublin, the Chancellor had sciatica, the Auditor had gout; the Chancellor accused a fellow Councillor of treason, the Treasurer accused the Chancellor of corruption; in Cork, Sir Warham St Leger cursed at the uselessness of having an Anglo-Irishman, Ormond, as Lord General of Munster, and having Anglo-Irish judges who were all related to traitors. Sir William Morgan asked to go home: his legs were swollen. Grey overworked. He ignored the advice of his predecessor, Sir Henry Sidney, that to keep healthy under colonial conditions one must give part of every day to sport.

The Queen chose this time to castigate the most reliable and successful of her officials, Maltby, who held Connaught, on information provided her personally by, of all people, the Countess of Desmond, wife of the rebel leader.

The country was now so anti-English that fort could communicate with fort only by disguising messengers as beggars.

Two bands sent out from Cork to seize cattle for food were seriously shaken up by the Seneschal of Imokilly.

And then in Raleigh's district, the country east of Cork, David Barry and his friends of the younger Anglo-Irish aristocracy gave signs of being about to join, openly, the rebels.

Raleigh, angry that in Munster no action had been taken by Ormond since Smerwick, and seeing that Barry needed quick handling and might profitably be handled by himself, rode off to Dublin and reported the situation to Grey and the Council. He returned with a commission to fight Barry and take Barry Court and Barry Island (on which Cobh now stands). Both he and Grey had acted behind Ormond's back; 'proper channels' had not yet acquired sanctity or even formulation.

On his way back to Cork, after passing through Youghal, Raleigh was in Barry country. He had with him two horsemen, four shot on horseback, his man and a guide. The Seneschal of Imokilly, with six horsemen and some kern, was waiting at a ford to ambush him.

Hooker:[1]

The captain being come towards the ford, the Seneschal spied him alone, his company being scattered behind, and very fiercely pursued him, and crossed him as he was to ride over the water, but yet he recovered the ford and was passed over.

The Irishman who was his guide, when he saw the captain thus alone and so narrowly distressed, he shifted for himself and fled into a broken castle fast by, there to save himself.

The captain being thus over the water, Henry Moile, riding alone about a bow's shot before the rest of his company, when he was in the middle of the ford his horse foundered and cast him down; and being afraid that the Seneschal's men would have followed him and have killed him, cried out to the captain to come and save his life; who not respecting the danger he himself was in, came unto him and recovered both him and his horse.

And then Moile, coveting with all haste to leap up, did it with such haste and vehemency that he quite overleapt the horse and fell into a mire fast by, and so his horse ran away and was taken by the enemy.

The captain nevertheless stayed still, and did abide for the coming of the residue of his company, of the four shot which as yet were not come forth, and for his man, Jenkin, who had about £200 in money about him, and sat upon his horse in the meanwhile, having his staff in one hand and his pistol charged in the other.

The Seneschal, who had so fiercely followed him upon spur, when he saw him to stand and tarry as it were for his coming, notwithstanding he was counted a man (as he was indeed) of great service, and having also a new supply of twelve horsemen and sundry shot come unto him, yet neither he nor any of them, being twenty to one, durst to give the onset upon him but only railed and used hard speeches unto him, until his men behind had recovered and were come unto him, and then without any further harm departed.

Raleigh, in a letter to Secretary Walsingham, wrote: 'The manner of my own behaviour I leave to the report of others, but the escape was strange to all men.'

5

Back from Dublin he was soon indignant because he was likely to lose Barry Court and Barry Island through Ormond.

Ormond, dark and handsome, had been Elizabeth's favourite, and she had once exasperated Sir Henry Sidney by demanding his exemption from taxes. Since the Norman conquest of Ireland he and his family, the Butlers, had owned north-east Munster; their traditional enemies, Desmond's family, the Geraldines, owned south-west Munster.

For several months three senior officials had been criticising Ormond to London, and Elizabeth was beginning to think he did little for much expense.

Raleigh also wrote to London, but intrigue came to him without natural ease.

Raleigh to Secretary Walsingham, 25 February 1581:[1]
The day after the writing of my letter to your Honour by Lieutenant Brigg news came that Davy Barry had broken and burned all his castles and entered publicly into the action of rebellion.

It pleased my Lord Deputy, at my being in Dublin (foreseeing whereunto this traitor was bent), to bestow on me the keeping of one of his castles called Barry Court and the island adjoining thereunto; which house he gave me in charge to keep to her Majesty's use, being a great strength to the country and a safety for all passengers between Cork and Youghal.

Notwithstanding, because my Lord General [Ormond] was presently to come up and Barry ready to go out (having before underground broken the foundations of the rest of his castles), I made stay to take his Barry Court, as well for that my Lord General should not allege that I crossed him in any service or did anything within his government without his privity, as also because it should not be said that the taking thereof was the hastening of Barry's rebellion.

But when my Lord came and Barry had burned all the rest, the Lord General, either meaning to keep it for himself – as I think all is too little for him – or else unwilling any Englishman should have anything, stayed the taking thereof so long, meaning to put a guard of his own in it, as it is, with the rest, defaced and spoiled.

I pray God her Majesty do not find that – what with the defence of his own country assaulted on all sides, what with the bearing and forbearing of his kindred, as all these traitors of this new rebellion are his own cousin-germans, what by reason of the incomparable hatred between him and the Geraldines, who will rather die a thousand deaths, enter into a million of mischiefs and seek succour of all nations, rather than they will ever be subdued by a Butler – that after her Majesty hath spent a hundred thousand pound more she shall at last be driven by too dear experience to send an English President [of Munster] to follow these malicious traitors with fire and sword, neither respecting the alliance nor the nation. Would God your Honour and her Majesty, as well as my poor self, understood how pitifully the service here goeth forward! Considering that this man, having now been Lord General of Munster now about two years, there are at this instant a thousand traitors more than there were the first day.

Would God the service of Sir Humphrey Gilbert might be rightly looked into: who, with the third part of the garrison now in Ireland, ended a rebellion not much inferior to this, in two months! Or would God his own behaviour were such in peace as it did not make his good service forgotten and hold him from the preferment he is worthy of! I take God to witness I speak it not for affection but to discharge my duty to her Majesty; for I never heard nor read of any man more feared than he is among the Irish nation. And I do assuredly know that the best about the Earl of Desmond, yea! and all the unbridled traitors of these parts, would come in here and yield themselves to the Queen's mercy, were it but known that he were come among them. The end shall prove this to be true.

And for mine own part, God is my judge, it grieveth me to receive her Majesty's pay (although God knows it be but a poor entertainment) to see her so much abused; and I will rather beg than live here to endure it. I would most willingly give over my charge – and did offer it to the Lord General, God is my judge – if I could, and serve her Majesty privately with a dozen or ten horse during the wars.

I beseech your Honour to take my bold writing in good part, protesting before him that knoweth the thoughts of all our hearts, that I write nothing but moved thereunto for the love I bear her Highness and for the furtherance of her service.

And further I humbly crave at your Honour's hands that you will reserve my letters to yourself, and if your Honour will promise me so much and give me leave, I will from time to time advertise your Honour truly of this estate. Myself being one that your Honour shall always find most ready to venture my life to do you all honour and service during life.

I beseech your Honour that I may by your means enjoy the keeping of this Barry Court and the island; or that it will please your Honour but to write to my Lord Deputy that he will confirm it unto me, whom I find most willing to do me good, being my honourable good Lord.

The war and the winter continued. Robbery with sword and fire had always been the recreation of the sons of Irish chiefs, and English law and order had brought more sword and more fire. All the officials in Ireland agreed that the native tribal society of elected chiefs and sub-chiefs, unruly and bloody in the uncertainties of democracy, had first to be 'planed smooth'; then a stable, centralised Tudor state could be emplanted, with hereditary nobility, hereditary land tenure, and reliable civil service.

Winter was the best time for this planing smooth, as Grey's secretary, Edmund Spenser, pointed out:[1] 'Then the trees are bare and naked, which use both to clothe and house the kern; the ground is cold and wet, which useth to be his bedding; the air is sharp and bitter to blow through his naked sides and legs; the kine are barren and without milk, which useth to be his only food . . . Towns there are none of which he may get spoil: they are all burned. Bread he hath none: he ploughed not in summer. Flesh he hath: but if he kill it in winter he shall want milk in summer, and shortly want life.'

However the English were not yet feeling successful. Grey complained to Walsingham of Ormond's inaction in Munster, and enclosed a letter he had had from Captain Raleigh which made detailed accusations (and tried again to get possession of Barry Court and Barry Island). In Ulster Grey was having to put up with the 'murders, stealths, rapes and other insolencies' of Turlough Lynagh O'Neill, having been refused additional troops in order to suppress him. He was instructed by Elizabeth to offer pardons to all the rebels in Ireland except one or two, because she was tired of the expense of fighting and planing smooth. He prayed earnestly to be recalled.

One in six of his troops had died or run away. The bands everywhere lacked clothes and were weak with cold. At Limerick and Cork they were virtually at the end of their victuals. At Youghal twelve of the garrison were said to have died of starvation.

Nevertheless, compared with the Irish rebels, the ill-clothed, ill-fed English conscripts (with the gaps in the bands filled by Irish who, conveniently, could be paid less) were relatively steady and well-disciplined, being well armed and well led, especially at captain level. Raleigh showed his own capacity when he was told by Ormond to fetch to Cork Lord and Lady Roche, who were suspected of disloyalty. According to the English story (there is no Irish record) the Seneschal and David Barry received information almost instantly and decided that with seven or eight hundred men they would ambush him.

Hooker:[1]

The captain perceiving and forethinking how dangerous his enterprise was against so noble a man in that country as the Lord Roche was, who was very well beloved, commanded upon a sudden all his men one and another, both horsemen and footmen, which in the whole were not above four score and ten persons, to be in a readiness upon the pain of death between ten and eleven of the clock of the same night.

At which time every man being in a readiness he took his journey and marched towards the Lord Roche's house, called Baillie in Harth, which is about twenty miles out of Cork, and came thither somewhat early in the morning.

At his coming he went forthwith to the castle gate.

The townsmen, when they saw their Lord's house and castle thus suddenly beset, they doubting the worst did arm about five hundred of themselves. Whereupon Captain Raleigh placed and bestowed his men in battle ray in the town itself, and marched again to the castle gate with certain of his officers and gentlemen of his band, as by name Michael Butler, James Fulford, Nicholas Wright, Arthur Barlow, Henry Swain, and Pinking Hughes. And they knocked again at the gate.

And after a while there came three or four of the said Lord Roche's gentlemen and demanded the cause of their coming. Unto whom the captain replied that he was come to speak with my Lord.

Which was offered he should, so that he would bring in with him but two or three of his gentlemen, which the captain was contented with. Yet in the end (but with much ado) he came in with all these few gentlemen before named.

When the captain was once come within the castle, and had entered into some speeches with the Lord Roche, he so handled the matter by devices and means that by little and little, and by some and some, he had gotten in within the iron doors or gate of the court lodge all his men. And then having the advantage he commanded his men to stand and guard the said gate that no man should pass in or out, and likewise charged every man to come into the hall with his piece well prepared, with two bullets.

The Lord Roche when he saw this, he was suddenly amazed and stricken at the heart with fear, but dissembling the same he set a good face upon the matter, and calling for meat requested the captain and the foresaid gentlemen to sit down, and to keep him company at dinner.

After dinner Raleigh told him why he had come and showed him his commission. He replied that he and Lady Roche neither could nor would go with him. Raleigh said that if they would not go with a good will they must go against their will.

At dusk they set off for Cork. The night was so dark and stormy, and the ambushed way 'so full of balks, hillocks, pits and rocks . . . that some by their often falls were not only hurt but also lost their armour and were marvellously spoiled'. Early in the morning he presented the Roches to Ormond.

He had brought his men back without a casualty (except for one John Whelan who had fallen so often that his foot afterwards rotted off), and he had made Lord Roche submit, without an undignified struggle, by a clean competence in the use of force.

7

With summer Ormond was sacked. Raleigh, appointed one of the commissioners to govern Munster in his place, left Cork and based himself on Lismore, thirty miles to the north-east. Meanwhile Desmond, David Barry and the Seneschal burned thirty-six 'towns', and Grey asked again to be recalled.

1. Sir Walter Raleigh, a miniature by Nicholas Hilliard

2. *a*) An Irish Chief at dinner

2. *b*) English soldiers returning from action against the Irish

From The Image of Ireland *by John Derrick* (*1581*)

Less than sixty out of five hundred had come for the Queen's pardon. Grey asked again and yet again to be recalled, and complained of his misery with troops dwindling in number 'hating and crying out for money', and the people starving as they walked. St Leger said that in Munster in six months 30,000 had died of starvation.

With August there was a rumour that Grey was to be recalled in the spring, and the Treasurer asked for his own recall as well. There was no money, and no wheat. St Leger took his wife and family to England, armed with a letter of recommendation to Leicester from Raleigh[1] – from, one would have thought, his junior.

In September Grey, who never ceased his exertions, left Leinster and Ulster to look after themselves and visited Munster. Raleigh returned to Cork and was confirmed by Grey in the possession of Barry Court and Barry Island, although, Grey said later, he did not like Raleigh. Three officials instantly complained that Grey had given traitors' lands to his favourites.

Grey rode great distances over Munster, and was then told that her Majesty thought the huge debt incurred in Ireland 'strange', and was instructed to consider how Ireland might be settled in some quietness. Moreover many of the bands were to be discharged.

The forces were cut down rapidly, and early in December Raleigh went home, along with many others. He carried official dispatches, and for his own use a couple of routine testimonials from the Acting Colonel of Munster. During his sixteen months in Ireland his name had never once been mentioned with either commendation or condemnation in any of the official letters or reports which have survived; the stories printed above may well have reached Court but they have reached us only through Hooker, who probably had them either from Raleigh himself or one of the officers who later returned to his service.

He left Ireland richer by ruined Barry Court and devastated Barry Island, but in no other way. He had neither tied to himself valuable friends nor given himself any reputation other than that of a captain over-active and on the make. When he had written to Leicester on behalf of St Leger, six months after the long letter to

Walsingham, it was still as a not very likeable, not very secure, not very trustworthy suppliant.

From Irish desolation he would step into the Christmas festivities of the Queen's Court at Westminster. He was in the Court hierarchy but on the lowest rung; he had been captain of one of the Queen's ships but on an unsuccessful voyage; he had been a captain in the Queen's army but in an expensive, unpopular and by no means finished war. The prospects of favourable notice were not good.

Moreover the Court had preoccupations. Jesuits and priests were coming into the country, in the official view agents for sedition, murder and foreign invasion. Campion and nine others had been dragged on hurdles to the gallows, but more and more were being smuggled in.

And there was the fantastic pantomime of the Queen's Frog Prince.

Part Three 1581-1592

I

The Queen's palace at Westminster stretched down the left-hand side of what is today Whitehall, looking like an Oxford or Cambridge college.

Near the top of the street were the courts and yards of 'Scotland', housing the bakehouse, spicery, poulterer's office, woodyard, and other departments under the Comptroller of the Queen's Household, Sir James Crofts. Crofts was a spy for Spain and regularly reported to Mendoza.

After Scotland was the gatehouse of the palace, much like that of St James's Palace, its contemporary. Through the gates was the Great Court, on the far side of which was the Great Hall – lofty roof, windows high in the walls with tapestries below – for dinner and supper and occasional plays. A passage past the doors of the Great Hall led to the Chapel and then to Whitehall Stairs and waiting wherries.

The Great Hall led into the Presence Chamber, large and high, with a gilt ceiling ornamented with the dates of battles. Here the Queen and her Councillors appeared usually in the late afternoon, most of the Court attended, and ambassadors and official visitors were presented.

Beyond the Presence Chamber was the smaller Privy Chamber, where Elizabeth usually breakfasted, dined and supped with her ladies and her half-dozen Maids of Honour dressed in white. The Maids, young and pretty, were expected to sing, play an instrument or two, speak a few languages, dance, converse, hunt and play cards, embroider, cook one or two specialities, and, in spite of lusty courtiers, remain maids. The Queen's women, Raleigh used to say, were 'like witches: they could do hurt, but they could do no good'.[1] They gossiped the Queen's secrets, such as they knew them, to Crofts or the nobleman, Lord Henry Howard, who also from this December reported regularly to Mendoza.

Entrance to the Privy Chamber was restricted to attendants on the Queen's person, her Councillors, and a few persons specially favoured. Gentlemen and Grooms of the Privy Chamber saw that no one entered who should not.

Beyond the Privy Chamber were the Privy Lodgings, the still more private apartments of the Queen. Her bedroom was low, dark and rather airless, with one window. The ceiling was gilt, the bed was of wooden inlay with silk covers, there was a great cushiony chair covered with cloth of gold, and next door a bathroom. Her library had books in Greek, Latin, French and Italian, bound mostly in red velvet. Nearly every room in the palace contained a musical instrument or two.

There were a vast number of knights, gentlemen and yeomen guarding or attending on the Queen. The most real guard were the 140 or so Yeomen of the Guard, in the uniform still worn by Beef-eaters of the Tower. Their captain was Sir Christopher Hatton. There were also Gentlemen Pensioners, who attended her on procession with gilt battle-axes and provided most of the tilters for the jousts held two or three times a year on the other side of the road. Arthur Gorges was already a Pensioner, George Carew was about to become one. Esquires of the Body, such as Raleigh, took charge of the Presence Chamber after 'All Night' at 9 p.m. and slept there. John Lyly was also one at this time (the ladies were still talking in the Euphuistic style of the novels Lyly had written for the feminine market). And all manner of pages, grooms and messengers, besides a great number of courtiers' own servants, dressed in their masters' liveries, cluttered the courtyards and the reed-matted passages and halls. The Queen's own palace staff numbered fifteen hundred. Most officers of the Court were provided with dinner and supper, and those who lodged there received bread, ale, candles and fuel as well.

Housekeeping was the responsibility of the Comptroller, but the rest of the running of the Court was done by the Lord Chamberlain, the Earl of Sussex, who was experienced and tolerant. He controlled staff from Captain of the Guard to rat-taker and musician, he controlled the presentation of petitions and ambassadors, and the

arrangements for progresses and revels, including the special festivities for this Christmas when there were to be five plays. He had had
put up, a few months before, a temporary banqueting hall to supplement the Great Hall. It was built of poles and painted canvas, and
had seats in tiers and a ceiling hung with foliage in which birds
fluttered and sometimes sang. It was a little past the Gatehouse and
fronted the road where the Inigo Jones Banqueting Hall stands today.

Behind it, next to the Great Court, was the square grass courtyard
known as the Preaching Place, with pulpit and sounding board in the
middle, and overlooked by the windows of the Council Chamber.

On the opposite side of the road from the Banqueting Hall was
the Tiltyard. This Christmas, for the special entertainment of Elizabeth's 'Frog', a few bears and mastiffs were brought to the Tiltyard
from Paris Garden across the river where baitings played to packed
houses every Wednesday and Sunday (the bear's teeth were blunted
and fresh mastiffs set on when the first tired; the skill of the showman
was in pleasing the audience with all-in-to-the-death fighting, and
yet separating the animals with iron rods in time for them to survive
and fight again another day).

The Queen watched shows from the Tiltyard Gallery, which she
reached from her Privy Gallery the other side of the road by walking
through the upper part of the Holbein Gate which spanned the road
at this point.

Beyond the Holbein Gate, on the right-hand side, was the sporting
part of the palace: the main covered Tennis Court, looking like a
Gothic chapel and standing where the Treasury is now, and where
Raleigh had his fray with Thomas Perrot; another covered tennis
court and two open ones; bowling alleys; a badminton court, and a
fine cockpit, the tallest building in the palace. Behind was St James's
Park with seats under the trees, artificial lake, and deer.

On the left side, beyond the Holbein Gate, was the Privy Garden –
painted columns surmounted by animals with gilded horns, and a
fountain and a sundial; and between the garden and the river were
the Privy Quarters, the Orchard and the Privy Stairs where the
Queen entered her barge.

The despot of this palace, now aged forty-eight, was tall, 'of such
state in her carriage as every motion of her seemed to bear majesty';

'compact in body'; 'well-favoured but high-nosed'; 'with great dignity of countenance, softened with sweetness'; 'the whole compass of her countenance somewhat long'; her eyes 'lively and sweet but short-sighted'; her face pale, her hair originally a reddish-gold; 'her hands, which she took care not to hide, of special beauty'; a fair performer on the virginals and lute; a stylish dancer of pavanes and galliards, a lover of English dances and a-maying; a fluent speaker of Latin, French and Italian, a reader of Greek; her voice the strident voice of an educated public woman, uncontradictable in its habit of power; a swearer; splendid in repartee; magnificent in public speech and ceremony; divine, or devilish, in power to touch a heart; hierarchical, intolerant of a subject rebelling even against an evil or non-English prince; masculine in words, feminine in action; devoted utterly to what she conceived to be the welfare of what she conceived to be England; liking to surround herself with men of calibre but keeping them to heel, trusting only her own judgment; to her officers mean, to her favourites generous with other people's money; a miser, a jewel addict; utterly without principle or honour as understood by men; not caring about differences of religion, but not prepared to share a subject's allegiance with the Pope or a Puritan conscience; her love affairs the scandal of Catholic Europe; 'with a membrane on her', or with some other oddity, 'which made her incapable of man, though for her delight she tried many'; unwilling to submit to a husband, but unable either as woman or politician to resist thinking of a husband; adoring games in which she was Queen of Beauty and Learning, for whom all men sighed; quick to eye a handsome man or a man of spunk.

2

The pantomime of Elizabeth's courtship by and of her 'Frog', the Duke of Anjou, brother of the French King and heir to his throne, was now in its sixth year. He was fifteen years younger than herself, pock-marked, bulbous-nosed, which mattered little; but also he lacked charm, was treacherous, and a Catholic.

The pantomime was Elizabeth's active defence of herself and her country, which were vulnerable on all sides. Ireland was an open door for Spanish invasion. In Scotland, a Jesuit disguised as a dentist was plotting an invasion under the Duke of Guise, which with all the Catholics in Scotland and England would sweep Mary Queen of Scots out of her prison and on to Elizabeth's throne. France was the traditional enemy and might at any time ally with Spain. Spain would one day insist on rescuing England from heresy and punishing her for Drake's circumnavigatory piracies. The Netherlands in either Spanish hands or French would be, like Ireland, a door for invasion.

Betrothal to her Frog was insurance against all these dangers. France would hesitate to act against her while there was a chance of winning England with a marriage; Spain would hesitate while there was a chance of a marriage uniting England and France.

On the other hand, to share her power with a husband, perhaps lose it; to introduce religious complications such as had bedevilled Mary; to find herself and England subject to France, would be intolerable.

Her Council, in their masculine way, wanted her either to marry or not to marry. She preferred doing both. For six years she had alternated between swearing marriage and objecting, raising conditions, postponing. She had recently made a public display of her firm intention to marry, giving Anjou a ring, a kiss and a promise, witnessed by the French ambassador; she was now trying 'underhand' (one of her favourite words) to rush him out of the country unmarried.

She had William of Orange demand his presence urgently in the Netherlands, where he had been offered the crown of the States in rebellion against Spain. She bribed his entourage to say he must not remain another day. She promised him money to help him in the Netherlands (he was bankrupt). She got her courtiers to tell him that if he stayed he would have to give her an expensive New Year's present.

But an elaborate fuss must be made of him, and the Court must have its most gorgeous Christmas season, to keep him happy and to soothe Elizabeth's heart, despairing at his imminent departure.

[45]

It was into this contrapuntal fuss that Raleigh entered with his dispatches.

Thomas Fuller (1606–1661):[1]
This Captain Raleigh coming out of Ireland to the English Court in good habit (his clothes being then a considerable part of his estate) found the Queen walking, till, meeting with a plashy place, she seemed to scruple going thereon. Presently Raleigh cast and spread his new plush cloak on the ground; whereon the Queen trod gently.

3

On New Year's Day Elizabeth received from Anjou allegorical jewels, including a shackle and a ship with sails spread, and in the afternoon there were, in his honour, 'barriers' in the Tiltyard, that is to say, a tournament of jousting on foot, with blunted pikes and swords: Leicester, Sussex, Anjou and three other Frenchmen challenging everyone else, from Lord Thomas Howard down to Ralph Lane and George Carew – but not Raleigh who, curiously, is not recorded as ever having jousted. Great splendour, and the public admitted to the stands at 12d each.

On this same New Year's Day Lord Treasurer Burghley wrote to Grey in Ireland that Captain Raleigh had described to her Majesty a scheme for putting the cost of some of the Munster troops on to the people of Munster instead of her own purse, and what did Grey think of it? Grey, by return, thought nothing of it.

On 1 February Elizabeth accompanied Anjou down the river to Gravesend. He was attended by Leicester and a hundred gentlemen, among them Raleigh. Now that Anjou was on his way, she doubled and redoubled her endearments. She showed him her ships at Rochester, and at Canterbury in tears waved him off with his escort and their three hundred serving men, to Sandwich, Flushing and Antwerp.

In due course, after banqueting and coronation, William of Orange making it clear that Anjou was crowned less for himself than for his royal brother and his prospective wife, Leicester and his train returned to England, hustled by a message from Elizabeth that they were spending too much money. Raleigh stayed behind a few days to receive from genial, frugal, patient William the Silent letters for Elizabeth, together with an oral message that the Netherlands relied utterly on her protection.

When he returned, at the end of February or the beginning of March, the Court was at Greenwich. The Queen was in a foul temper, angry with her handsome but plumped and red-faced Leicester, who had married a second time, and missing her 'Frog'.

He presented his message. For a few days after his return Ireland was much discussed by the Councillors and by the Queen: the shortage of victuals, Grey's faults, Ormond's dilatoriness, which amounted almost to treachery; and Raleigh, named as one of the witnesses against Ormond, probably gave his views on all three matters. A very few months later, his views on policy in Ireland were being noted by Burghley as though of serious importance: first, the lesser lords should be brought on the English side; second, the English soldiers should be punctually paid and supplied so they did not prey on and antagonise the local population.

It was in these days of 1582, at the age of twenty-eight, that he came fully into Elizabeth's eye, and there burgeoned.

Aubrey:[1]
He was a tall, handsome and bold man... He had a most remarkable aspect, an exceeding high forehead, long-faced, and sour eye-lidded, a kind of pig-eye. His beard turned up naturally... His voice was small.

Raleigh to the Queen:
> Sought by the world, and hath the world disdained
> Is she, my heart, for whom thou dost endure,
> Unto whose grace, sith Kings have not obtained,
> Sweet is thy choice, though loss of life be sour.
> Yet to the man, whose youth such pains must prove,
> No better end than that which comes by Love.

Steer then thy course unto the port of death,
Sith thy hard hap no better hap may find,
Where when thou shalt unlade thy latest breath,
Envy herself shall swim to save thy mind,
  Whose body sunk in search to gain that shore,
  Where many a Prince had perished before.

And yet, my heart, it might have been foreseen,
Sith skilful medicine mends each kind of grief;
Then in my breast full safely hadst thou been.
But thou, my heart, wouldst never me believe,
  Who told thee true when first thou didst aspire,
  Death was the end of every such desire.

Fuller:[1]

[He] found some hopes of the Queen's favour reflecting upon him.
This made him write in a glass window, obvious to the Queen's eye:
  'Fain would I climb, yet fear to fall.'
  Her Majesty, either espying or being shown it, did underwrite:
'If thy heart fails thee, climb not at all.'

Raleigh to the Queen:
    Those eyes which set my fancy on a fire,
    Those crisped hairs, which hold my heart in chains,
    Those dainty hands, which conquered my desire,
    That wit, which of my thoughts doth hold the reins!

    Those eyes for clearness do the stars surpass,
    Those hairs obscure the brightness of the sun,
    Those hands more white than ever ivory was,
    That wit even to the skies hath glory won!

    O eyes that pierce our hearts without remorse,
    O hairs of right that wear a royal crown,
    O hands that conquer more than Caesar's force,
    O wit that turns huge kingdoms upside down!

[48]

Then Love be judge, what heart may thee withstand?
Such eyes, such hair, such wit, and such a hand!

Sir Robert Naunton (1563–1635):[1]
True it is, he had gotten the Queen's ear in a trice, and she began to
be taken with his elocution, and loved to hear his reasons to her
demands. And the truth is, she took him for a kind of oracle, which
nettled them all.

4

One of those nettled was the Vice-Chamberlain and Captain of the
Guard, Sir Christopher Hatton. He had first taken Elizabeth with
his dancing, and then held her affection with courtship and common-
sense. In the early forties, he was still active in her love-games; and
she called him her 'Sheep', her 'Mutton', her 'Bell-Wether', her
'Pecora Campi'.

She was now calling Raleigh anything connected with water.
'Walter Raleigh' was pronounced 'Water Rawly', but her nick-
name was probably more than a pun and fitted with the grey-blue
eyes, the unidiosyncratic face, and the movement of his mind, and
perhaps of his body.

Hatton kept away from Court and in October 1582 sent his friend,
Sir Thomas Heneage, to offer the Queen as she was about to hunt
at Windsor symbolic jewels: a book (Hatton swears . . .), a bodkin
(. . . he will kill himself . . .), and a tiny bucket (. . . if there is not
less of Wa'ter Raleigh).

Elizabeth was delighted and said that Pecora Campi was so dear
to her that she was sending him a bird, which with the rainbow had
once brought the good tidings and covenant that there should be no
more destruction by Water.

Two months later Hatton was still ruffled. He sent her a tiny fish-
tank (Water creatures should be constrained).

Heneage to Hatton, December 1582:[1]
The fine 'fish-prison' . . . I presented immediately to the delightful
hands of her sacred Majesty, who . . . hath willed me to write unto
you that the Water and the creatures therein do content her nothing
so well as you ween, her food having been ever more of flesh than of
fish, and her opinion steadfast that flesh is more wholesome.

Raleigh to the Queen:

> Those eyes that hold the hand of every heart,
> Those hands that hold the heart of every eye,
> That wit that goes beyond all nature's art,
> That sense so deep, for wisdom to descry!
> > That eye, that hand, that wit, that heavenly sense,
> > All these doth show my mistress' excellence.
>
> O eyes that pierce into the purest heart,
> O hands that hold the highest hearts in thrall,
> O wit that weighs the depth of all desert,
> O sense that shows the secret sweet of all!
> > The heaven of heavens with heavenly powers preserve
> > thee,
> > Love but thyself, and give me leave to serve thee.
>
> To serve, to live, to look upon those eyes,
> To look, to live, to kiss that heavenly hand,
> To sound that wit, that doth amaze the wise,
> To know that sense no sense can understand!
> > To understand that all the world may know,
> > Such wit, such sense, eyes, hands, there are no moe.

5

Elizabeth's income from customs, crown lands, etc. was only about
£250,000 a year, which had to cover her own expenses and all the
normal expenses of government. Taxes were raised only for the

special expenditures of war and did not fully cover them. She made both ends meet by selling Crown property, borrowing, fining Roman Catholics, and investing in privateering and trading companies – she had earned £250,000 from Drake's voyage round the world.

She could not spend money on those she favoured, so she appointed them to profitable posts, or squeezed property for them out of the Church (of which, after all, she was the head) or the estates of traitors, or gave them monopolies (Parliament had shown dislike of this last practice). In return she expected them to dance continual attendance on her and, as she gradually increased their responsibilities, to work as heads of government departments.

Early in this first year of favourable notice, Raleigh was given command of a band in Ireland (over Grey's 'I like neither his carriage nor his company'), but was required to remain at Court and appoint a substitute. This transaction would have brought him a few pounds a year, but very few.

Not until a year later did he receive a couple of leases extracted by the Queen from All Souls' College, Oxford, and a wine 'monopoly': he was made licenser of the retail wine trade, responsible for controlling quality and price (if French wines were bought at £11 the tun or under they were not to be sold above 16d a gallon), and for this he received the revenue from the licences, a little over £1,000 a year, of which £400 went to his agent, Richard Brown.[1]

But he had already spent £2,000[2] on building a ship of 200 tons (600 tons by our reckoning), the *Bark Raleigh*, which he intended should sail in a fleet being prepared by Gilbert. Favour must have improved his credit and probably brought him presents from those for whom he said a word to the Queen – although on the only three occasions in 1583 when he is known to have said a needed word there were probably no presents.

One occasion was a small kindness for John Dee, who had been asking for years for a paid and leisured post as reward for his scientific labours. Dee had been the theorist behind all English geographical exploration for the past twenty years and more, including a new search for a north-west passage being planned by the youngest Gilbert, Adrian, together with Raleigh. He had expounded the

Queen's rights to the North American continent, he was her scientific adviser, and her astrologer. He had just made extensive calculations which showed that England's calendar should jump ten days, like Pope Gregory's, to bring it into step with the sun and moon, and the government had prepared the necessary proclamation.

Dr John Dee, Private Diary, 18 April 1583:[1]
The Queen went from Richmond towards Greenwich, and at her going on horseback, being new up, she called for me by Mr Raleigh, his putting her in mind, and she said: '*Quod defertur non aufertur,*' and gave me her right hand to kiss.

'What is deferred is not put off for ever.' But John Dee waited another twelve years for a post, and England's calendar – the bishops refusing to have truck with a reform originated in the Vatican – remained for another century-and-a-half ten days behind that of Catholic Europe.

On another occasion Raleigh was asked by Burghley (who also asked Hatton) to intercede with the Queen for the Earl of Oxford, who was no friend of Raleigh's. A year before, Oxford had had the worst of a duel with the uncle of Anne Vavasour, and then had him set upon. The Queen had banned him the Court. Raleigh spoke to her, but when he wrote back to Burghley[2] it was in the same uncertain tones as when he had been a captain writing to Walsingham. A few days later Oxford was received by the Queen while the Court was staying at Burghley's house, 'Theobalds', in Hertfordshire. At 'Theobalds' Raleigh shared a group of two or three rooms with Arthur Gorges, Fulke Greville and others, while next door Heneage had a room to himself, and Walsingham the next room to Heneage.[3] Raleigh was of only slight status.

The other needed word was for Humphrey Gilbert, who was making a desperate attempt to found a colony in America before his patent expired in 1584. In 1582, in order to raise money, Gilbert had sold to Catholics some millions of acres in unexplored America, many Catholics wanting to escape the stricter regulations and higher fines for recusancy with which Elizabeth had countered the Pope's and the Jesuits' encouragement of invasion, rebellion and her own assassination. He had raised another £1,000 or so from merchants of Southampton, who were looking for new fields, their trade with Venice having declined, and a thousand or two more from his relations; but the project was still under-capitalised. Gilbert, however, planned his colony in happy detail: the government, the size of the villages, the schools, the rents, the tithes for the churches, the labour code.

Then in February 1583 he was told by Secretary Walsingham, who was more impressed by a scheme of Christopher Carlile's which had stronger backing by Bristol and London merchants, that he had been forbidden to go 'as a man noted of no good hap by sea', a euphemism for an incompetent naval commander. Raleigh was not going himself; his function was to attend the Queen. But it was through him, it must be assumed, that the ban was lifted from Gilbert.

Raleigh to Gilbert, 17 March 1583:[1]
Brother,

I have sent you a token from her Majesty, an anchor guided by a lady, as you see; and farther, her Highness willed me to send you word that she wished you as great good hap and safety to your ship, as if she herself were there in person; desiring you to have care of yourself, as of that which she tendereth; and therefore, for her sake, you must provide for it accordingly.

Farther, she commandeth that you leave your picture with me.

For the rest I leave till our meeting, or to the report of this bearer, who would needs be the messenger of this good news.

So I commit you to the will and protection of God, who send us such life or death as he shall please or hath appointed.

Your true brother . . .

6

Gilbert should have sailed in April but he did not get off until June. Within two days the *Bark Raleigh*, which made up half the tonnage of the expedition, returned home infected, it was said, with a contagious disease. The remainder, although short of victuals and although it was late in the season, took the northern route, to Newfoundland, on which Gilbert had decided. The *Bark Raleigh* may have been infected only with dislike of his decision.

At the end of August, when Raleigh was with the Court at Oatlands, in Surrey, the first letters came from Newfoundland.

Gilbert had had a sod and turf presented to himself in token of formal possession, had rented to the English, French, Spanish and Portuguese fishermen plots for drying their fish (plots they already used), and before sailing on south for the mainland had been handsomely revictualled by them: 'Be of good cheer, for if there were no better expectation it were a very rich demesne, the country being very good and full of all sorts of victual.'

A Hungarian geographer, Parmenius, wrote to the younger Hakluyt with less enthusiasm: 'What shall I say, my good Hakluyt, when I see nothing but a very wilderness?'

At the end of September the *Golden Hind* limped into Dartmouth. No landing had been made on the mainland. The biggest ship, the *Delight* (Parmenius on board, and also a mysterious parcel of ore to which Gilbert had attached importance), had gone down, chiefly through ill-discipline. In a wild storm the smallest, the *Squirrel* of 8 tons, grossly overloaded, had almost certainly gone down also, with Gilbert. He had refused to transfer to the safer *Hind* because it was being said he was afraid of the sea. All afternoon the company of the *Hind* saw him sitting aloft with a book in his hand, and each time they were within hailing distance he shouted through the storm something like: 'We are as near to heaven by sea as by land' – which punned 'heaven' with 'haven', and perhaps palled with repetition.

Immediately Sir John Gilbert made plans to exploit Humphrey's claim to Newfoundland, but they came to nothing. Adrian meanwhile received a patent to look for a north-west passage, with Raleigh an associate, and Raleigh himself prepared ships to explore the mainland to which Humphrey had failed to stake claim by occupation and for which his patent would expire in a few more months.

But before it expired, Elizabeth gave Raleigh a six-year patent for himself.

[54]

Patent:[1]

Elizabeth by the grace of God of England, France and Ireland Queen, Defender of the Faith, etc. To all people to whom these presents come, greeting.

Know ye that of our especial grace, certain science, and mere action, we have given and granted, and by these presents for us, our heirs and successors do give and grant to our trusty and well-beloved servant Walter Raleigh Esquire, and to his heirs and assigns for ever, free liberty and licence from time to time, and at all times for ever hereafter, to discover, search, find out, and view such remote, heathen and barbarous lands, countries and territories, not actually possessed of any Christian Prince, nor inhabited by Christian people, as to him his heirs and assigns, and to every or any of them shall seem good, and the same to have, hold, occupy and enjoy to him his heirs and assigns for ever, with all prerogatives, franchises and pre-eminences, thereto or thereabouts both by sea and land . . .

[*The patent goes on to reserve to the Crown a fifth part of any gold or silver ore obtained in the country, gives Raleigh exclusive rights and powers to a distance of 600 miles from any spot where his associates 'within six years next ensuing make their dwellings or abidings', and threatens expulsion 'out of our allegiance and protection' if restitution is not made for any robbings or spoilings of the subjects of friendly states.*]

In witness whereof, we have caused these our letters to be made Patents, Witness ourselves, at Westminster the five and twenty day of March, in the six and twentieth of our reign.

Elizabeth.

7

Raleigh also gained a London headquarters for himself. The Queen leased to him part of Durham House in the Strand. It belonged to the see of Durham but the Crown had had the use of it for many years. Its courts stretched down the steep hill to the river, and with its gardens and orchards from the present-day entrance to Shell-Mex House to Durham House Street.

The Strand frontage consisted of a gatehouse, with tenements, Durham House 'rents', packed either side. Within were the Outer Court, and then the Inner, and the marble-pillared hall and the chapel.

To the west were York House, usually occupied by the Lord Keeper of the Seal, with a gatehouse and York rents, and, beyond, the 'Bell', the 'Lion', the 'Reindeer', a brewery, and a crowd of smaller properties. Turning off where Northumberland Avenue is now was Hartshorn Lane, from which the eleven-year-old Ben Jonson walked down past the palace every morning to Westminster School.

To the east was Arundel House, its courts surrounded by low-timbered buildings like a farm. Further east, between St Clement Danes and the river, was Leicester's house.

Opposite Durham House were the 'Black Bull', and in either direction tenements and other taverns, and a little to the east Burghley House, brick, with a turret at each corner.

From the river Durham House was a Norman fortress, rising sheer out of the Thames where now is the inner boundary of the Embankment Gardens. The river makes a right-angle turn at this point, so from Durham House you saw on your right the river frontage of Whitehall Palace and Westminster Hall; down-river you saw London Bridge and the turrets of the Tower.

Aubrey:[1]
Durham House was a noble palace . . . I well remember his study, which was a little turret that looked into and over the Thames, and had the prospect which is pleasant perhaps as any in the world, and which not only refreshes the eye-sight but cheers the spirits, and (to my mind) I believe enlarges an ingenious man's thoughts.

Durham House, in none too good repair, and old-fashioned compared with the new houses of the great, which had much glass and many chimneys, was the base for Raleigh's London activities as long as Elizabeth lived. There is no record of any entertainment there more elaborate than a small dinner-party, or of any grandeur of furnishing or decoration, or of very great troops of servants: at the end of the century, a married man, he had there about forty people and twenty horses. Apart from servants in the modern sense, the gentlemen in his service lived there, or were in and out: Thomas Hariot, mathematician and astronomer, employed to teach Raleigh and his captains navigation; later, Lawrence Keymis, fellow of Balliol; lesser men like Carew Raleigh's step-son, Charles Thynne, and John Pearson who copied manuscripts for Raleigh; and gentlemen who captained his ships – Jacob Whiddon; Michael Butler, his lieutenant in Ireland, who had captained the *Bark Raleigh* when it turned back from Gilbert's voyage; Philip Amadas who was to be its next captain; and Arthur Barlow, who had been on the Lord Roche exploit in Ireland and was about to captain the little *Dorothy*.

It was on the leads of Durham House that Thomas Hariot with a 12-foot instrument observed the position of the Pole Star over several years.[1] Seamen calculated their latitude from observations of the Pole Star or the sun, but there might be a whole degree of difference between the two methods. Hariot provided Raleigh's ships with new tables which made sun and star agree 'like sister and brother'.[2]

The instruments used by sailors were hard to read even to the nearest half-degree; for Raleigh's ships Hariot improved the design of the instruments, laid down rules for their use, made instruments agree 'like husband and wife'.

Sea-charts ignored the curve of the earth's surface and so gave quite incorrect compass bearings. He gave Raleigh's ships rules for making chart and compass agree 'like master and mate'.

The three 'marriages' made by Hariot were certainly necessary: the most experienced navigators could be off the rocks of Ushant when they thought they were a hundred miles away off the Scillies. But Hariot could do little about the calculation of longitude as long as a ship's timepiece was not an eighteenth-century chronometer but an inaccurate spring-clock or an hour-glass, worn and ill-made.

Moreover the very simplest arithmetic was difficult for either a seaman or an educated gentleman. Arabic numerals had been replacing the Roman for twenty or thirty years, but even Lord Treasurer Burghley preferred to translate them back into Roman. There are only half a dozen examples of Raleigh's addition extant, but there is a mistake in one of them.[3]

8

He was now in a better position to raise the funds for an exploratory expedition. He had been given the right to issue export licences for a certain amount of woollen cloth (Burghley, Walsingham and other leading officials had similar rights; a proportion of the fees went to the Queen); and his finances were being handled by a London merchant, William Sanderson, who had married Raleigh's sister's daughter, Margaret Snedell.

Raleigh gave his two ships in the Thames, probably the *Bark Raleigh* and the *Dorothy*, their last instructions, and wrote confirmatory letters which they picked up in Devon before sailing for America at the end of April 1584.

The same week as they sailed, he had stolen from him in London 'a jewel worth £80, a hatband of pearls worth £30, and 5 yards of silk, called damask, worth £3'.[1] He dressed, according to his portraits, with a jewelled splendour, but not with a greater splendour than some contemporary noblemen (his silver armour and white feathers are paralleled in portraits of Essex, Southampton and Sussex), nor so great as was alleged later by a Jesuit:[2] the shoes of 'the darling of the English Cleopatra' were not worth 6,600 gold pieces. He loved jewels but he did not amass them: most of the money that came into his hands was quickly employed on his enterprises.

His own resources and the sums he could raise from shareholders were too slight for colonisation on the scale he thought necessary; it was a matter, he said, for the Crown. While his ships were away and he prepared a bigger follow-up expedition, he employed the younger Hakluyt to write a pamphlet which would stress to the Queen the value of American colonies – strategically, as bases from which to attack Spanish shipping and settlements; economically, for their products, including probably copper, and their demand for English woollens, and the possibility of a trans-American route to China; socially, for their absorption of the unemployed and the Puritans; and above all for extending the kingdom of the Reformed Religion.

Meanwhile Elizabeth, 'a forlorn widow robbed of her dearest treasure', mourned her 'Frog' who had died in sudden agony after two years of treacherous leadership of the Netherland States; and she soon mourned a greater man.

William the Silent, for whose assassination many material and spiritual rewards had been promised by Spaniards and Jesuits, had been shot in the throat by an assassin soon after Raleigh left him in 1582, and there had been three attempts on his life in the following two years. He had at last been successfully murdered. The Protestant leaders of France, Scotland and the Netherlands had now all been assassinated. In England a new plot to assassinate Elizabeth had been uncovered only a few months back.

During the summer Raleigh awaited his ships and tried in vain to buy 'Hayes' where he was born.

In mid-September Amadas and Barlow were home, full of enthusiasm and with products of the country they had been directed to explore, which was called, it was thought, Wingandacon, and was 'a most pleasant and fertile ground'. They had had friendly contacts with the natives, and brought back two of them, Manteo and Wanchese.

They had sailed to the West Indies, and then north to Cape Hatteras and the latitude in which the homebound treasure fleets turned east towards the Azores and Spain.

On 2 July they had found shoal water 'where we smelled so sweet and so strong a smell, as if we had been in the midst of some delicate garden'. They landed on what turned out to be one of a long string of banks and islands close to the mainland (the North Carolina Banks), very sandy at the shore but very fertile. Grapes grew to the water's edge, covering every shrub and climbing to the tree-tops. The woods had 'the very highest and reddest cedars of the world ... and many other of excellent smell and quality'. When they climbed a little hill and shot off an arquebus 'such a flock of cranes (of the most part white) arose under us, with such a cry redoubled by many echoes, as if an army of men had shouted together'.

On the third day natives appeared, proved friendly and trustworthy and were anxious to trade. Twenty skins worth a crown each were obtained for a tin dish, fifty for a copper kettle. Knives exchanged well; a sword would have fetched almost anything but they would not part with swords. The king's brother offered a great box of pearls for some arms and armour, but they pretended they attached no value to pearls until they found out where they came from. Prospects of gold and silver were doubtful, but the king's brother wore a copper-looking plate on his head, and the women wore in their ears copper-looking pendants.

Barlow was set to writing an account of Wingandacon to gain support for a colony. It was not only the fertility that had impressed him. He and some others had visited an Indian village where they had been entertained with the most generous and thoughtful kindness: 'We found the people most gentle, loving, and faithful, void of all guile and treason, and such as lived after the manner of the golden age.'

This village on Roanoke Island was about three miles north of the present town of Manteo, named after one of the Indians brought to England. Wanchese also has a town named after him, a little further south. The village is now under water, but clay tobacco pipes and fragments of pottery from it are in the Fort Raleigh museum nearby.

In October Raleigh presented Hakluyt's treatise to the Queen, and brought Manteo and Wanchese to Court.

Leopold von Wedel (a tourist from Pomerania), Journal 18 October 1584:[1]
He allowed us to see them. In face and figure they were like white Moors. Normally they wear no shirt, just a wild animal skin across the shoulders, and a piece of fur over the privies, but now they were dressed in brown taffeta. No one could understand what they said, and altogether they looked very childish and uncouth.

Elizabeth was benevolent to her favourite's project but not to the extent of taking over responsibility for it, or investing anything like the £40,000 she had just lent the Levant Company to take up a trading concession from the Sultan of Turkey. The Levant Company would renew England's eastern trade and make a sound profit. Raleigh's colony might bring no profit and much expense.

9

In view of the Queen's danger from assassination Parliament met a few weeks later and for the first time Raleigh was a member.

He introduced a Bill by which Parliament would confirm his patent for Wingandacon. It was referred to a committee of Drake, Grenville, Sidney, Walsingham and others, and was then passed by the Commons with a proviso that he was not to press ships, nor was he to ship to the colony criminals or debtors. But it was not proceeded with in the Lords: his patent had been given him under the Queen's prerogative, and she never in her life admitted that Parliament had the right to derogate from her prerogative by so much as imposing a proviso. Raleigh proceeded with his preparations.

Parliament also, for the safety of the Queen and the realm, introduced the death penalty for the harbouring of Jesuits or priests, and expressed its disappointment that, in spite of the danger in which she stood, the Queen would not name her successor. However, she liked no decision she might regret, and preferred that no heir to her Majesty should compete for the attention of her subjects and of foreign powers.

The woman's majesty was very great. It was not only that she liked ceremony and thought it politically desirable. Sovereignty was an Idea, absolute. A Sovereign was analogous to a Divinity. Her elder statesmen delighted in her as an intelligent rooted-in-England woman, tore their hair at her vacillations and her susceptible heart, and genuflected without being servile or ridiculous to the Goddess Sovereign.

Von Wedel, who watched Elizabeth at dinner in the Presence Chamber at Greenwich Palace on 27 December 1584 – she dined there alone on certain feast days:[1]
To the right of the table stood noblemen, for instance Lord Charles Howard . . . the Earl of Leicester . . . the Lord Treasurer and . . . the Earl of Oxford . . . There was also Christopher Hatton, the captain of the bodyguard, who is said to have been the Queen's

lover after Leicester . . . If she summoned one of them, as often happened – as a rule, she talks with scarcely a break – he had to kneel until she commanded him to rise. Then he made a low bow and retired, and when he came to the centre of the room he bowed again . . .

When the first dishes had been removed and others put on the table, the Queen did not stay much longer. She rose . . . and turned her back upon the table, and two bishops stepped forward and said grace. After them came three of the noblemen . . . with a large covered bowl of silver gilt, and two with a towel. The five of them advanced to the Queen and knelt down before her. While two held the bowl, a third raised the cover and poured water over the Queen's hands . . . Before washing she handed a ring to the Chamberlain . . . and afterwards put it on again.

Then she took an earl's son by his cloak and stepped with him to the bow-window, where he knelt before her and was a long time in conversation with her.

When he had gone she took a cushion and sat down on the floor, and summoned another young gentleman, who likewise knelt and talked with her.

On his leaving she called a countess, who like the gentlemen knelt before her.

Then dancing began, and ladies and gentlemen took hands as they do in Germany . . . In this first dance only the highest in rank took part, no longer young. When it was over, the young men laid aside their rapiers and cloaks, and in doublet and hose invited the ladies to the galliard . . .

During the dancing the Queen summoned young and old to come and talk with her. They all knelt to her, and she chatted in a very friendly way, making jokes.

She said to a captain named Raleigh, pointing with her finger at his face, that there was a smut on it, and was going to wipe it off with her handkerchief; but before she could he wiped it off himself. She was said to love this gentleman now beyond all the others; and this may be true, because two years ago he could scarcely keep one servant, and now with her bounty he can keep five hundred.

Raleigh to the Queen:
> Praised be Diana's fair and harmless light;
> Praised be the dew wherewith she moists the ground;
> Praised be her beams, the glory of the night;
> Praised be her power, by which all powers abound.
>
> Praised be her nymphs, with whom she decks the woods;
> Praised be her knights, in whom true honour lives;
> Praised be that force, by which she moves the floods;
> Let that Diana shine which all these gives.
>
> In heaven Queen she is among the spheres;
> She mistress-like makes all things to be pure;
> Eternity in her oft change she bears;
> She beauty is; by her the fair endure.
>
> Time wears her not: she doth his chariot guide;
> Mortality below her orb is placed;
> By her the virtues of the stars down slide;
> In her is virtue's perfect image cast.
>
> A knowledge pure it is her worth to know:
> With Circes let him dwell that think not so.

On the Twelfth Day of Christmas she knighted him, and graciously allowed Wingandacon to be named Virginia.* The divine attribute of Virginity had been added with safety to Elizabeth only recently, since she had passed the age of child-bearing; added principally by Raleigh to whom virginity and other absolutes appealed, and who as 'Ocean' liked to identify her with the virgin Moon-Goddess.

He had a seal made for himself, inscribed around: *Propria Insignia Walteri Ralegh Militis Domini Gubernatoris Virginiae* ('The arms of

---

* Hariot, who was studying the language, may already have been persuaded by Manteo and Wanchese that 'Wingandacon' was not the name of the country, but meant 'You wear good clothes'. Raleigh mentioned the original mistake in *The History of the World*, Book I, Chapter VIII, Sect. 15, Sub-sect. 5.

Walter Raleigh, knight, Lord and Governor of Virginia'), and within, his arms surmounted by a roebuck and underwritten '*Amore et Virtute*'.[1] His '*virtus*' – strength, purity and grace – flowered in love of the Queen, and the Queen's love:

> Praised be her power, by which all powers abound . . .
> She mistress-like makes all things to be pure . . .
> She beauty is, by her the fair endure . . .
> By her the virtues of the stars down slide;
> In her is virtue's perfect image cast.
> A knowledge pure it is her worth to know.

10

Favour did not command respect. The Vice-Chancellor and Senate of the University of Cambridge had been unimpressed by Mr Raleigh and were no more impressed by Sir Walter. They had themselves issued wine-licences in Cambridge and showed no concern when the wife of one of Raleigh's five licensed vintners was put into 'sundry swoons and passions' by hostile undergraduates.

He wrote courteously to the Vice-Chancellor; had no reply. His vintner was jailed by the Vice-Chancellor. He said he would refer the matter to the Lord Treasurer; had still no reply.

Raleigh to the Vice-Chancellor and others, the Senate of the University of Cambridge, 20 February 1585:[2]
Mr Vice-Chancellor,

I cannot a little marvel at your peremptory and proud manner of dealing. I was content to use all manner of courtesy towards you . . . but I perceive that my reasonable or rather too submiss dealing hath bred in you a proceeding insufferable. You have committed a poor man to the prison having done nothing but warranted by the Great Seal of England, your Seals supposing a privilege by Charter. I do not know that any man, or any men, or society, would take so much upon them, before trial made.

But, as I reverence the place of which you are the governors, so

I will not willingly take any wrong or disgrace from you. And I am assured my Lord Treasurer, who may command me, will be indifferent in this case. For the matter so much concerneth the validity of my patent elsewhere, as well as in your University, as I will try the uttermost of my right, as well for this one, which I was content to be satisfied withal, as for all the other four.

And so, having thought you would have vouchsafed an answer of my last letters, I end.

Your friend as you shall give cause.

To the eye of the University the letter of the favourite must have confirmed that he was not to be feared: in the political world he was a man only of words, he had written three letters without taking action.

When the matter was at last referred for a decision, it was declared[1] that 'by usage and charters from her Majesty' the University had the right to nominate vintners in Cambridge; fines upon vintners, if any, should go to Raleigh. The vintner he had licensed was kept in prison for nearly two years.

II

The Queen, Walsingham and others were 'adventurers' in the expedition Raleigh now had in preparation, but most of the money was his own.

There were to be about six hundred men, half of them seamen; Sir Richard Grenville in charge; Amadas, second-in-command on the naval side, and Ralph Lane, who had waited twenty years for a chance, second-in-command on the military side, and in charge of the colony; Thomas Hariot, in charge of economic and anthropological survey; one John White, for maps and drawings; and treasurers, factors, brickmakers, apothecaries . . .

The Spaniards, who had now planted forts in Florida for the sole purpose of preventing colonisation on the mainland by any other nation, were watching the preparations as usual. Mendoza, however, had to report to Philip from Paris, because he had been expelled from London for implication in a plot to murder Elizabeth.

[65]

The fleet sailed from Plymouth on 9 April 1585 (after the *Roebuck* had privateered a French ship in the Channel), was scattered by storms but continued on its way: the Queen's *Tiger*, Raleigh's *Roebuck* of 140 tons, the *Lion* 100 tons, the *Elizabeth* 50 tons, Raleigh's *Dorothy* smaller still, and two small pinnaces which could be carried on deck.

A month later Spain made war a degree more actual by seizing all the English merchant ships in her ports, of which there were more than usual since there was famine in Spain and Portugal and they had been offered special protection to bring corn. The crews were thrown into prison or to the galleys, and the cannon taken for an armada in preparation at Cadiz. Sooner or later Spain would attempt to invade.

The City, which as a whole had opposed courtier-backed privateering for fear that Spain would take reprisals on their trade, now urged as much privateering as possible, and joined in. The industry began to be capitalised on a firm basis. Ships went off in dozens to pick up what they could round the coast of Spain, and Raleigh was commissioned to send the ships which he had made ready to follow Grenville, to Newfoundland instead, there to take all the Spanish ships fishing on the banks. They brought back seventeen ships, with six hundred men, and five other ships as well, making a profit of a few hundred per cent on the voyage.

Meanwhile Hatton was offended again. When the Court stayed in the Archbishop of Canterbury's palace at Croydon, the room which should have been his was occupied by Raleigh, who no longer had to share a room as at Burghley's home two years before. This time Hatton sent the Queen through Heneage a true lover's knot. She spoke bitterly of Raleigh, Heneage told him: 'She had rather see him hanged than equal him to you, or that the world should think him so.' [1]

Whether or not Raleigh was as true a lover as Hatton, he may have expressed his feeling more privately. His name never appeared in the list at New Year of those who gave the Queen a present and received one back: Hatton always gave something of rather excessive value. Raleigh's pose was that of the silent lover.

Raleigh to the Queen:

Wrong not, dear Empress of my heart,
The merit of true passion,
With thinking that he feels no smart
That sues for no compassion:
Since, if my plaints serve not to prove
The conquest of your beauty,
It comes not from defect of love,
But from excess of duty.

For, knowing that I sue to serve
A saint of such perfection,
As all desire, but none deserve,
A place in her affection,
I rather choose to want relief
Than venture the revealing:
Where glory recommends the grief,
Despair distrusts the healing.

Thus those desires that aim too high
For any mortal lover,
When reason cannot make them die,
Discretion will them cover.
Yet, when discretion doth bereave
The plaints that they should utter,
Then your discretion may perceive
That silence is a suitor.

Silence in love bewrays more woe
Than words, though ne'er so witty:
A beggar that is dumb, you know,
Deserveth double pity.
Then misconceive not, dearest heart,
My true though secret passion:
He smartest most that hides his smart
And sues for no compassion.

[67]

Puttenham was to say in *The Art of English Poesy*, published in 1589: 'For ditty and amorous ode, I find Sir Walter Raleigh's vein most lofty, insolent, and passionate.'

I2

The summer opened with Raleigh receiving the lease of a manor, of no special importance, ragged by Elizabeth out of the old Bishop of Bath and Wells for marrying a very young girl.[1]

In the next few months, after three years of favour and apprenticeship, he was appointed to posts which made him the most powerful man in the west of England: he was made Lord Warden of the Stannaries, Lord Lieutenant of Cornwall, Vice-Admiral of Cornwall and Devon.

Cornwall and Devon were the likeliest area for Spanish raids and invasion: Raleigh was in naval charge of both, in military charge of Cornwall. As Warden of the Stannaries he was in charge of the tin industry which was of great value and importance: even the Turks, pressing west upon Europe and east upon Persia, used Cornish tin for their bronze guns. The tin could not be sold to London merchants or Flemish or Italian or other agents until, tested and stamped by the Lord Warden's officers, it had paid £2 a thousand-weight to the Queen.

The Stannaries, covering most of Cornwall and a little of Devon, were a kingdom within the kingdom, subject to their own courts and their own parliament except in matters of land, life and limb.

The miners earned £3 a year in hot, stuffy, damp, dangerous, underground workings, and were the poorest and toughest men in England, with the most taverns per head, the shortest working day (commonly four hours), and the most holidays.

This community, squabbling over mining boundaries and watercourses (the streams washed the ore, drove the stampers, worked the bellows which roared up the fires for the melting, and could easily be diverted from one tinwork to another), over theft and debt and impure tin and smuggled tin, referred their disputes either to their courts or to the Vice-Warden(Raleigh appointed his elder brother, Carew), and then if necessary, but rarely, to the Lord Warden. Their parliaments met every seven or eight years; the parliament for Cornwall sat indoors, that for Devon on Crocken Tor, on Dartmoor. For military purposes the tinners were mustered by the Warden, separately from the other men of Devon and Cornwall who were under their Lord Lieutenant.

Routine administration was handled by Carew Raleigh; Raleigh himself handled relations with the Crown, problems referred to him by the Privy Council, and the defence of his own jurisdiction and the tinners' rights.

Richard Carew (1555–1620):[1]

Your ears and mouth have ever been open to hear and deliver our grievances, and your feet and hands ready to go and work their redress, and that, not only always as a magistrate, of yourself, but also very often as a suitor and solicitor of others of the highest place.

A letter survives in which he asked the Devon Justices not to demand from some tinners a contribution towards a private bridge, 'which is overburdensome to poor men in regard of their daily travail and disbursements about the mines'.[2] As with the Cambridge vintner, his letter implies a hankering after Justice, a faith that an appropriate person or body will see that Justice is done, and a slowness in his use of Court contacts to enforce his own contention. If he had handled Lord Roche in this way, without first securing complete superiority of power and then demonstrating his will to use it, he would never have brought him to Cork.

His appointment as Lord Warden brought the inevitable criticism.

'A. B.' to Lord Treasurer Burghley, 7 July 1586:[3]

Her Majesty and you have placed Sir Walter Raleigh as Lord Warden of the Stannaries, but amongst so rough and mutinous a multitude, 10,000 or 12,000, the most strong men of England, it were meet their governor were one whom the most part well accounted of, using some familiarity, and abiding amongst them. Whereas no man is more hated than him; none cursed more daily by the poor, of whom infinite numbers are brought to extreme poverty through the gift of the cloth to him. His pride is intolerable, without regard to any, as the world knows; and as for dwelling amongst them, he neither does nor means it, having no place of abode; so that in time of service, this head must either fight without a body, or else the members will cut off such a head.

Fuller:[1]
Sir Walter was wont to say:

'If any man accuseth me to my face, I will answer him with my mouth, but my tail is good enough to return an answer to such who traduceth me behind my back.'

The letter of 'A. B.' is the earliest reference to Raleigh as widely hated and intolerably proud. His licence to export cloth had not brought infinite numbers to poverty – it was a licence to export, not to prevent export – but it is true that at this time there was distress in the cloth industry. Spanish reprisals and the dislocation of trade on the continent had hit very hard the export of English cloth, for which the Merchant Adventurers held a monopoly except for such licensees as Raleigh. For the last seventeen years the nation's trade had boomed, but now for seventeen years trade slumped, and the licensees were obnoxious competitors in a contracting market. Raleigh's agent, against whom the Merchant Adventurers of Exeter laid a complaint, and Raleigh himself, were scapegoats for the state of trade.

13

He went down to take over his posts and was entertained by the Plymouth City Council.

At the end of September one of the smaller ships brought news from Virginia. The expedition had collected cattle and stores in the West Indies, but at Virginia the *Tiger* had struck a shoal, and the stores had been ruined by sea-water. More were needed.

3. *a*) The manner of their fishing

3. *b*) The true form of their houses

Water colour drawings of Indians by John White, made during or soon after the 1585 expedition to Virginia

4. *a*) Houses in trees

4. *b*) Ewaipanoma

4. *c*) Amazons coupling

4. *d*) The city of Manoa

A few days later the *Tiger* was in, with letters from Lane full of
delight with Virginia, but complaining of Grenville's high-handed-
ness; and in another few days Grenville himself was in, with a prize
which he had boarded from a boat knocked up out of chests, which
sank as they left it. The prize covered the whole expenses of the
expedition, but Grenville did his best to depreciate it in view of
the customs, the tenth due on all prizes to the Lord Admiral, and
the shares of other adventurers. He had come home himself, leaving Lane and a hundred men on Roanoke, because the anchorage
was not safe enough for a base against the treasure fleets and the
Indies.

On his way out, Grenville had lingered picking up what he could
in the Indies, so not until August had Lane built a little star-shaped
fort on Roanoke Island. Grenville had rowed around the neighbourhood, and treated the natives, he felt, with proper firmness: one of
them had stolen a silver cup, so he sent Amadas with a party to burn
their village and crops.

He would be delighted to go again early in 1586, with supplies,
and Raleigh put preparations in hand.

Captain John Davis, meanwhile, had returned from looking for
the North-West Passage, under Adrian Gilbert's patent. He had
given the name of 'Mount Raleigh' to a 'brave mountain, cliffs
orient as gold' on the east coast of Greenland.

Raleigh was having trouble at this time with Leicester, who had
been sent to help the leaderless Netherland States against Spain. As
security for repayment of her expenses, the States were allowing
Elizabeth to garrison Flushing and other ports with English troops;
which she did, but with troops which she left moneyless, foodless,
tattered, since she was short of money and did not intend them to
fight the Spaniards. With the ports she would make as if to buy her
peace with Spain: she would dangle them in front of Spain's eyes
and at least postpone Spanish aggression. She used her Comptroller,
Sir James Crofts, as a go-between and said nothing to her Council
or to Leicester.

But Leicester wanted to fight. He demanded reinforcements of
his wretched troops, and as well miners from Raleigh's Stannaries to
make fortifications and mine the enemy's. And against categorical

instructions he let himself be sworn-in Governor-General of the States, so committing England officially to their support and upsetting Elizabeth's intrigue. She pulverised him: he must eat his oath in public or she would reduce him to the zero from which she had raised him.

Leicester's friends blamed the cataclysm on the intolerable Raleigh, for whose miners Leicester was still waiting. Raleigh could afford to have him unfriendly, but not bitterly hostile.

Raleigh to Leicester, 29 March 1586:[1]

You wrote unto me in your last letters for pioneers to be sent over; whereupon I moved her Majesty, and found her very willing, in so much as order was given for a commission; but since, the matter is stayed. I know not for what cause.

Also, according as your Lordship desired, I spake for one Jukes for the office of the Bakehouse, and the matter well liked.

In aught else your Lordship shall find me most assured to my power to perform all offices of love, honour and service towards you. But I have been of late very pestilent reported in this place to be rather a drawer back than a furtherer of the action where you govern ... Your Lordship doth well understand my affection towards Spain, and how I have consumed the best part of my fortune, hating the tyrannous prosperity of that estate, and it were strange and monstrous that I should become an enemy to my country and conscience ...

I humbly beseech you, let no poetical scribe work your Lordship by any device to doubt that I am a hollow and cold servant to the action, or a mean well-willer and follower of your own ...

PS: The Queen is in very good terms with you, and thanks be to God, well pacified; and you are again her 'Sweet Robin'.

He asked to carry one of the Queen's dispatches to Leicester. She would not let him go; instead she made Walsingham assure Leicester that Raleigh had spoken for him as strongly as any of his declared friends.[2]

Leicester was not clever but he had a natural gift for accumulating power, by exploiting his influence with the Queen and by getting official posts filled with his nominees. Raleigh had no such natural gift, but he had not ceased to arouse jealousy.

Aubrey:[1]
His naeve was that he was damnably proud . . . He was such a person (every way) that . . . a prince would rather be afraid of than ashamed of. He had that awfulness and ascendancy in his aspect over other mortals.

Edmund Bohun (1645–1699):[2]
Tarleton, the best comedian of these times in England . . . when a pleasant play he had made was acting before her Majesty, he pointed at Sir Walter Raleigh, and said:
'See, the Knave commands the Queen!'
For which she corrected him with a frown. Yet he had the confidence to add, that he was of too much and too intolerable a power.

There is no incident on record which exemplifies his damnable pride. Perhaps, speaking and acting as dedicated servant of the Queen he was exasperatingly magistral like many dedicated servants. Perhaps his reputation suffered because it was to nobody's advantage to defend it: he identified himself with no vested interest and attached to himself no following outside his family and a few employees.

Sir John Harington (1561?–1612); 'Paulus' = Raleigh:[3]
>Proud Paulus, late advanced to high degree,
>Expects that I should now his follower be.
>Glad I would be to follow one's direction
>By whom my honest suits might have protection.
>But I sue Don Fernando's heir for land –
>Against so great a peer he dare not stand.
>A bishop sues me for my tithes – that's worse,
>He dares not venture on a bishop's curse.
>Serjeant Erifilus bears me old grudges –
>Yea but, saith Paulus, serjeants may be judges.
>Pure Cinna o'er my head would beg my lease –
>Who? My lord . . .? Man, oh hold your peace.

Rich widow Lesbia for a slander sues me –
Tush, for a woman's cause he must refuse me.
Then farewell frost: Paulus, henceforth excuse me,
For you, that are yourself thralled to so many,
Shall never be my good Lord, if I have any.

Neither is there any incident which exemplifies his 'intolerable power'. But he was 'Ocean' – shifting, ungraspable, disquieting.

Harington:[1]
No man more servile, no man more submiss,
Than to our Sovereign Lady Paulus is.
He doth extol her speech, admire her feature,
He calls himself her vassal, and her creature.
Thus while he daubs his speech with flattery's plaster,
And calls himself her slave, he grows our master.
Still getting what he list without control,
By singing this old song, *re mi fa sol.*

14

Early in April he sent off to Virginia a 100-ton ship with supplies and a fortnight later three ships under Grenville with more supplies and more men.

On other enterprises he sent out in June the pinnace *Dorothy* on a privateering expedition of the Earl of Cumberland's, and the *Serpent* and the *Mary Spark* to privateer at the Azores. There they fought twenty-four Spaniards for thirty-two hours and took three prizes and a valuable prisoner, Don Pedro Sarmiento de Gamboa, Governor of a colony planted by the Spaniards in Patagonia to protect the Straits of Magellan.

On 27 July Drake came into Plymouth. He had sailed to the West Indies the previous year with twenty-five ships, and had agreed to drop in on Virginia if he could, with slaves and anything useful that had come his way. He returned with loot sacked from Cartagena,

San Domingo and elsewhere (not enough to pay the expenses of the expedition) – and with the whole Virginia colony: 108 men, less four dead and three left behind.

Lane's men had built houses by the star-shaped fort on Roanoke; they had explored inland, and seventy miles north to Chesapeake Bay, where they thought the colony should be moved. Lane was enthusiastic; White had drawn his maps and sketched people, animals, plants; and Hariot had collected specimens, made notes, astonished the Indians with his 'perspective glass' and preached to them in their own language. The four ships sent out in April had not yet arrived, but Drake could have spared them stores. Then why had they come home?

Relations with the Indians had been difficult. In spite of some being impressed by Hariot's optical instruments (it is not known for certain what they were), some by the religious services, and others by the extraordinary way that death had descended on villages visited by the Englishmen (carrying measles or the common cold); in spite of there being no woman trouble (Hariot declared the colonists were not attracted), there had been scrapping, and finally if the colonists had not attacked first they would have been wiped out. Manteo remained loyal, but Wanchese deserted.

And they had been short of food. After the first twenty days of their own stores, they had lived on the Indians' hospitality, which had worn thin with the winter. The colonists had not even fished for themselves.

They had expected relief by the beginning of April. When it did not come, they feared that the war with Spain would prevent it ever coming. So they planted crops, which were within a fortnight of harvest when Drake with his twenty-five ships arrived on 10 June. He offered negro and Indian slaves as extra labour, he offered ships, supplies, navigators. They had decided to stay until August and were supplied accordingly by Drake, but a furious storm from 13 to 16 June swept some of the ships to sea, including the one Drake was leaving them, which was already filled with stores and had some of Lane's men on board.

Drake offered still another, larger, ship, and supplies and a navigator to help them explore further the Chesapeake Bay area; but he insisted that the ship was not to be brought into the sound, it must lie off shore. Roanoke was indeed admirably close to the route of the treasure fleet but impossible as a permanent base from which to raid it.

Lane's company then asked to be taken home, and 'for fear they should be left behind, left all things confusedly, as if they had been chased from thence by a mighty army; and no doubt they were, for the hand of God came upon them for the cruelty and outrages committed by some of them against the native inhabitants of that country'.

In the hurry and in difficulty with the treacherous seas, many charts, books, writings, specimens, even pearls, were thrown overboard by Drake's sailors. And they did not wait for three men who were on trek.

Some of the colonists, home after a year of hard lying and no gold, spread rude stories about the country and its people, but Hariot gave Raleigh for publication a description of the Indians and a thorough-going survey of the possibilities.

As export goods there were flax and hemp, for which there was a ready demand; pitch, tar, and turpentine (North Carolina became known as the Turpentine State); cedarwood (before the year was out Raleigh had given the Earl of Northumberland a bed of cedarwood); dyes, of which the cloth industry was in great need; root and bark of the sassafras tree, for malaria and syphilis; wines, furs, pearls, silk (Hariot praised a grass from which a kind of silk could be made, and thought incorrectly that there were silkworms); copper and iron (smelting of iron in England had already wasted most of the forests: it would be better to mine and smelt in America).

Hariot described the products on which colonists could live. There were maize (grown more easily and of greater yield than wheat; and ale and bread could be made from it); plentiful peas and beans (a great part of the Elizabethans' diet); groundnuts; a great variety of fruits, fowls, beasts and fish.

The potato was said in Gerard's *Herbal* of 1597, dedicated to Raleigh, to be a Virginian product (it is an important product of North Carolina today); but it is believed now that if Hariot brought home any potatoes he took them from the kitchens of Drake's ships, which had been further south.

Hariot certainly brought the blessed Uppowoc with him, which he and the others had smoked, like the Indians, through pipes of clay. Uppowoc was *nicotiana rustica*, which Raleigh learned to cure and smoked himself. *Nicotiana tabacum*, of which Drake brought back considerable quantities from the West Indies, was the better tobacco to contemporary taste and is also to ours. The U.S.S.R. and Poland smoke some *nicotiana rustica* but the rest of the world smokes *nicotiana tabacum*. Tobacco was already respected in Europe for its believed medicinal properties, but it was rarely smoked, and then as a cigar. It was the fashion of smoking, and especially of pipe-smoking, that came from Raleigh. Within twelve years universal pipe-smoking became an English oddity noted by foreign visitors.

Raleigh made Elizabeth have a puff. There were instant whispers that he was killing her, but she made her Maids have a puff too. He bet her that he could weigh tobacco smoke, and won the bet by subtracting the weight of the ash from the weight of the original tobacco. He smoked a silver pipe constantly. The old servant who poured a mug of ale over him to put out the fire is claimed both by a house he had later in England (Sherborne) and by a house he had later in Ireland (Youghal).

15

The autumn and winter held other excitements besides Raleigh's pipe-smoking. In mid-August the bells rang for the capture of Anthony Babington and other young Catholic gentlemen who had planned to murder Elizabeth, rescue Mary Queen of Scots, and plant her on the throne with the help of a Spanish invasion – Parma was to land with troops from the Netherlands as soon as Elizabeth was killed.

Elizabeth had many Catholics at her Court, and there were many throughout the country. Raleigh's secretary, William Langharne, was a Catholic and had been thought of by the conspirators as a route for correspondence with Mary, since Raleigh was friendly with Sir Amyas Paulet, Mary's jailor.[1]

Mary herself had blessed Babington's plot, and her letters blessing it, smuggled out in false-bottomed beer-barrels (supplied for the purpose by Walsingham's spies) were copied for Walsingham and the Council. Parliament petitioned that she be executed. Elizabeth wavered for a few days and then brought herself to duplex action, signing the warrant and then showing sincere anger and grief when it was carried out. Bells rang, bonfires blazed.

Puritans as well as Catholics were causing trouble. They were not a small expungable minority, and when Whitgift demanded from the clergy strict obedience to the 39 Articles a number denied episcopal authority, emulating Dr Robert Browne of Norwich. The Brownists increased, and the bishops were abused as never before or since by Martin Mar-prelate. Persecution of the Puritans became official policy.

Meanwhile in the Netherlands, in one of the brief actions in the war Elizabeth was trying not to fight, the earnest and principled Sir Philip Sidney, born in the same year as Raleigh but with better connections, so shining in the eyes of his generation that he still dazzles, had been wounded through gallantly not wearing thigh-armour; and then died (a story of Aubrey's) through honourably serving his pretty wife; leaving debts, incurred with the highest motives, which ruined his father-in-law, Walsingham.

Raleigh was in the funeral procession to St Paul's and wrote, as did others, an elegy. He was probably not a familiar of Sidney's; he spoke of his 'love that envy in thy life suppressed', and his sixty lines of praise, which have been much admired, were forced – their enormous earnestness contains signs that he was still chafed, perhaps unconsciously, by Sidney's connections and the special glory attributed to Sidney's not very extraordinary actions.

Raleigh:

> . . . to sharp wars sweet honour did thee call,
> Thy country's love, religion, and thy friends,
> (Of worthy men the marks, the lives and ends),
> And her defence, for whom we labour all . . .

Drawn was thy race, aright from princely line,
Nor less than such (by gifts that nature gave,
The common mother that all creatures have)
Doth virtue show, and princely lineage shine.
A king gave thee thy name . . .

The kingly godfather was England's principal enemy, Philip II.

A month later Leicester (Sidney's uncle) was home, sick of the rich burghers and the inglorious war, and with him his stepson, the Earl of Essex, just nineteen, tall, fair-skinned, delicate of head on a neck bent forwards, with fine hands, impetuous, blooded in battle, not caring much how he was dressed or barbered, cogitative at meals, of literary tastes. Elizabeth, who was fifty-four, immediately behaved as if she were in love with him, and Essex as if he were her adored and adoring heir.

Charles Cavendish to the Countess of Shrewsbury:[1]
Sir Walter Raleigh is in wonderful declination, yet labours to underprop himself by my Lord Treasurer and his friends. I see he is courteously used by my Lord and his friends, but I doubt the end, considering how he hath handled himself in his former pride, and surely now groweth so humble towards everyone, as considering his former insolency he committeth over-great baseness, and is thought he will never rise again.

Raleigh, from a poem by Philippe Desportes:
Like to a hermit poor, in place obscure
I mean to spend my days of endless doubt,
To wail such woes as time cannot recure,
Where none but Love shall ever find me out.

My food shall be of care and sorrow made;
My drink nought else but tears fall'n from mine eyes;
And for my light, in such obscured shade,
The flames shall serve which from my heart arise.

A gown of grief my body shall attire,
And broken hope the staff of all my stay;
Of late repentance, linked with long desire,
Shall be the couch whereon my limbs I'll lay.

And at my gate Despair shall linger still,
To let in Death when Love and Fortune will.

Set to music by Alfonso Ferrabosco, 'Like to a hermit poor' became a popular song, hackneyed almost to death by the time Pepys and Samuel Butler mentioned it in the 1660's.[1]

16

The Governor of Patagonia, who had been taken prisoner for Raleigh by the *Serpent* and the *Mary Spark*, suggested that his captor become a paid agent for Spain, since the future of a favourite was uncertain.[2] The suggestion was taken up: it would be a useful opening for counter-espionage or twilight diplomacy, whichever Elizabeth required, so with her connivance Sarmiento was released to put his scheme before Philip. Nothing came of it except that Sarmiento escaped without ransom.

Raleigh was no millionaire, but he was no 'hermit poor'. In Ireland he had been granted 42,000 acres of land from Desmond's confiscated estates in County Cork and County Waterford, which he had to settle with English families. Now he received from Babington's estates some manors and lands in the Midlands.[3] To improve relations with Leicester he put on a great show in the Tiltyard, presenting glamorously the general's exploits in the Netherlands, and took part himself.[4] And he tackled Virginia again.

Grenville had left a dozen-and-a-half men at Roanoke when he found Lane and his colonists gone; not enough to defend themselves, but he had seen this time only a few Indians (one of whom he brought home; the Indian was baptised at Bideford the following year, christened 'Raleigh', and died). A new expedition was to go under John White, the map-maker and artist of the 1585–1586 colony – for good or ill not a martial man this time, nor a plunder-hunter. White was to take 150 genuine settlers, including women and children, and set up the city of Raleigh on the shores of the splendid and safe Chesapeake Bay. Every man who went would receive 500 acres, and more if he invested money. Early in May 1587 they sailed from Plymouth.

In June Raleigh had the pleasure of seeing launched at Deptford the 800-ton *Ark Raleigh*, which had innovations of his own (it is not known what they were). He sold her to the Queen for £5,000 and she became the first *Ark Royal*.

The Queen found Essex autocratic and a great resenter. The boy wanted to be rid of his rival. But Raleigh was a man, and she made him Captain of the Guard so that at all times, as of duty, he could be within a few yards of her.

Essex to Edward Dyer, 21 July 1587:[1]
Things have fallen out very strangely against me since last being with you. Yesternight the Queen came to Worth Hall . . . She came to speak of Raleigh, and it seemed she could not well endure any thing to be spoken against him; and taking hold of one word, 'disdain', she said there was no such cause why I should disdain him.

This speech troubled me so much that as near as I could I described unto her what he had been and what he was, and then I did let her see whether I had cause to disdain his competition of love, or whether I could have comfort to give myself over to the service of a mistress that was in awe of such a man.

I spake, what of grief, and choler, as much against him as I could, and I think he standing at the door might very well hear the worse that I spoke of himself.

In the end I saw she was resolved to defend him, and to cross me . . . I told her . . . I had no joy to be in any place but loathe to be near about her when I knew my affection so much thrown down, and such a wretch as Raleigh highly esteemed of her.

To this she made no answer, but turned away to my Lady of Warwick.

This strange alteration is by Raleigh's means, and the Queen that hath tried all other ways now will see whether she can by these hard courses drive me to be friends with Raleigh, which rather shall drive me to many other extremities.

17

In the autumn White was back from Virginia. He had left the colony without its leader because, he said, the whole colony had insisted he come to hasten supplies, trusting no one else. He had not set the colony on Chesapeake Bay as directed; they were at Lane's old fort on Roanoke, because the seamen had refused to take them further, anxious to get on with privateering.

He reported that on Roanoke his settlers had looked for the men left by Grenville and found the bones of one. Lane's fort, except the earthworks which had been thrown down, was in order. They had found deer feeding on melons which had grown all over the ground-floor rooms of the houses, but the houses were soon habitable and extra ones built.

Unfortunately one of the settlers had wandered off a couple of miles catching crabs, and Indians shot a dozen arrows into him, killed him with wooden swords, and beat his head to pieces. To avenge his death they had attacked the Indian village, which, unknown to them, had been abandoned and was being at that moment pillaged by Manteo's tribe, so they had shot their friends by mistake.

Manteo had been christened on Wednesday 13 August, and by Raleigh's instructions named Lord of Roanoke. The following Monday a child had been born to White's daughter, Eleanor Dare, and on the Sunday she was christened 'Virginia'.

White had left for England three days after the christening, with a promise by the settlers that they would look after the chattels he left behind.

Raleigh said he would send a pinnace immediately, and a proper fleet to reach Virginia the next summer. Grenville prepared the fleet at Bideford in his own country of north Devon, but what happened about the pinnace is not known: there was already a 'stop' on ships leaving England.

Philip had been preparing an Armada for two years. His crusade had been blessed by the Pope (it was to be subsidised by him only if successful), and now it was invigorated by the martyr blood of Mary Queen of Scots. Moreover it had sharper point for Philip now that it could not put Mary on the English throne and might put himself.

In England it was thought that Drake had so destroyed Philip's stores in his April beard-singeing raid on Cadiz that there could be no invasion until the following year. In fact Philip made good the damage very quickly, and if some ships he needed from the Mediterranean had arrived, his Armada would have sailed in September and found the Channel empty of Elizabeth's ships except for a pinnace or two.

Elizabeth was desperately short of money. She could get no loan abroad (the Netherlands, which had been a lender, had become a borrower) and scarcely at home because of the business depression. Spain had stopped English trade with Portugal, Barbary, France, Flanders, Hamburg and the States – and the only trade with Spain was in Scottish ships, or ships registered as Scottish. She still hoped to gain time by bargaining with Philip over the Netherlands, where poor Leicester had been sent again, his men starving until they streamed incontinently home, but her Council persuaded her also to stop merchant shipping from leaving the country and to put her fighting ships in order.

Seven days after Raleigh saw White he attended a Council of War. It included Grey, Grenville, Ralph Lane (now to be Muster-General of the Forces), the governors of Guernsey and the Isle of Wight, and Elizabeth's two greatest soldiers, Sir John Norris and Sir Roger Williams. Leicester had quarrelled with these last two in the Netherlands and dispensed with their services. Williams was a Fluellen, 'Black John Norris' scarred and intractable. Raleigh had spoken to the Queen in Norris's defence when he was abused by Leicester.

Raleigh had been riding around the east, south and west of England improving fortifications (probably with Hariot's help on theory – fortifications are a subject on which Hariot has left papers), and he is said to have prepared the memorandum on land defences which was discussed by the Council of War. It was thought that the Spaniards would try to master a harbour before venturing far up the Channel, that Plymouth and Portland therefore needed strengthening, and also the Isle of Wight, while Dover, Margate and the Thames were the likely invasion points for Parma's troops from the Netherlands.

Immediately after the Council Raleigh hurried down to the west to levy troops and do what he could about arms and ammunition. He left Court the day before Leicester arrived back, and was therefore assumed to be avoiding him.

The fleet got to sea in December, but by January it was back again and the Channel was undefended. January was Philip's new date-line. But Santa Cruz, his greatest soldier who was to lead the Armada, died, and the sailing had to be postponed again while the Duke of Medina Sidonia took over the huge unprecedented enterprise and prayed Philip to appoint someone else.

In England the economies were countermanded, and Lord Charles Howard of Effingham, formerly Lord Chamberlain and now Lord Admiral of the Fleet, was in February on watch in the Channel.

Lord Admiral Howard to Burghley, 28 February 1588:[1]
I protest before God, and as my soul shall answer for it, that I think there were never in any place in the world worthier ships than these are, for so many. And as few as we are, if the King of Spain's forces be not hundreds we will make good sport with them.

And I pray you tell her Majesty from me that her money was well given for the *Ark Raleigh*, for I think her the odd ship in the world for all conditions; and truly I think there can be no great ship make me change and go out of her.

We can see no sail, great or small, but how far soever they be off, we fetch them and speak with them . . .

From aboard her Majesty's ship the *Ark*.

18

The seven or eight ships for Virginia were to have sailed by the end of March but there was still a stop on shipping, as the Vice-Admiral of Devon and Cornwall reminded his half-brother, the Deputy Vice-Admiral of Devon.

Raleigh to Sir John Gilbert, 27 February 1588:[1]
Sir,

Hearing of late that there is little regard taken of the general restraint made heretofore by the Lords of the Council of shipping and mariners, but that every man provideth to go for Newfoundland and other places at their pleasure . . . I thought good therefore to put you in mind to have special care that none pass without special order from the Lords of the Council . . .

Your loving brother,
W. Raleigh.

PS: Such as I acquainted you withal to whom I have given leave you may let them steal away.

The Council must have heard about the postcript: on 31 March they ordered Grenville to 'forbear his intended voyage'. Again Raleigh must have tried to save the day, for a week later Grenville was told that one or two of the smallest ships, if Drake did not want them for the country's defence, might be sent to Virginia, but Grenville himself must not leave the country.

So on 22 April John White and two small ships, of 30 and 25 tons, with crews not required by Drake, and supplies and a few men and women settlers, set sail. But the crews chased every ship they saw, and on 22 May they were back in England; some had been killed, some were wounded, they had gained nothing and got nowhere.

The same week the Armada, after the entire company of 30,000 men had confessed and communicated, sailed out of Lisbon. Pope Sixtus V conferred England upon Philip.

Howard with the Queen's ships went to Plymouth to join Drake and the forty private ships under his command. Howard thought the Queen still did not realise the danger (she was continuing her secret peace negotiations), and a month later had to write to her: 'For the love of Jesus Christ, Madam, awake and see the villainous treasons round about you, against your Majesty and the realm.'

Raleigh had been organising the 2,000 men of Cornwall, and wains and horses to carry them wherever there might be a landing; both horse and foot needed more armour but there was no more in the county.

Gales scattered the Armada; it gathered again at the north-west tip of Spain, and on 12 July sailed finally for England.

Seven days later it was sighted off Cornwall by the *Golden Hind*. The news was beaconed across the country just in time for an already signed discharge of the musters to be cancelled.[1]

Next morning, Howard in the *Ark*, and three other ships, ran along the rear line of the Armada firing into each galleon three or four shots to the Spaniards' one.

The Armada's crescent moved undamaged into the Channel. The *Roebuck* was sent back to Torbay with a captured galleon, and then sent after the fleet with powder taken off it, the fleet already being short. The *Roebuck* also rustled out of the galleon fourteen or fifteen coffers containing 'cloth of gold and other rich furniture', for which inquiries were still being made many months later.

Every little ship that would float came out of Lyme, Weymouth, Poole and the Isle of Wight, to watch, fight, or snap up a trifle. The Armada, lacking pilots who knew the Channel, with half as many seamen to a ship as the English, in ships less manœuvrable, with 2,000 guns in all but fewer guns to a ship and less heavy, reached Calais virtually intact; but forced out of Calais by fireships and shot at from dawn to dusk, it could not convey Parma's invasion barges from the Netherlands.

Raleigh was sent to Howard with the Queen's tactical instructions (she thought Howard should have closed with the Spaniards and boarded; Raleigh believed Howard right to have done no such thing[2]), but by the time he reached it, the fleet, which had been chasing the Spaniards for three days without any powder to fire a shot, was already turning back from the North Sea, short also of food and infected with pestilence. Raleigh prophesied that the

Armada would make for Denmark, refit, and then return to invade. But it fumbled a way north as if to round Scotland. He and Grenville were ordered to Ireland to prevent a landing.

His work on the land defences had never been tested, and the order to Ireland was soon countermanded. His memorable contribution to the victory was a single prodigious sentence of celebration.

Raleigh:[1]
Their navy, which they termed invincible, consisting of 240 sail of ships, not only of their own kingdom, but strengthened with the greatest argosies, Portugal carracks, Florentines and huge hulks of other countries, were by thirty of her Majesty's own ships of war, and a few of our own merchants, by the wise, valiant and most advantageous conduction of the Lord Charles Howard, High Admiral of England, beaten and shuffled together, even from the Lizard in Cornwall, first to Portland – where they shamefully left Don Pedro de Valdes, with his mighty ship – from Portland to Calais, where they lost Hugo de Moncado with the galliasse of which he was captain – and from Calais, driven with squibs from their anchors: were chased out of the sight of England, round about Scotland and Ireland,

where, for the sympathy of their barbarous religion, hoping to find succour and assistance, a great part of them were crushed against the rocks, and those other that landed, being very many in number, were notwithstanding broken, slain and taken, and so sent from village to village, coupled in halters to be shipped into England,

where her Majesty, of her princely and invincible disposition disdaining to put them to death, and scorning either to retain or entertain them, they were all sent back again to their countries, to witness and recount the worthy achievements of their invincible and dreadful navy,

of which the number of soldiers, the fearful burthen of their ships, the commanders' names of every squadron, with all their magazines of provisions, were put in print, as an army and navy unresistible and disdaining prevention:

with all which so great and terrible an ostentation, they did not in all their sailing round about England so much as sink or take one ship, bark, pinnace, or cockboat of ours, or ever burned so much as one sheepcote of this land.

19

England rejoiced and there was a thanksgiving service at St Paul's; seamen died of the pestilence, commanders were quizzed over their accounts; Howard and Drake quarrelled; Leicester died, and the Queen grieved and sold his property to recover what she was owed. Essex, who had been given a military post beyond his years, pursued his quarrel with Raleigh; Elizabeth held fast to both men and prevented a duel.[1]

It was not through Essex that Raleigh would one day lose favour. Elizabeth Throgmorton appeared for the first time, on 1 January 1589, on the list of those who gave the Queen New Year presents. She gave 'two ruffs of lawn cut-work made', and received back 'in gilt plate 15 oz. 3 qrs.' She had been sworn of the Privy Chamber four years before, just before the evening of Court dancing when Elizabeth moved to wipe a smut from Raleigh's face. She was twenty-three, an orphan with a fortune of only £500, which was on loan to a nobleman. Her father, Sir Nicholas Throgmorton, had served Henry VIII and Edward VI as a soldier; under Mary had defended himself with vigour against a charge of treason; and for Elizabeth had been ambassador to France. She was a woman of formidable determination, but in her letters the spelling is so unpredictable that scholars have deduced that she was also a woman of charm.

It is not known when she first became Raleigh's mistress. He was now thirty-four and, it is believed, never yet married.

Aubrey:[2]
He loved a wench well; and one time, getting up one of the Maids of Honour up against a tree in a wood . . . who seemed at first boarding to be something fearful of her honour, and modest, she cried:
'Sweet Sir Walter, what do you ask? Will you undo me? Nay, sweet Sir Walter! Sweet Sir Walter! Sir Walter!'

[88]

At last, as the danger and the pleasure at the same time grew higher, she cried in the ecstasy:
'Swisser Swatter Swisser Swatter!'

He was perhaps not a man for marriage. He wrote a reply to a poem by young Christopher Marlowe, whose *Dr Faustus* had been acted in Armada year, and *Tamburlaine* the year before.

Raleigh, 'The Nymph's Reply to the Passionate Shepherd':

> If all the world and love were young,
> And truth in every shepherd's tongue,
> Those pretty pleasures might me move
> To live with thee and be thy love.
>
> But Time drives flocks from field to fold,
> When rivers rage and rocks grow cold;
> And Philomel becometh dumb;
> The rest complains of cares to come.
>
> The flowers do fade, and wanton fields
> To wayward Winter reckoning yields;
> A honey tongue, a heart of gall,
> Is fancy's spring, but sorrow's fall.
>
> Thy gowns, thy shows, thy beds of roses,
> Thy cap, thy kirtle, and thy posies,
> Soon break, soon wither, soon forgotten,
> In folly ripe, in reason rotten.
>
> Thy belt of straw and ivy-buds,
> Thy coral clasps and amber studs –
> All these in me no means can move
> To come to thee, and be thy love.
>
> But could youth last, and love still breed;
> Had joys no date, nor age no need;
> Then these delights my mind might move
> To live with thee, and be thy love.

Nevertheless it was in the year that was just opening, 1589, that he first tried to get possession of Sherborne Castle in Dorset, as if it were time he had a country seat and founded a family.

The families out in Virginia received no relief this year. Extra backing for the city of Raleigh came from a group of London merchants in exchange for rights of free trade for seven years, and Raleigh gave £100 for the use of the settlers and for teaching the Indians Christianity; but if ships were sent they did not reach Virginia. There was no official restraint on shipping in 1589, but it was in much demand for a great invasion of Portugal, inspired by the Armada victory.

The privateers were active on normal business. The *Roebuck* brought in a Flemish ship, which Raleigh said was really an enemy ship since it carried goods for Spain; two French ships were brought in, and Raleigh and his captains were instructed by the Council to 'offer no further cause of grief' to the subjects of the French king; at least one Spanish ship from the Indies was taken, perhaps more.

And he had two fine quarrels, one with Brown, who he thought was cheating him over the wine licences, and one with Sir Roger Williams about the ownership of a prize taken off Portugal. Although Williams said that Raleigh had 'belied the Ark of Noah, which was the best ship that ever was', Raleigh won the case before the Council, and moreover was given by the Queen a gold chain. Williams himself had nearly lost his head for helping Essex take part in the abortive invasion of Portugal, by 130 ships and 15,000 men, financed as a joint-stock enterprise (Raleigh was one of the adventurers). Essex was frowned on, and given no chain, and became pettish.

But he was quickly in favour again, and Raleigh out, quite far out it seemed. He was given leave of absence to look to his estates in Munster where, as in Virginia, he was trying to plant a colony. The gossips said that Essex had 'chased Raleigh from the Court and confined him in Ireland'.[1]

Raleigh:
> Like truthless dreams, so are my joys expired,
> And past return are all my dandled days,

My love misled, and fancy quite retired:
Of all which past, the sorrow only stays.

My lost delights, now clean from sight of land,
Have left me all alone in unknown ways,
My mind to woe, my life in Fortune's hand:
Of all which past, the sorrow only stays.

As in a country strange without companion,
I only wail the wrong of death's delays,
Whose sweet spring spent, whose summer well nigh done:
Of all which past, the sorrow only stays.

Whom care forewarns, ere age and winter cold,
To haste me hence to find my fortune's fold.

20

Raleigh's estate stretched from Youghal at the mouth of the Black-water up both sides of the river, an area ten or twelve miles long and four or five broad, for which he paid a little over £200 a year.

It was good soil, but, said the surveyors, was 'long overgrown with deep grass, and in most places with heath, brambles and furze'. Munster in fact was 'so barren, both of man and beast, that whoso-ever did travel . . . should not meet man, woman or child, saving in cities or towns, nor yet see any beast, save foxes, wolves, or other ravening creatures'.

According to the rules on which the confiscated estates were rented to English 'undertakers', he was required to people his area with 86 English families and have no Irish anywhere on his land. Undertakers pointed out to prospective settlers that they could keep better house in Ireland for £50 a year than in England for £200; and that for £100 they could buy 60 milch cows, 300 ewes, 20 pigs, and a good team of horses, and the rent for 400 acres would be only £10 a year. But there was no rush to the Irish colonies.

Against the intention of the scheme, some undertakers sold out to Catholics or rented to Irish. In a few years Raleigh had 50 Irish families on his land, but he had also settled 120 Englishmen and had done better than most. He brought Cornish miners to exploit the minerals, drained bogs, and started an industry in supplying the vineyards of the Azores and elsewhere with wine casks.

He probably had a hand in introducing the potato to Ireland around this time; within fifty years it was grown there more widely than anywhere else, having the advantage of not being laid waste as easily as above-ground crops. He is often said to have introduced also a yellow wallflower from the Azores and a cherry from the Canaries.

He made two homes in Ireland – one at the southern end of his estate at Youghal, where he is believed to have lived in a simple house not much bigger than 'Hayes', and the other at the northern end, in Lismore Castle, sheer to the Blackwater, with views up-river and down. From Youghal and Lismore he planned the development of his estate, and made verses for his queen-goddess-sweetheart.

Raleigh:

'As you went to Walsingham,
   To that holy land,
Met you not with my true love
   By the way as you went?'

'How shall I know your true love,
   That have met many one
As I went to the holy land,
   That have come, that have gone?'

'She is neither white nor brown
   But as the heavens fair.
There is none hath a form so divine,
   In the earth or the air.'

'Such an one did I meet, good sir,
   Such an angelic face,

[92]

Who like a Queen, like a nymph, did appear
    By her gait, by her grace.'

'She hath left me here all alone,
    All alone as unknown,
Who sometimes did me lead with herself
    And me loved as her own.'

'What's the cause that she leave you alone,
    And a new way doth take,
Who loved you once as her own
    And her joy did you make?'

'I have loved her all my youth,
    But now old as you see,
Love likes not the falling fruit
    From the withered tree.'

'Know that love is a careless child
    And forgets promise past,
He is blind, he is deaf, when he list,
    And in faith never fast.

'His desire is a dureless content
    And a trustless joy.
He is won with a world of despair,
    And is lost with a toy.'

'Of womankind such indeed is the love,
    Or the word "love" abused,
Under which many childish desires
    And conceits are excused.

'But Love is a durable fire
    In the mind ever burning,
Never sick, never old, never dead,
    From itself never turning.'

21

A neighbour of Raleigh's, thirty miles beyond Lismore, was Grey's secretary, Edmund Spenser ('a little man, wore short hair, a little band and little cuffs'), now deputy clerk to the Council of Munster. Spenser was an undertaker with 3,000 acres and at Kilcolman an old castle on a knoll, which looked across a little crescent-shaped lake and his well-wooded well-watered country to the mountains. *A Shepheardes Calender* had made a reputation for him before he came to Ireland, and Sidney had been his patron. Raleigh called on him and they read to each other the poems they had in hand.

Spenser, 'Colin Clout's Come Home Again':
>. . . His song was all a lamentable lay,
>Of great unkindness, and of usage hard,
>Of Cynthia the lady of the sea,
>Which from her presence faultless him debarred.
>And ever and anon with singults rife,
>He cried out, to make his undersong:
>'Ah, my love's Queen, and goddess of my life,
>Who shall me pity, when thou dost me wrong?' . . .

Spenser read to Raleigh from the first three books of *The Faerie Queene*, the third including an episode where Belphoebe (Elizabeth) cured with 'divine tobacco', or some other drug, the wounds of Timias (Raleigh).

Raleigh, too, had earlier been at work on a very long poem or sequence of poems, called *The Ocean's Love to Cynthia*, and read it to Spenser. Spenser said, equivocally, that it lulled his senses 'in slumber of delight', and that Raleigh would do better with martial themes. *The Ocean's Love to Cynthia* is lost, but a poem has been discovered recently which may have been added at about this time as an envoi, affectionate, unstrained, musical.

Raleigh for the Queen:[1]
>Now we have present made
>To Cynthia, Phoebe, Flora,

Diana, and Aurora,
Beauty that cannot fade.

A flower of love's own planting,
A pattern kept by nature
For beauty, form and stature
When she would frame a darling.

She as the valley of Peru
Whose summer ever lasteth,
Time conquering, all she mastereth
By being always new.

As elemental fire
Whose food and flame consumes not,
Or as the passion ends not
Of virtue's true desire,

So her celestial frame
And quintessential mind,
Which heavens together bind,
Shall ever be the same.

Then to her servants leave her,
Love, nature and perfection.
Princess of world's affection,
Our praises but deceive her.

If Love could find a quill
Drawn from an angel's wing,
Or did the Muses sing
That pretty wanton's will,

Perchance he could indite
To please all other sense,
But love's and woe's expense
Sorrow can only write.

[95]

22

It is clear from the fourth book of *The Faerie Queene* that Raleigh had offended Elizabeth by making love, but to whom? Timias, low-born squire, adorer of Belphoebe and defender of the virtue of young women, is fairly certainly Raleigh.[1] Belphoebe is quite certainly Elizabeth in her virginal aspect. But who is Amoret?

Amoret was carried away by Lust to a cave. Timias fought Lust to rescue her but Lust used her body as a shield against Timias's sword. Lust's blood soiled Amoret, and Timias accidentally wounded her. Belphoebe came and chased away Lust. When Belphoebe returned she found Timias tending the unconscious Amoret: 'From her fair eyes wiping the dewy wet, Which softly stealed, and kissing them atween, and handling soft the hurts, which she did get'. Belphoebe was 'filled with deep disdain, and great indignity', and almost killed them on the spot. ' "Is this the faith -?" she said, and said no more, But turned her face, and fled away for evermore.' Timias retired to a hut in the forest where he waxed 'pale and wan, All overgrown with rude and rugged hair'. Amoret was taken charge of by Arthur, the perfect knight, but they both became involved with Slander. Timias was vastly comforted by the lamentations of a dove in whose notes he heard his own name (presumably Wa'er, Wa'er), and by looking at a ruby shaped like a heart, which Belphoebe had once given him. The dove carried the ruby to Belphoebe and effected a reconciliation.

There was indeed a reconciliation with Elizabeth because in a few weeks Raleigh returned to Court and took Spenser with him. Amoret is still a mystery; she might have been in this part of *The Faerie Queene* Bess Throgmorton or some other lady about the Court, or more probably the less virginal side of Elizabeth herself – Amoret was the twin sister of Belphoebe, but while Belphoebe had been brought up virginally by Diana, Amoret had been brought up by Venus. Raleigh may have been making more passionate approaches to Elizabeth than hitherto (Leicester was dead; Essex's success demanded competitive action), and the Virgin was affronted.

Raleigh and Spenser sailed through appalling seas to Penzance and rode up to London, England seeming sublime to Spenser after the colonies. Raleigh presented him and *The Faerie Queene* to Elizabeth who, in abounding health, was dancing six or seven galliards in a morning, and playing on the virginals and singing. She liked the poem.

On 1 December the first three books were entered at Stationers' Hall. At Raleigh's request Spenser wrote an explanation of what he meant by his allegory, which he dedicated to the 'Queen of England, France, and Ireland, and of Virginia'. He added dedicatory sonnets to everyone who could possibly be of service to him, including one to Raleigh: 'To thee that art the summer's nightingale, Thy sovereign Goddess's most dear delight'. But Raleigh was now only her second dearest delight.

Officials were seeming obstructive. There was litigation over the lease of Lismore, and the Lord Deputy was not interfering on his behalf.

Raleigh to Sir George Carew, who was in Ireland, 28 December 1589:[1]
Cousin George,

For my retreat from Court it was upon good cause to take order for my prize. If in Ireland they think that I am not worth the respecting they shall much deceive themselves. I am in place to be believed not inferior to any man, to pleasure or displeasure the greatest; and my opinion is so received and believed as I can anger the best of them. And, therefore, if the Deputy be not ready to stead me as I have been to defend him – be it as it may . . .

I look for you here this spring, and if possible I may, I will return with you. The Queen thinks that George Carew longs to see her; and therefore see her.

Farewell, noble George, my chosen friend and kinsman, from whom nor time, nor fortune, nor adversity, shall ever sever me.

Love for his cousin, bluster for his enemy, and intuition of adversity. But in due course Elizabeth ordered Lord Deputy Sir William Fitzwilliam to quash the suit of his opponent in the Lismore litigation. He endeared himself further to Fitzwilliam by offering the Privy Council to raise in Ireland a hundred foot and fifty horse, well mounted and armed; they would protect his own estates and the families on them, otherwise undefended, and would be paid from the budget of the Lord Deputy. The offer was not accepted.

23

At last in 1590 an expedition went off to Virginia after the welfare of the settlers of whom nothing had been heard for three years.

In early August John White with two ships sailed up the Carolina Banks; having privateered for some months around the Indies they were late in the year and the hurricane season was beginning.

On Roanoke they found the colonists gone, and 'Croatoan' carved on a tree. It had been agreed that the colonists would carve the name of their destination if they left Roanoke, and also a cross if they were in trouble. There was no cross. White found his own three chests of belongings, which had been buried in the sand and later dug up, his books, pictures and maps lying around sodden by rain, and his armour almost eaten through with rust.

Croatoan Island was fifty miles south; Manteo's people lived there. Before White could set out, the ships had been tossed by storms, cables broken, anchors lost. One ship went home; the other, with White, decided to go south to the Indies, try to winter there, and then both privateer and search again in Virginia. But again weather was too much for them; they were blown to the Azores, and in October they were in Plymouth.

The lost colonists were not seen again. They were not wiped out by the Spaniards, who instead had to concentrate on safeguarding the passage of treasure. Later on, early in the seventeenth century, it was being said in Jamestown that they had been killed by Indians, all except four men, two boys and a girl who were made slaves.

The Croatoans (known today as the Lumbee tribe) have light complexions and rounded features and have shown signs of a European stubbornness: in the nineteenth century they clung to their franchise and their schools better than most Indians; in 1958 they routed with shot-guns a rally of the Ku-Klux-Klan.[1] All this has been attributed to possible interbreeding with the lost colonists, or with pirates in the seventeenth and eighteenth centuries, or with stranded sailors even before 1584 (Amadas and Barlow had noticed children with very fine auburn and chestnut-coloured hair).

The first all-white American baby, White's grand-daughter Virginia Dare, grew up, according to a nineteenth-century poet, into a white doe, Winona, and was shot by her Indian lover. She has been transmogrified by the twentieth century, at Elizabeth City, the nearest airport to Roanoke, into a squarefaced fireproof 'Virginia Dare Hotel'.

24

At the time when White in Virginia was searching for his daughter and her baby, at Court the Queen was noting a plumpness in Philip Sidney's pretty widow. When Essex confessed that he had secretly married her, Elizabeth was angry for his faithlessness and deceit, and as much for his stupidity in marrying an undowered nonentity. He kept his wife away from Court, and the Queen calmed down.

Unknown to Elizabeth, her second most dear delight had been urging on Bess Throgmorton 'such delights, As will shorten tedious nights'.

Raleigh, 'On his Mistress Serena' (it was with 'Serena' that Timias became involved later in The Faerie Queene):

> Nature, that washed her hands in milk
> And had forgot to dry them,
> Instead of earth took snow and silk
> At Love's request, to try them
> If she a mistress could compose
> To please Love's fancy out of those.

Her eyes he would should be of light,
A violet breath, and lips of jelly,
Her hair not black nor over-bright,
And of the softest down her belly;
As for her inside he'ld have it
Only of wantonness and wit.

At Love's entreaty, such a one
Nature made, but with her beauty
She hath framed a heart of stone,
So as Love, by ill destiny,
Must die for her whom Nature gave him,
Because her darling would not save him.

But Time, which Nature doth despise,
And rudely gives her love the lie,
Makes Hope a fool and Sorrow wise,
His hands doth neither wash nor dry,
But, being made of steel and rust,
Turns snow and silk and milk to dust.

The light, the belly, lips and breath,
He dims, discolours, and destroys;
With those he feeds (but fills not) Death
Which sometimes were the food of Joys;
Yea, Time doth dull each lively wit,
And dries all wantonness with it.

O cruel Time! which takes in trust
Our youth, our joys, and all we have,
And pays us but with age and dust;
Who in the dark and silent grave,
When we have wandered all our ways,
Shuts up the story of our days.

In June 1591 Bess Throgmorton became pregnant.[1]

25

Elizabeth at last promised to allow him out of her kingdom. He was to go as Vice-Admiral of an expedition under Lord Thomas Howard, a nephew of Lord Henry Howard, who was himself second cousin of Lord Charles Howard of Effingham. No treasure fleet had sailed in 1590; at least one had to sail in 1591 if Philip was to remain solvent. Five of the Queen's ships (two of them victualled by Raleigh), with the *Bark Raleigh*, and some supply ships and pinnaces were to wait for it at the Azores.

But when the time came, Elizabeth would not part with him. Grenville must go instead.

Philip had prepared an armada to cover the last lap of the treasure route, from the Azores to Spain. False rumours of this armada, and the finding of Spanish pinnaces in the Channel, sent England into another alarm of invasion. Shipping was stopped, and Raleigh sent post-haste to the west to see to Cornish defences and advise the Governor of the Scillies. He rode down with Carew Raleigh, and near Blandford in Dorset they committed a sin which locally was not forgotten: they commandeered the parson's horse to serve as a post-horse.[1]

Philip was well informed of Lord Thomas Howard's plans, and at the Azores his armada surprised the English ships. Raleigh had sent a pinnace to warn them but it arrived too late. However, all escaped, except Grenville in the *Revenge*.

The *Revenge* was the first ship of the Queen's to fall into Spanish hands. To counter criticism in England and propaganda boasting by Spain, Raleigh wrote an account of the fight in which he first admitted Grenville's error in not running away ('notwithstanding, out of the greatness of his mind he could not be persuaded'), and then gave the *Revenge* and his cousin their immortality.

Raleigh, A report of the truth of the fight about the Isles of Azores, this last summer, betwixt the Revenge, *one of her Majesty's ships, and an armada of the King of Spain:*

... All the powder of the *Revenge* to the last barrel was now spent, all her pikes broken, forty of her best men slain, and most part of the rest hurt. In the beginning of the fight she had but one hundred free from sickness, and fourscore and ten sick, laid in hold upon the ballast. A small troupe to man such a ship, and a weak garrison to resist so mighty an army. By those hundred all was sustained, the volleys, boardings, and enterings of fifteen ships of war, besides those which beat her at large. On the contrary, the Spanish were always supplied with soldiers brought from every squadron: all manner of arms and powder at will. Unto ours there remained no comfort at all, no hope, no supply either of ships, men or weapons; the masts all beaten over board, all her tackle out asunder, her upper work altogether razed, and in effect evened she was with the water, but the very foundation or bottom of a ship, nothing being left overhead either for flight or defence.

Sir Richard finding himself in this distress, and unable any longer to make resistance, having endured in this fifteen hours fight, the assault of fifteen several armadoes, all by turns aboard him, and by estimation eight hundred shot of great artillery, besides many assaults and entries; and that himself and the ship must needs be possessed by the enemy, who were now all cast in a ring round about him; the *Revenge* not able to move one way or other, but as she was moved with the waves and billow of the sea: commanded the Master Gunner, whom he knew to be a most resolute man, to split and sink the ship, that thereby nothing might remain of glory or victory to the Spaniards: seeing in so many hours fight, and with so great a navy they were not able to take her, having had fifteen hours time, fifteen thousand men, and fifty and three sail of men-of-war to perform it withal.

Against the will of Grenville, dying of his wounds, the ship was surrendered to the Spaniards. But the other English ships took five prizes while at sea, providing on balance a small profit.

Simultaneously with Lord Thomas Howard's voyage, Raleigh was an adventurer, with eleven others, in a privateering enterprise which captured bullion and merchandise valued at £31,150. Of this, one-third, £10,383, went to the mariners instead of wages; £3,015 (*sic*) to the Lord Admiral as his 'tenth'; £1,600 to the Queen's customs; £1,200 to the cost of bringing the goods from the west to London. This left £14,952 to be divided among the owners of the ships and the victuallers, who had invested something under £8,000. 'All which,' said Raleigh, 'amounted not to the increase of one for one, which is a small return. We might have gotten more to have sent them afishing.'[1]

26

One of his official duties was to attend executions of Catholic priests condemned for treason, as on 10 December 1591 when the twenty-nine-year-old Oliver Plasden was dragged to the gallows.

Relation of Father James Young:[2]
Oliver Plasden, priest, born by Fleet Bridge, in London, was next put into the cart, who prayed for the Queen and the whole realm, which when Sir Walter Raleigh heard, 'What,' said he, 'dost thou think as thou prayest?'

'Otherwise,' quoth he, 'I expect no salvation at God's hands.'

'Then thou dost acknowledge her for thy lawful Queen?' said Raleigh.

'I do sincerely.'

'Wouldst thou defend her,' quoth Raleigh, 'against all her foreign and domestical enemies, if so thou were able?'

'I would,' said Plasden, 'to the uttermost of my power, and so I would counsel all men who would be persuaded by me.'

The people hearing this, began to speak one to another: 'There is no cause why this honest man should die. He would never say thus at death, except he thought so in his heart.'

Then Raleigh said: 'How happened it that yesterday before the judges thou wouldst not say thus much? Then thou hadst not come thus far. I know, good people,' said Raleigh, turning himself, 'her Majesty desireth no more at these men's hands, than that which this man hath now confessed. Mr Sheriff,' said he, 'I will presently go to the Court, let him be stayed.'

Which when Topcliffe heard [Topcliffe, chief hunter of Jesuits and priests, a Balliol man, was fifty-nine at this time]: 'I pray you,' saith he, 'suffer me to offer him one question, and anon you shall hear that I will convince him to be a traitor.' Then he said: 'Plasden, in thy conscience, before all this assembly, tell me thy judgment. If the King of Spain or the Pope would come into this country by force for no other end precisely, but by his canonical law,' for so he spake, 'to establish that faith which thou believest and which thou thinkest to be the true Catholic faith as you call it, tell me, wouldst thou resist them?'

'I am a priest,' quoth he, 'and therefore may not fight.'

'Although thou mayst not fight, wouldst thou give counsel to others who would fight to defend her Majesty?'

'I would,' said the priest, 'counsel all men to maintain the right of their prince.'

'He saith marvellous well,' quoth Raleigh. 'No more. I will presently post to the Queen. I know she will be glad of this plain dealing.'

'Then,' said Topcliffe, 'let me say but one word unto him,' which was granted. 'Thou sayest, Plasden,' quoth he, 'that thou wouldst counsel all to defend the Queen's right, but tell me, dost thou think that the Queen hath any right to maintain this religion, and to forbid yours?'

'No,' said the priest.

'Then thou thinkest not,' quoth he, 'to defend the Queen against the Pope, if he would come to establish thy religion; speak, what sayest thou to this? I charge thee before God.'

'I am a Catholic priest,' quoth he, 'therefore I would never fight nor counsel others to fight against my religion, for that were to deny my faith. O Christ,' saith he, looking up to heaven and kissing the rope, 'I will never deny thee for a thousand lives.'

Then lo! they cried, he was a traitor, and the cart was drawn away, and he, by the word of Raleigh, was suffered to hang until he was dead; then he was drawn and quartered after their custom.

It was not long before this that Raleigh tried to help the imprisoned John Udall,[1] who also had been condemned for treason.

Udall, however, was a Puritan. His crime was that he had criticised the bishops; it was held that since the bishops were the creatures of the Queen, he had criticised the Queen – treason. But he was not executed, he died in prison.

Raleigh probably shared with every other official a readiness to be paid for the help he gave to people in trouble (as for getting a pardon for Bainham in 1601) but he had other motives than, for example, Essex. While Essex helped Puritans and others chiefly to increase his own power and the difficulties of the Administration, Raleigh seems to have been moved by quick (perhaps over-quick) sympathy. He helped a number of small men to prise their rights out of the Treasury, and he was the spokesman of others to the Queen. 'When, Sir Walter, will you cease to be a beggar?' 'When your gracious Majesty ceases to be a benefactor.'

The persecuted Catholics, caught between Queen and Pope, had not disrupted the defences in Armada year as they might, but their absence of disloyalty went unnoticed. Persecution increased, largely because of propaganda for rebellion and invasion which issued violently from Catholics abroad, in particular from Raleigh's Oxford contemporary, the Jesuit Robert Parsons. Parsons attacked the Queen and every official for whom he could find a stick and a strong Latin sentence. He found both for Raleigh.

Robert Parsons:[1]
Certainly if the school of atheism of Sir Walter Raleigh flourishes a little longer – which he is well known to hold in his house, with a certain necromantic astrologer as teacher, in order that considerable numbers of noble youths may spend their time making fun of both the old law of Moses and the new of the Lord Christ, with brilliant witticisms and jokes, and laughing at them among themselves – if, let me say, this school should take root and strength, and Raleigh himself be chosen for the Council and thus rule in state matters (which all expect – with good reason since following Leicester and Hatton he holds the chief place about the Queen, and almost from the ranks in Ireland we see him made a principal and powerful man, thanks solely to the Queen, having shown no merit), what (let me say) shall we have to expect but that at some time or another we shall

[105]

actually see a proclamation drawn up by that Magus and Epicurus, Raleigh's teacher, and published in the name of the Queen, by which every single divine being, the immortality of every soul, and the expectation of another life, are distinctly, clearly, briefly and without circumlocution denied, and all would be accused of treason (as if they were disturbers of the realm) who against a doctrine of that kind (so sweet and easy in the wallowing vices of the flesh) raised scruples or made trouble.

This is the earliest statement of the belief that Raleigh was an atheist and that Hariot dabbled in necromancy.

27

Essex meanwhile had been in France fighting for Henry of Navarre, now Henry IV, against his Catholic rebels, and knighting for good-will and Essex's own glory (he knighted twenty-four). The English soldiers sickened, starved, drifted home, and Essex himself was back at Court for Christmas.

At Court, Burghley's second son, Robert Cecil, small, somewhat humped, deprecating, was now a member of the Council, and Secretary in all but name. Essex opposed Burghley and Cecil in everything, and of course Raleigh.

Raleigh, in 1592, was at last to be an Admiral, in full command of an expedition of thirteen ships to attack the silver fleet and sack Panama. In February he went down to the west to supervise preparations. Sherborne, a posting station about halfway there, was always a stopping place, but this time he could regard himself as tenant of Sherborne Castle. Elizabeth had kept the see of Salisbury vacant for three years, waiting for a candidate who would lease Sherborne to her so that she could hand it on to Raleigh. A suitable candidate had at last appeared. Raleigh gave Elizabeth a ring in appreciation of 'making the bishop'.[1] The rent he would have to pay the see was £230 a year.

A blow fell. As before, she needed him by her. Frobisher was to sail instead. It was difficult to get men to follow Frobisher: he was a good seaman but a martinet, and he had made a fool of himself over black stone.

It was a worrying time. Robert Cecil was pressing Raleigh, already fully committed in the voyage, to commit himself deeper still, with nothing in black-and-white as to what he would get back for it, and himself not in charge.[1]

Moreover he had been several months married to Bess,[2] and it was ceasing to be a secret.

Raleigh to Sir Robert Cecil, 10 March 1592:[3]
I mean not to come away, as they say I will, for fear of a marriage, and I know not what. If any such things were, I would have imparted it unto yourself before any man living; and, therefore, I pray believe it not, and I beseech you to suppress, what you can, any such malicious report.

For I protest before God there is none on the face of the earth that I would be fastened unto.

Before the end of the month a boy was born. He was christened Damerei,[4] and Essex was one of the godfathers. A month later Bess returned to Court as a Maid of Honour.

Raleigh sailed with his fleet. He was to take it some way and then hand over to Frobisher. He had recommended that the sacking of Panama should be abandoned, and when, on the very voyage, he heard from an Englishman escaped from Spain that no treasure fleet was to sail that year, he decided to concentrate on the great Portuguese carracks due from the East Indies in July or August. He disposed Frobisher's squadron close to the Spanish coast, and a squadron under Sir John Burrough at the Azores.

By the end of May, Elizabeth knew the secret, or some of it; Raleigh was back in London, in Cecil's custody, and the Treasury added up how much he owed the Queen.

Early in June he was confined to Durham House,[5] with cousin George Carew, newly made Lieutenant-General of the Ordnance, as his keeper, and Bess was put in the custody of Heneage. Nevertheless the assignment to him by the Queen of the lease of

Sherborne was officially completed in June, as if his disgrace was not mortal.

A month later, when Elizabeth came up the Thames in the royal barge and disembarked at Blackfriars, he was watching from his turret three-quarters of a mile away.

Arthur Gorges to Cecil, 26 July 1592:[1]
Sir Walter Raleigh having gazed and sighed a long time at his study window, from whence he might discern the barges and boats about the Blackfriars Stairs, suddenly he brake out into a great distemper, and sware that his enemies had of purpose brought her Majesty thither, to break his gall sunder with Tantalus' torment . . .

And as a man transported with passion, he sware to Sir George Carew that he would disguise himself and get into a pair of oars to ease his mind but with a sight of the Queen; or else, he protested, his heart would break. But the trusty Jailor . . . flatly refused to permit him . . .

Upon this dispute they fell out to choleric outrageous words; with striving and struggling at the doors . . . and in the fury of the conflict the Jailor had his new periwig torn off his crown . . . At last they had gotten out their daggers, which when I saw I played the stickler between them, and so purchased such a rap on the knuckles that I wished both their pates broken.

And so with much ado they stayed their brawl to see my bloodied fingers . . .

As yet I cannot reconcile them by any persuasions . . . Good sir, let nobody know thereof, for I fear Sir W. Raleigh will shortly grow to be Orlando Furioso if the bright Angelica persevere against him a little longer.
PS: . . . I could wish her Majesty knew.

Elizabeth knew her *Orlando Furioso* in the original, had been given the previous year an English translation by Sir John Harington, and had probably seen at Court, the last Christmas, the play Greene made from it. Not harrowed by the idea of Raleigh Furioso, she confined him more closely.

Sir Arthur Throgmorton, Diary, 7 August 1592:[1]
Ma sœur s'en alla à la Tour, et Sir W. Raleigh.

It was to be several years before Raleigh, in any extant record, referred to Bess with affection.

I

The Tower – by a Swiss tourist who was shown round by one of Raleigh's Yeomen of the Guard:[1]

We were put in charge of a guardsman who was to act as guide round the sights. We first of all entered an armoury where were many shields, weapons and pikes . . . In this apartment we made the first gratuity to a keeper in attendance, three shillings.

We were then led into another chamber in which they showed us the ten-span long barrel which belonged to the late King Henry, the Queen's father . . . Here we made the second gratuity.

In another room we saw an incredible number of arrows . . . and from this room we went to another full of armour . . . There we gave largesse for the third time.

Having descended a little and entered another apartment we saw a number of small field-pieces, set on wheels . . . and here we made the fourth gratuity.

From here we made for another portion or floor of the castle, up a spiral staircase, and entered a large hall in which Julius Caesar, the first emperor, is supposed to have dined. Thence we came to the guardroom; in the dungeon we saw the ropes used to rack malefactors . . . Afterwards in another room we were shown a very ancient tapestry . . . Here we gave the fifth gratuity.

Then we climbed the tower erected by Julius Caesar; it was high, and sixteen great pieces on wheels stood there, which could fire a distance. Here we made the sixth gratuity.

Descending again we entered the Mint . . . There we made the seventh gratuity.

We then proceeded to the Lieutenant's apartments, where we saw the axe which is carried before the judge at a trial . . . We were then shown the iron gate, and having gone round the castle we came to a grating through which criminals are led . . .

We likewise saw six lions and lionesses in this stronghold, in separate wooden cages, and two were over a hundred years old. And if I remember, one was named Edward, and one of the lionesses Elizabeth ... And but for a little a lion might have caught one of the party's servants, for it could get its claws through the bars of the cage.

And having, now for the eighth time, made a gratuity to the guardsman, we returned to our hostel.

From the Tower, Raleigh:

> My body in the walls captived
> Feels not the wounds of spiteful envy;
> But my thralled mind, of liberty deprived,
> Fast fettered in her ancient memory,
> Doth nought behold but Sorrow's dying face.
> Such prison erst was so delightful
> As it desired no other dwelling place,
> But time's effects and destinies despiteful
> Have changed both my keeper and my fare.
> Love's fire and beauty's light I then had store;
> But now, close kept, as captives wonted are,
> That food, that heat, that light, I find no more.
>
> Despair bolts up my doors, and I alone
> Speak to dead walls: but those hear not my moan.

From the Tower, Bess to Sir Moyle Finch:[1]
I assure you truly I never desired nor never would desire my liberty without the good liking nor advising of Sir W. R. It is not this imprisonment, if I bought it with my life, that should make me think it long if it should do him harm to speak of my delivery.

From the Tower, Raleigh to Cecil:[2]
My heart was never broken till this day that I hear the Queen goes away so far off, whom I have followed so many years with so great love and desire, in so many journeys, and am now left behind her, in a dark prison all alone.

While she was yet near at hand, that I might hear of her once in two or three days my sorrows were the less: but even now my heart is cast into the depths of all misery. I that was wont to behold her riding like Alexander, hunting like Diana, walking like Venus, the gentle wind blowing her fair hair about her pure cheeks, like a nymph; sometime sitting in the shade like a goddess; sometime singing like an angel; sometime playing like Orpheus.

Behold the sorrow of this world! Once amiss hath bereaved me of all.

From the Tower, Raleigh to Lord Admiral Howard:[1]
I beseech your Lordship not to offend her Majesty any farther by suing for me . . . I only desire that I may be stayed no one hour from the extremity that either law or precedent can avow.

And, if that be too little, would God it were withal concluded that I might feed the lions as I go by, to save labour.

2

For a shipping man the Tower was inconvenient. One of his captains had taken a prize loaded with 106,000 fish: there was trouble because it was said to belong to a neutral. Two prizes were sent back by Frobisher and Burrough, a Biscayan with £6,000-worth of ironware, and a Brazilian with sugar (privateered sugar was building London's refineries): the cargoes had to be sold, mariners and soldiers paid, decisions taken on what to do with the ships.

And then into Dartmouth was brought a Portuguese carrack, the *Madre de Dios*, taken at the Azores by Burrough in the *Roebuck* and, in consort with him, privateers of the Earl of Cumberland. She was the largest ship that had ever entered an English port, seven decks high, the most valuable single prize ever taken, with 537 tons of pepper, cloves, cinnamon, cochineal, mace and nutmegs, and as well jewels, gold, ebony, carpets and oriental silks. She lifted Raleigh out of impotence.

[113]

Raleigh to Burghley:[1]
My promise was not to buy my bondage but my liberty . . .

Her Majesty's adventure will come but to the tenth part. Which of £200,000 (such, I think, is the value of the carrack) her Majesty's part will be £20,000 . . . Instead of this £20,000 if I had made it £100,000 and done injury to none but myself I hope it may be thought that it proceedeth from a faithful mind and a true desire to serve her. Fourscore thousand pounds is more than ever a man presented her Majesty as yet . . .

From this unsavoury dungeon . . .

But the upper decks and the personal effects of passengers and crew had already been pillaged by the seamen, as was their customary right, and it was not known how much further the pillage had gone. The merchants and gentlemen of the west and from London, mad for bargains in jewels, silks and spices, were swarming on the seamen. Urgently commissioners were appointed to preserve what was left and search out what had been taken. Cecil was sent down to help them, and Raleigh was brought out of the Tower, less than two months after he went in, and was sent down too.

Raleigh to Burghley, from Dartmouth, 21 September 1592:[2]
I dare give the Queen ten thousand pounds sterling for that which is gained by Sir Robert Cecil's coming down; which, I protest before the living God, I speak of truth, without affection of partiality, for (God is my judge) he hath more rifled my ship than all the rest.

Cecil to Heneage, also from Dartmouth, 21 September 1592:[3]
I assure you, sir, his poor servants to the number of 140 goodly men, and all the mariners, came to him with such shouts and joy as I never saw a man more troubled to quiet them in my life.

But his heart is broken, for he is very extremely pensive, longer than he is busied, in which he can toil terribly.

But if you did hear him rage at the spoils, finding all the short wares utterly devoured, you would laugh as I do, which I cannot choose.

The meeting between him and Sir John Gilbert was with tears on

Sir John's part; but he, belike finding that it is known that he hath a keeper, whensoever he is saluted with congratulations for liberty he doth answer: 'No, I am still the Queen of England's poor captive.'

After some months while the Queen and Burghley calculated what method of division between Raleigh's associates and Cumberland's would give most to Elizabeth without discouraging adventurers from future adventuring, Raleigh and his group received back £24,000 out of their investment of £26,000, Cumberland received £36,000 against an investment of £19,000, the City of London £12,000 against £6,000. The Queen, for her investment of £1,800 and the loan of two ships, took about £80,000.

He said that for a loss of £2,000 he had risked all his estate and paid interest on £11,000 he had borrowed. But he had back his freedom. Later Bess was released. No more is heard of Damerei.

3

In London there was plague, and so many deaths that tolling for burial was forbidden. Howling dogs compensated for silence of bells: dogs abandoned by plague-fleers wandered until caught by the dog-catchers, or yelped and starved in the locked houses. The theatres were closed. Shakespeare occupied himself with *Venus and Adonis*, and then in *Love's Labour's Lost* dug at courtiers who swore celibacy but could not keep away from women.*

Raleigh was meeting business snags. He was involved in disputes over two more neutral ships his men had taken, and the authorities were suppressing one of his Irish industries, the making of staves for wine-casks. The little industry supported a number of colonising families, and in time would have made his woods less thick for the hiding of wild Irishmen. But he was exporting the staves to the

---

* It is widely held that a free-speculating group around Raleigh was known by the name of 'the School of Night', that *Love's Labour's Lost* was directed especially against it, and that there was violent literary war between the Raleigh group and the Essex-Southampton group. The cryptological arguments for these beliefs are ingenious, but hard evidence is still scarce.

Azores, a former Portuguese possession and therefore now Spanish: the Council forbade him to trade with the enemy.

He had a chance to show himself still the responsible servant of the Queen, almost before her eyes, when Parliament met to vote money for defence (Spain was preparing another invasion fleet). He spoke vigorously in favour of the money proposals 'not only (he protested) to please the Queen, to whom he was infinitely bound above his deserts, but for the necessity he both saw and knew'. He described the great strength of Spain – supplied with ships by Denmark and Norway, having ports in France and the Low Countries, and allied with Papist nobles in Scotland – and England's great shipping losses and reduction of trade at the hands of Spain. It had been objected that it was not the time to ask for more money.

Sir Simonds D'Ewes (1602–1650) – The House of Commons, 7 March 1593, afternoon:[1]

Sir Walter Raleigh said: 'I can see no reason that the suspicion of discontentment should cross the provision for the present danger. The time is now more dangerous than it was in '88, for then the Spaniard which came from Spain was to pass dangerous seas, and had no place of retreat or relief if he failed. But now he hath in Brittany great store of shipping, a landing place in Scotland, and men and horses there as good as we have any. But for the difficulty in getting the subsidy, I think it seems more difficult by speaking than it would be in gathering.'

Now stood up two or three to have spoken, striving who might speak first. Then the Speaker propounds it as an Order in the House in such a case for him to ask the parties that would speak, on which side they would speak, whether with him that spake next before or against him: and the party that speaketh against the last speaker is to be heard first. And so it was ruled.

The Commons were developing their procedures and, moreover, their principles. When the Lords invited them to a joint discussion of a proposal by the Lords for a larger subsidy than the Commons intended, Francis Bacon said that on principle the invitation must be refused. The money proposals became deadlocked. Raleigh resolved the difficulty by proposing that the two Houses confer on the general question of the danger and the subsidy, without any mention of the Lords' proposal, to which the Commons (after asking him to repeat his proposal because they could not hear him) agreed happily.

He wanted to please the Queen but he opposed the bill of Whitgift, her 'little black husband', to amend the 'Act to retain the Queen's Majesty's subjects within their due obedience', which had been passed twelve years before as an anti-Catholic measure. It was still assumed that all Catholics hoped, like Parsons, that the Pope would invade, and considered, like Parsons, that the murder of Elizabeth would not only be justified by the Papal Bull but was a duty; the amendment however strengthened the measures against the Puritans as well.

H. Townshend (1577–c. 1620) – The House of Commons, 4 April 1593:[1]
Sir Walter Raleigh said: 'In my conceit the Brownists are worthy to be rooted out of a Common-wealth; but what danger may grow to our selves if this law pass, it were fit to be considered. For it is to be feared that men not guilty will be included in it; and that law is hard that taketh life, or sendeth into banishment, where men's intentions shall be judged by a jury, and they shall be judges what another means. But that law that is against a fact, that is but just, and punish the fact as severely as you will.

'If two or three thousand Brownists meet at the seaside, at whose charge shall they be transported? Or whither will you send them? I am sorry for it: I am afraid there is near twenty thousand of them in England. And when they be gone, who shall maintain their wives and children?'

His speeches were always clear, his points tabulated almost under (a), (b), (c) and left at that, as when he supported a Bill to reduce the number of foreigners setting up shop in England. There had been ill-feeling against them, and in London rioting, but the Bill met some opposition.

D'Ewes, 23 March:
Raleigh: Whereas it is pretended that for strangers it is against

[117]

charity, against honour, against profit to expel them, in my opinion it is no matter of charity to relieve them. For first, such as fly hither have forsaken their own king. And religion is no pretext for them, for we have no Dutchmen here but such as came from those provinces where the Gospel is preached, and here they live disliking our Church.

For honour, it is honour to use strangers as we be used amongst strangers; and it is lightness in a commonwealth, yea baseness in a nation, to give a liberty to another nation which we cannot receive again. In Antwerp where our intercourse was most we were never suffered to have a tailor or a shoemaker to dwell there . . .

And for profit, they . . . pay nothing, yet eat out our profits, and supplant our nation. Custom indeed they pay, paying fifteen pence where we pay twelve pence, but they are discharged of subsidies . . .

The Dutchman by his policy hath gotten trading with all the world into his hands, yea he is now entering into the trade of Scarborough fishing, and the fishing of the Newfound-lands, which is the stay of the West Countries. They are the people that maintain the King of Spain in his greatness . . .

And so to conclude, in the whole cause I see no matter of honour, no matter of charity, no profit in relieving them.

He was speaking in a popular cause but soon, almost accidentally, he was in worse repute than ever.

4

The dramatist, Thomas Kyd, at a loose end while the theatres were closed, had written inflammatory leaflets against the foreign shopkeepers and he was arrested for fomenting trouble. In his rooms were found papers which denied the divinity of Christ. He said they were the property of Christopher Marlowe. A spy then told the Council that Marlowe had boasted he had 'read the atheist lecture to Sir Walter Raleigh and others', and had said 'that Moses was but a juggler, that one Hariot, being Sir Walter Raleigh's man, can do more than he'.[1] Marlowe had also said 'that Christ was a bastard and his mother dishonest . . . ; and the sacraments would have been much better administered in a tobacco pipe'. His blasphemies may have publicised Durham House as a 'school of atheism' as effectively as the propaganda of the Jesuits.

When Marlowe was killed in odd circumstances a few days after being called before the Council it was taken as a divine judgment which should also have fallen elsewhere.

As for Raleigh's own atheism, the records show that he dabbled in medicine and in chemical experiments; that he was facile in swearing by 'God' as if the word had rather less meaning for him than 'Fortune' or 'Time'; and that some of his company were scientists and others iconoclastic hooligans.

And further that he was given to mental sports of a kind which frightened the dogmatic. For example, he summarised a work by Sextus Empiricus on scepticism, which argued that it was not possible to say that one's impressions of the world were more true than anyone else's, or even than animals', since many animals see or smell better than men, and have brains which serve their purposes as satisfactorily as men's serve theirs. 'The sceptic,' his summary says, 'doth neither affirm, neither deny any position; but doubteth of it, and opposeth his reasons against that which is affirmed or denied, to justify his not consenting.'

There is a record of a conversation in which he acted the sceptic, 'not consenting'. It was one evening at the house of Sir George Trenchard, the Sheriff of Dorset.

Rev. Ralph Ironside, Minister of Winterbotham:[2]
Towards the end of supper some loose speeches of Mr Carew Raleigh's being gently reproved by Sir Ralph Horsey in these words, '*Colloquia prava corrumpunt bones mores* [Evil words corrupt good morals]', Mr Raleigh demands of me what danger he might incur by such speeches.

Whereunto I answered: 'The wages of sin is death.'

And he making light of death as being common to all, sinner and righteous, I inferred further that as that life which is the gift of God

[119]

through Jesus Christ is life eternal, so that death which is properly the wages of sin is death eternal, both of the body and of the soul also.

'Soul!' quoth Mr Carew Raleigh, 'what is that?'

'Better it were,' said I, 'that we would be careful how the souls might be saved than to be curious in finding out their essence.'

And so keeping silence, Sir Walter requests me that for their instruction I would answer to the question that before by his brother was proposed unto me.

'I have been,' said he, 'a scholar some time in Oxford, I have answered under a Bachelor of Arts, and had talk with divers, yet hitherunto in this point (to wit, what the reasonable soul of man is) have I not by any been resolved. They tell us it is *primus motor*, the first mover, in a man, etc.'

Unto this – after I had replied that howsoever the soul were *fons et principuum*, the fountain, beginning and cause of motion in us – yet the first mover was the brain or heart.

I was again urged to show my opinion, and hearing Sir Walter tell of his dispute and scholarship some time in Oxford, I cited the general definition of *anima* out of Aristotle 2 *de Anima* cap. 1, and thence *a subiecto proprio* deduced the special definition of the soul reasonable, that it was *actus primus corporis organici animantis humani vitam habentis in potentia* [the initial driving force of the organic matter of a human being having potential life].

It was misliked of Sir Walter as obscure and intricate. And I withal yielded that though it could not unto him, as being learned, yet it might seem obscure to the most present, and therefore had rather say with divines plainly that the reasonable soul is a spiritual and immortal substance breathed into man by God, whereby he lives and moves and understandeth, and so is distinguished from other creatures.

'Yes, but what is that spiritual and immortal substance breathed into man, etc.?' saith Sir Walter.

'The soul,' quoth I.

'Nay, then,' saith he, 'you answer not like a scholar.'

Hereupon I endeavoured to prove that it was scholarship, nay in such disputes as these, usual and necessary to run *in circulum* . . .

'But we have principles in our mathematics,' saith Sir Walter, 'as *totum est minus quamlibet sua parte*, and ask me of it, and I can show in the table, in the window, in a man, the whole being bigger than the parts of it.'

I replied first that he showed *quod est*, not *quid est*, that it was but not what it was; secondly, that such demonstrations as that were against the nature of a man's soul, being a spirit, for as things being sensible were subject to the sense, so man's soul being insensible was to be discerned by the spirit. Nothing more certain in the world than that there is a God, yet being a spirit, to subject him to the sense otherwise than perfected it is impossible.

'Marry,' quoth Sir Walter, 'these two be alike, for neither could I learn hitherto what God is,' Mr Fitzjames answering that Aristotle should say he was *ens, encium*.

I answered, that . . . God was *ens entium*, a thing of things, having being of himself, and giving being to all creatures, it was most certain, and confirmed by God himself unto Moses.

'Yea, but what is this *ens entium*?' saith Sir Walter.

I answered, 'It is God.'

And being disliked as before, Sir Walter wished that grace might be said.

'For that,' quoth he, 'is better than this disputation.'

The Rev. Ironside noted down the conversation because he feared that Raleigh was giving the lie to the Soul. If the conversation had turned differently Raleigh would have taken the part of the Soul and given the lie to the supper table.

Raleigh, 'The Lie':

> Go, Soul, the body's guest,
> Upon a thankless errand;
> Fear not to touch the best:
> The truth shall be thy warrant;
> Go, since I needs must die,
> And give the world the lie.

Say to the Court it glows
And shines like rotten wood;
Say to the Church it shows
What's good and doth no good.
If Church and Court reply,
Then give them both the lie . . .

Tell zeal it wants devotion;
Tell love it is but lust;
Tell time it is but motion;
Tell flesh it is but dust.
And wish them not reply,
For thou must give the lie . . .

Tell wit how much it wrangles
In tickle points of niceness;
Tell wisdom she entangles
Herself in over-wiseness.
And when they do reply,
Straight give them both the lie.

Tell physic of her boldness;
Tell skill it is pretension;
Tell charity of coldness;
Tell law it is contention.
And as they do reply,
So give them still the lie.

Tell arts they have no soundness,
But vary by esteeming;
Tell schools they want profoundness,
And stand too much on seeming.
If arts and schools reply,
Give arts and schools the lie.

Tell faith it's fled the city;
Tell how the country erreth;
Tell manhood shakes off pity;
Tell virtues least preferred.
And if they do reply,
Spare not to give the lie.

So when thou hast, as I
Commandeth thee, done blabbing –
Although to give the lie
Deserves no less than stabbing –
Stab at thee he that will,
No stab the Soul can kill.

5

Bess had been pregnant since early in 1593. They were living mostly at Sherborne Castle, but Raleigh was at Durham House to deal with a Stannary case and to get, after some months' delay, a permit to sell his Irish pipe-staves in England. In London plague was so bad the City decided to build a pest-house with any profit beyond 100 per cent which they made out of the *Madre de Dios*.

At Sherborne Raleigh had been repairing and trying to make comfortable his powerful and complete Norman castle. It had four huge three-storeyed towers. The 'great lodging', which was in the middle of the court, was 'very strong and full of vaults'. There were drawbridges and a moat. In London too he had elected to live in a Norman castle, and in Ireland he had spent money on his near-Norman castle at Lismore. But this summer, within a year of taking Bess to Sherborne, he abandoned work on the Castle and began to build for her a more convenient modern house in the grounds. He compensated himself by giving it a great many hexagonal towers.

It was a mild and fertile spot, facing south over the river, a little to the east of stone-built Sherborne, not far from where the main road from London to Plymouth crossed the road from Weymouth and Portland to Bath. It was twenty miles to Portland Castle, of which he was Captain, and forty to Bath where he had just taken the waters: 'I am worse for the Bath, not the better.' He had complained the previous year of his 'lame legs and lamer lungs'.

The threat of invasion brought him duties, but he may have dealt with them without leaving Dorset: a hundred men had to be ready in Cornwall to be rushed to the Scillies if the Scilly beacons were seen, and men had to be ready for Portland, which he reported was without cannon.

Meanwhile he continued his siege of Elizabeth with a new, long and last outpouring of *The Ocean's Love to Cynthia*. In 138 stanzas of memory and complaint he reminded Elizabeth that he had sucked love of her with his mother's milk; that for twelve years he had devoted himself lovingly to her service; that she had been for him 'heaven on earth transparent'. Now she had made him 'th' example in love's story'.

Raleigh, '*The Ocean's Love to Cynthia*':
> But as a body violently slain
> Retaineth warmth although the sprite be gone,
> And by a power in nature moves again
> Till it be laid below the fatal stone;
>
> Or as the earth, even in cold winter days,
> Left for a time by her life-giving sun,
> Doth by the power remaining of his rays
> Produce some green, though not as it hath done;
>
> Or as a wheel, forced by the falling stream,
> Although the course be turned some other way,
> Doth for a time go round upon the beam,
> Till, wanting strength to move, it stands at stay:
>
> So my forsaken heart, my withered mind,
> Widow of all the joys it once possessed,
> My hopes clean out of sight with forced wind,
> To kingdoms strange, to lands far-off addressed,

Alone, forsaken, friendless on the shore,
With many wounds, with death's cold pangs embraced,
Writes in the dust, as one that could no more,
Whom love, and time, and fortune, had defaced;

Of things so great, so long, so manifold,
With means so weak, the soul even then depicting
The weal, the woe, the passages of old,
And worlds of thoughts described by one last sighing;

As if, when after Phoebus is descended,
And leaves a light much like the last day's dawning,
And, every toil and labour wholly ended,
Each living creature draweth to his resting,

We should begin by such a parting light
To write the story of all ages past,
And end the same before the approaching night.

He had already meditated, then, a history of the world.

6

But his most urgent interest was Guiana.

He was intent on wresting some of the New World for England.
North America he had tried to colonise; Central America he had
planned in 1592 to raid in force, as Drake and Hawkins shortly
would; South America was occupied by the Spaniards in the north-
west, but not in Guiana. Guiana became his passion.

It had fabulous possibilities. There was a persistent Indian story of
a king who, after his body had been smeared with an oily substance,
rolled in gold-dust and then bathed in a lake among the mountains.
It was believed that this Golden Man, 'El Dorado', was the Inca
himself who with some of his people had fled eastward from Peru and
had founded across the Andes a new empire at least as rich as the old.

Twenty Spanish expeditions had tried to find El Dorado. They burned Indians and tore them to pieces with dogs to get information; or used them as porters, with chain from neck-ring to neck-ring, and cut off the heads of the exhausted to save fiddling with the chain. With incomparable endurance they crossed the Andes and explored the vast western watersheds of the Orinoco and the Amazon, and the main rivers themselves.

All the Indian information seemed now to point to an area which was unexplored, Guiana. It is a mountainous slab of territory which has the Orinoco flowing three or four hundred miles along its western side and five hundred miles along its northern. Today it is largely in Venezuela.

In the last ten years three expeditions had been made by an aged Spanish soldier, Antonio Berrio, who thought he had narrowed the site down to the upper reaches of the River Caroni, a tributary which enters the Orinoco from the south. He had made his head-quarters on the island of Trinidad, at the mouth of the Orinoco.

Raleigh, who wanted to know at least how far the Caroni was from the sea, sent off Captain Whiddon to reconnoitre. He was determined to go himself with a larger expedition, in which both Cecil and Lord Admiral Howard were prepared to invest, before Spain added El Dorado to her empire.

But there were distractions. At Court there were to be some new Privy Councillors, and he would have liked to be one of them in spite of opposition by the Essex faction. And Bess (with a four-month-old baby, 'Wat') did not want him to go to Guiana: behind his back she asked Cecil not to help him.[1] And he was finding the Bishop of Salisbury difficult about leasing him another manor or two he wanted at Sherborne; the bishop was bothered about his late payment of rent and the reports of his atheism. There was even a commission to investigate atheism in the Sherborne neighbourhood, at which the Rev. Ralph Ironside submitted his report of the supper-table conversation of the previous year. The Vicar of Blandford told how, three years before, the Raleigh brothers had taken his horse, which he needed in order to get to Blandford to preach next day, and Carew Raleigh had told him the horse would be there first and could preach instead.[2]

A more refreshing distraction was the capture of a Jesuit at a house nearby, 'an Irishman and a notable stout villain, and I think can say much'. Raleigh visited him in prison and, like his mother visiting Alice Prest, found himself moved. However, at the execution he thought that Father Cornelius abused the customary right to make his peace with the world, the Jesuit's behaviour and speech coming close to propaganda; so he stopped him several times from speaking, and Father Cornelius was thrown off the ladder without finishing his prayer for the conversion of the Queen.[1]

By midsummer his Guiana plans were at a standstill. Instead he was involved in defence against the Spaniards, who had fortified Brest, preliminary, it was assumed, to invasion. He served a few weeks under Howard watching for them in the Channel, unable to sleep at night with the tossing, and worried about plague, which had left London and was now everywhere else, including Sherborne: 'My Bess is on one way sent; her son, another way; and I am in great trouble therewith.'

And then one of his ships captured Spanish dispatches from South America. Berrio had sent a fourth expedition, which had gone up the tributary Caroni to within a league of the edge of El Dorado, and the dispatches indicated the route.

Whiddon came back. Some of his men had been killed by Berrio, but he had brought back an Indian who could be trained as an interpreter, and he thought the Caroni was quite near the mouth of the Orinoco.

In December Raleigh received his commission from Elizabeth, on much the same lines as his patent for Virginia, except that he was authorised to 'offend the King of Spain'. And he was addressed, not as 'our trusty and well-beloved servant', but as 'our servant'.

At the end of January 1595, he was in Devon, with Hariot who would be in charge of his affairs in his absence, and Keymis who was to come as one of his captains, and Sanderson, his financial agent. Bess came down to see him off and to check, no doubt, on his cabin with its handsome bed (green silk hangings, and gilded legs carved like dolphins) and its trunk of books. He embarked, after a row with Sanderson, at midnight on 5 February.[2]

I am in hope, ere it be long, to hear from him, though not for long
time to see him. In which time I shall fly to you in all my cumbers, as
to the surest staff I trust to in Sir Walter's absence.

Within another two days there was news. He had come, about
three weeks before, on six Portuguese ships laden with fish; he had
taken a little fish and some wine and water from each, and let them
go. One had since been taken as a prize by someone else and sent into
Plymouth; its coxswain said Raleigh had been 'merry and in good
health', and he and his ships had made off SSW.

7

By the time Bess had this news Raleigh was approaching Trinidad.
He explored and mapped the coast, noting the lake of asphalt and
the oyster-trees. Two Indians came out in a canoe, one of whom
had worked for Whiddon the previous year. Soon others came, and
were given presents and told about '*Ezrabeta cassipuna aquerewena*',
Elizabeth the great princess. Two were afterwards hanged and quartered by the Spaniards.

Soon Spaniards sent by Berrio to find what the English were
about were drinking Raleigh's wine and giving him information.
When he had exhausted their usefulness he killed them and any
others he could catch, in order to leave as few enemies behind him as
possible when he went inland, and to avenge Whiddon's men.

He captured Berrio, seventy-five years of age, 'very valiant and
liberal . . . and of a great heart', and treated him hospitably. He told
him he was on his way to Virginia, and had called at Trinidad only
for victuals and refreshment. During two or three weeks he drew
him out about the country and its tribes, and was shown the report of
a Spaniard who had actually visited Manoa, the capital city of El
Dorado; it had taken him a day and a half to walk from the entrance
of the city to the Inca's palace.

When he told Berrio that he intended to find El Dorado and
Manoa himself, the old man was 'stricken into a great melancholy
and sadness'.

Raleigh had been waiting at Trinidad for Sir Amyas Preston, but Preston with whom he had quarrelled over a prize some years before, still had not arrived. Without waiting any longer he left Berrio prisoner and set out to find a way through the Orinoco delta. He had sixty men in a galley, which he had made from the smallest of his ships; thirty in the ships' boats and a wherry; and ten in his barge. All the larger ships would have stuck on the bar. After a day or two in the delta they were lost, in spite of an Indian pilot.

Raleigh, 'The Discovery of Guiana':
And if God had not sent us another help, we might have wandered a whole year in that labyrinth of rivers, ere we had found any way, either out or in, especially after we were past the ebbing and flowing, which was in four days, for I know that all the earth doth not yield the like confluence of streams and branches the one crossing the other so many times, and all so fair and large, and so like one to another as no man can tell which to take. And if we went by the sun or compass hoping thereby to go directly one way or other, yet that way we were also carried in a circle amongst multitudes of islands, and every island so bordered with high trees, as no man could see any further than the breadth of the river, or length of the breach.

They captured an old Indian from a tribe which lived in trees; he knew the streams well, but the galley went aground. Then the gentlemen had to take turns with the men at rowing because of the violent current. They were all exhausted by the heat. They drank the thick river water, shot birds and collected fruit, but they were down to their last ration of bread. The old man found them relief at last, after a row up a side-stream which took thirteen hours instead of his promised three.

Then they lost a negro who went swimming and was eaten by a crocodile. Just as they were again at their last gasp they captured two canoes loaded with cassava bread.

Only once did they see some Spaniards, in a canoe. They lost them but caught their Indian pilot, who told Raleigh of places where the Spaniards got gold.

Announcing himself the enemy of the Spaniards and not eating the various Indians he seized in his journey up-river, as they had been told by the Spaniards to expect, he was brought food and drink wherever he went and provided continually with fresh pilots. He visited the chiefs in their villages and caroused with them until some of his captains were 'reasonable pleasant'. He was meticulous in giving presents. He saw that the Indians were not robbed, 'a very impatient work', and that the young women were not molested – which was much easier, although they were attractive and came among them 'without deceit and stark naked', one of them sophisticated and very like a society woman he knew in England. The Indians told him the antidotes for their arrow-poisons, which he was sure they had never told a Spaniard.

At last they reached the town of Morequito, and sent a pilot for the old chief, Topiawari. The Spaniards had recently led Topiawari around in chains for seventeen days until he ransomed himself with a hundred plates of gold; and they had killed his predecessor.

Raleigh, 'The Discovery of Guiana':
The next day following, before noon he came to us on foot from his house, which was fourteen English miles (himself being 110 years old), and returned on foot the same day, and with him many of the borderers, with many women and children, that came to wonder at our nation, and to bring us down victual . . .

After this old king had rested a while in a little tent that I caused to be set up, I began by my interpreter to discourse with him of the death of his predecessor, and afterwards of the Spaniards, and ere I went any farther I made him know the cause of my coming thither, whose servant I was, and that the Queen's pleasure was, I should undertake the voyage for their defence, and to deliver them from the tyranny of the Spaniards, dilating at large (as I had done before to those of Trinidad) her Majesty's greatness, her justice, her charity to all oppressed nations, with as many of the rest of her beauties and virtues, as I either could express, or they conceive.

All which being with great admiration attentively heard, and marvellously admired, I began to sound the old man as touching Guiana, and the state thereof . . .

He told me that himself and his people with all those down the river towards the sea, as far as Emeria . . . were of Guiana, but that they called themselves Orinocoponi, because they bordered the great river of Orinoco, and that all the nations between the river and those mountains in sight called Wacarima, were of the same cast and appellation; and that on the other side of those mountains of Wacarima there was a large plain . . . called the valley of Amariocapana, in all that valley the people were also of the ancient Guianians.

I asked what nations those were which inhabited on the further side of those mountains, beyond the valley of Amariocapana.

He answered with a great sigh . . . that he remembered in his father's lifetime when he was very old, and himself a young man, that there came down into that large valley of Guiana, a nation from so far off as the sun slept (for such were his own words), with so great a multitude as they could not be numbered nor resisted, and that they wore large coats, and hats of crimson colour, which colour he expressed by showing a piece of red wood wherewith my tent was supported, and that they were called Oreiones and Epuremei, those that had slain and rooted out so many of the ancient people as there were leaves in the wood upon all the trees, and had now made themselves lords of all . . .

And farther told me that those Epuremei had built a great town called Macureguarai, at the said mountain foot, at the beginning of the great plains of Guiana, which have no end; and that their houses have many rooms, one over the other, and that therein the great king of the Oreiones and Epuremei kept three thousand men to defend the borders against them, and withal daily to invade and slay them, but that of late years since the Christians offered to invade his territories, and those frontiers, they were all at peace, and traded one with another . . . each one holding the Spaniard for a common enemy.

After he had answered thus far, he desired leave to depart, saying that he had far to go, that he was old and weak, and was every day called for by death, which was also his own phrase. I desired him to rest with us that night, but I could not entreat him.

[131]

8

Next morning they started to row up to where the Orinoco was joined by the Caroni. They could hear in the distance the great roar of the Caroni falls but the journey took them two days.

The Caroni had risen four or five feet and it was impossible to row up towards El Dorado. He therefore sent a party to look for a silver mine said to be near the river, while he with a few others marched overland to see the falls.

Raleigh, 'The Discovery of Guiana':

When we ran to the tops of the first hills of the plains adjoining to the river, we beheld that wonderful breach of waters which ran down Caroni, and might from that mountain see the river how it ran in three parts, above twenty miles off, and there appeared some ten or twelve overfalls in sight, every one as high over the other as a church tower, which fell with that fury, that the rebound of waters made it seem, as if it had been all covered over with a shower of rain, and in some places we took it at the first for a smoke that had risen over some great town.

For mine own part I was well persuaded from thence to have returned, being a very ill footman, but the rest were all so desirous to go near the said strange thunder of waters as they drew me on little by little, till we came into the next valley, where we might better discern the same.

I never saw a more beautiful country, nor more lively prospects, hills so raised here and there over the valleys, the river winding into divers branches, the plains adjoining without bush or stubble, all fair green grass, the ground of hard sand easy to march on, either for horse or foot, the deer crossing in every path, the birds towards the evening singing on every tree with a thousand different tunes, cranes and herons of white, crimson and carnation perching on the river's side, the air fresh with a gentle easterly wind, and every stone that we stooped to take up promised either gold or silver by his complexion.

They had nothing but their daggers to chip out bits of the rock here and there, and it was hard as flint. The men carried away stones they picked up, convinced that the glittering was gold; and Whiddon and the surgeon brought Raleigh some stones like sapphires.

The rains were coming down now in terrible gusts – 'the shirts were washed on our backs ten times in a day' – and the river raged and overflowed. They had been a month away from their ships, and Berrio, he knew, was expecting reinforcements from elsewhere in South America and also from Spain; it was time to return.

At Morequito he sent off again to Topiawari, this time to discuss practical action.

Raleigh, 'The Discovery of Guiana':
After he had rested a while in my tent, I shut out all but ourselves and my interpreter, and told him that I knew that both the Epuremei and the Spaniards were enemies to him, his country and nation . . . and therefore I desired him to instruct me what he could, both of the passage into the golden parts of Guiana and to the civil towns and apparelled people of Inca.

He gave me an answer to this effect. First, that he did not perceive that I meant to go onwards towards the city of Manoa, for neither the time of the year served, neither could he perceive any sufficient numbers for such an enterprise . . .

He told me farther that four days journey from his town was Macureguarai, and that those were the next and nearest subjects of Inca and of the Epuremei, and the first town of apparelled and rich people, and that all those plates of gold which were scattered among the borderers and carried to other nations far and near, came from the said Macureguarai and were there made, but that those of the land within were far finer, and were fashioned after the image of men, beasts, birds and fishes.

I asked him whether he thought that those companies that I had there with me were sufficient to take that town or no; he told me that he thought they were.

I then asked him whether he would assist me with guides, and some companies of his people to join with us; he answered that he would go himself with all the borderers, if the rivers did remain fordable, upon this condition: that I would leave with him till my return again fifty soldiers, which he undertook to victual . . .

When I had given him reason that I could not at this time leave him such a company, he then . . . prayed us to defer it till the next year, when he would undertake to draw in all the borderers to serve us.

Topiawari gave him one of his sons to take to England and Raleigh left with him Francis Sparrow, a twenty-five-year-old servant of one of his captains, to draw what maps he could of the area, and to take some trading goods into Guiana to spy the land; and also Hugh Godwin, a fifteen-year-old boy of his own, to learn the language.

The return journey was made in thunder and heavy rain. As they went down-river in their small boats, with their hearts cold, he said, at the rage and increase of Orinoco, they explored the south bank, stopped to look at a mine and a mountain of crystal, although Raleigh was unable to walk all the way to either; and called on a chief who had promised to guide them. They found the chief's village all drunk as beggars 'and the pots walking from one to another without rest'.

They had a feast of armadillo meat, and with speed and absence of labour bounced down the river.

At the sea they had to pass through several miles of storm and shoal, but 'being all very sober and melancholy, one faintly cheering another to show courage', they put themselves to God's keeping and finally reached the ships.

9

Reaching the ships he was back in the civilised world of book-keeping. He had handed out in gold coins bearing the sacred head of Elizabeth more gold than he had received. In order to cover the cost of the expedition he decided to attack some of the Spanish coastal towns west of Trinidad. At the first two he got little, at the third a drubbing. He lost, according to the Spaniards, seventy-five men.

On the credit side, he could map the way to El Dorado, or most of it, and as well to mines in the borderlands; he had made friends

5. *a*) Raleigh and his son
Wat, 1602, by an
unknown artist

5. *b*) Elizabeth Raleigh, a
little later, attributed
to Marc Ghaeraedts
the Younger

6. *a*) Queen Elizabeth, painted on chicken skin

6. *b*) Sir Robert Cecil, 1602, by an unknown artist

6. *c*) James I by Marc Ghaeraedts the Younger

6. *d*) Prince Henry by an unknown artist

with the borderland Indians and could count on their future help; he had four casks of what he hoped was gold ore, as well as the men's private pieces of stone; and apart from the fighting, he had lost only one man, the negro, and none by sickness.

On arrival in England he put forward his plan. The Queen should send out a few hundred men, build one or two forts, and accept the sovereignty which the chiefs bordering Guiana were ready to accord her. In addition, the Emperor of Guiana itself, the Inca, would pay her, he was sure, a tribute of a hundred thousand pounds a year to defend him against the Spaniards. With English help the Spaniards could be driven out and the old Indian prophecy fulfilled, that the 'Inga' would be restored to his throne west of the Andes by people from 'Inga-land'.

Raleigh, 'The Discovery of Guiana':
The West Indies were first offered her Majesty's grandfather by Columbus, a stranger, in whom there might be doubt of deceit, and besides it was then thought incredible that there were such and so many islands and regions never written of before. This Empire is made known to her Majesty by her own vassal, and by him that oweth to her more duty than an ordinary subject . . .

Guiana is a country that hath yet her maidenhead, never sacked, turned, nor wrought, the face of the earth hath not been torn, nor the virtue and salt of the soil spent by manurance, the graves not been opened for gold, the mines not broken with sledges, nor their images pulled down out of their temples . . . The common soldier shall here fight for gold, and pay himself instead of pence, with plates of half a foot broad, whereas he breaketh his bones in other wars for provant and penury. Those commanders and chieftains, that shoot at honour, and abundance, shall find here more rich and beautiful cities, more temples adorned with golden images, more sepulchres filled with treasure, than either Cortez found in Mexico, or Pizarro in Peru.

In London he put Hariot to work on a map, to be shown the Queen, and himself went down to Sherborne to finish 'The Discovery of the Large, **Rich** and Beautiful Empire of Guiana, with a

Relation of the great and Golden City of Manoa (which the Spaniards call El Dorado)'.

Raleigh to Cecil, from Sherborne, 13 November 1595:[1]
You may perceive by this Relation that it is no dream which I have reported of Guiana . . . You find that there are, besides gold, both diamonds and pearl . . . and there is enough for all the world if we have the grace. But we must cast so many doubts; and this dolt and that gull must be satisfied, or else all is nothing. If the Spaniards had been so blockish and slothful, we had not feared now their power.

He was back in the world of scepticism as well as book-keeping. The glittering stones were tested by a London alderman and an official of the Mint and declared to be marcasite. The public which had once been caught by Frobisher and his black stone said that the little gold Raleigh had brought back was bought probably in the Barbary States. Perhaps he had never crossed the seas at all, but hidden himself in Cornwall.

His tall stories were laughed at – oyster-bearing trees, tree-living men, Amazons (he had inquired into their military and coupling habits, and thought they would have an altogether special feeling for a Virgin Queen), and Ewaipanoma, the men with 'their eyes in their shoulders, and their mouths in the middle of their breasts' (he had been told of them by Topiawari's son).

He did what he could to counter the slanders, not only for practical reasons but because he had himself been deeply moved by his experiences: 'Sir Walter Raleigh . . . goes daily to hear sermons, because he hath seen the wonders of the Lord in the deep. 'Tis much commended and spoken of.'[2]

He emphasised that he had himself seen neither an Amazon nor an Ewaipanoma: he was reporting what he had been told. He protested: 'There are stranger things to be seen in the world than are between London and Staines.'[3] And he was right about both the oyster-trees (in Trinidad, oysters cling to mangroves and when the water is low can be gathered like fruit) and the tree-living men (some of the delta Indians move their nests up and down as the Orinoco rises and falls). He said that, of course, those stones the alderman tested were marcasite: he had told the men so himself. But his own ore, assayed by Westwood, and Bulmar, and Dimoke of Goldsmiths' Hall, and Palmer, the Comptroller of the Mint, gave a very high proportion of gold.

But no one's opinion mattered if he could convince the Queen. Without ever being able to speak to her in person he had to make her see herself as Empress of Guiana. A poet he patronised, George Chapman, whose Homer was to give Keats a vision of a new kingdom, tried to inspire her: 'Go forth upon the waters and create A golden world in this our iron age'.[1] And she could create it, Raleigh submitted in a new treatise he caused to be written, quite cheaply.[2]

She should send – instead of soldiers – technicians and military advisers so that the Incas and the borderers, in alliance, could build a modern army capable of doing all the fighting for themselves. Potential rulers among the tribes should be brought to England, educated, trained, married to English women, and then sent back to senior positions in the great new Indian state, which would practise Christianity, be skilled in all the arts of England, and owe allegiance to Elizabeth. Elizabeth would receive tribute, as was just, England would make an honest profit from Indian trade, and there would be no reliance on loot.

Because an advanced country should not conquer a backward; it should be its partner in development. Christian nations had no right to invade primitive peoples simply because they were not Christians, not even if they maltreated Christian missionaries and traders. This view might be wrong, but there was authority for it in the Bible, and the treatise cited many texts. In fact it spoke as if the Bible, not Elizabeth, were now 'heaven on earth transparent'.

His proposals were not approved.

10

It was an unfortunate time to put forward an imperial project. While he had been away, four Spanish galleys with a hundred men in each had rowed across from Brittany to Cornwall, burned Mousehole and

Penzance, and celebrated on English soil, at leisure, a thanksgiving Mass. They successfully made the invasion danger seem real and urgent. So while he let no one forget Guiana, and sent out Keymis to make sure Guiana did not forget him, he shared the general pre-occupation.

Newsletter, Rowland White to Sir Robert Sidney, 4 March 1596:[1]
Sir Walter Raleigh hath been very often very private with the Earl of Essex and is the mediator of a peace between him and Sir Robert Cecil, who likewise hath been private with him. Sir Walter alleges how much good may grow by it. The Queen's continual unquietness will turn to contentments. Dispatches for all matters of war and peace for the safety of the land will go forward to the hurt of the common enemies.

The common enemies had assembled biscuit in their ports for 10,000 men, which meant a greater armada than in '88. In reply, England mustered the men in the coastal counties, and for the first time – centralised government having come of age – the muster returns were made on printed forms.

Raleigh said the Spaniards should be attacked. There were always dangers in being on the defensive.

Raleigh, Spanish Alarum:
First, all winds that bring the Spanish fleet out of Spain, if they have any part of the south, keep all ships upon the coast of England within harbour . . .

Secondly, it is very probable that the enemy will first make offer where he hath no intent to take land . . . hereby causing us to march from one county to another . . .

Thirdly, it is very unlikely that any prince of judgment or counsel will offer invasion where there is neither assurance nor hope of party. Now if there be any already disposed to alteration and rebellion it will be found most dangerous to suffer expected succours to come within sight . . .

Fourthly, it is to be considered that those who are to bear the greatest burden of the war, are not such as have received the greatest profit of peace . . . There will not want in those times enough of such as will persuade in this manner, 'Let the rich fight for themselves' . . . Such will be the encouragement to despoil in these hopeless people that murder, robbery, rapine and all other dangerous insolency will be . . . universal . . .

Fifthly, the home defence and war abroad have great difference, the invader putting confidence in his own valour, having no retreat, the other that knoweth by flight how to escape death . . . It is also great advantage that the invader hath in this, that the one hath hope by victory to command countries, to spoil towns, to enjoy other men's wives and daughters, when as the most part of those that defend must either die for 8*d* wages or if he live with many wounds, perchance beg all his life after . . .

Sixthly, there can be no greater dishonour to a prince and kingdom than to be invaded. It holdeth the neighbour princes and allies in neutrality, because it resteth in the chance of a battle whether we shall retain freedom or be brought to vassalage . . . It impoverisheth the Estate in general by the conveyance of treasure out of the land, whereof the greatest part being in the hands of foreigners the very bruit hath already blown away great abundance.

In any case, he said, experience showed that it was only a lucky chance when a fleet gave warning of the enemy's approach, as in '88, and that an army could rarely prevent a landing.

It was agreed to attack. A grand expedition, augmented by ships from the Netherlands, would destroy the armada before it left Spain and, to pay expenses, would afterwards capture the West Indian treasure fleet or the East Indian carracks.

In March Raleigh was hustling up and down the Thames with Lord Admiral Howard getting ready the ships, while Essex at Plymouth got ready the army. His new relationship with Essex suffered by the suspicions of distance.

Essex to Cecil, from Plymouth, 28 April 1596:[1]
I beg that Sir Walter Raleigh may be hastened away.

Raleigh to Cecil, from the Thames, 4 May:[1]
The wind is so strong as it is impossible to turn down or to warp down, or to tow down.

I cannot write to our Generals at this time, for the poursuivant found me in a country village, a mile from Gravesend, hunting after runaway mariners, and dragging in the mire from ale-house to ale-house, and could get no paper, but that the poursuivant had this.

Essex to Cecil, from Plymouth, 12 May:[2]
Sir Walter Raleigh with the rest of our fleet is not come, and yet he hath had (if the winds be the same there that they are here) all the wished winds he could desire.

Raleigh to Cecil, from the Channel, 13 May:[3]
Some seven or eight sail of the Fleet, who being all like to perish on Wednesday, after midnight they were driven to let slip all their cables and anchors. I humbly beseech your Honour to cause letters to be written to the Mayor of Dover to send a boat of the town to save the said cables and anchors, having all buoys upon them.

Anthony Bacon to Francis Bacon, from Plymouth:[4]
Sir Walter Raleigh's slackness and stay by the way is not thought to be upon sloth, but upon pregnant design.

When he arrived at Plymouth (egregious Charles Chester[5] with him) he quarrelled, 'at table in drink', with Sir Francis Vere, Marshal of the Army, over precedence. It was settled by Raleigh having precedence at meetings on water, Vere on land, but not before Bess's brother, Arthur Throgmorton, 'a hot-headed youth', had 'desborded in such words as my Lords commanded him from the table' and dismissed him the army.[6]

The company settled down. Howard and Essex had a little trouble over their relative importances, Howard snipping Essex's over-prominent name out of a joint-letter; but Raleigh behaved with correctness.

Anthony Standen to Anthony Bacon, 30 May:[1]
Sir Walter Raleigh's carriage to my Lord of Essex is with the cunningest respect and deepest humility that ever I saw or have trowed.

I I

Raleigh commanded a squadron, as did Essex, Howard, and Lord Thomas Howard. The four of them composed the Council of War.

The prime object had become changed to an attack on the city of Cadiz, although Elizabeth had categorically forbidden it: every soldier would get loot, she would get nothing.

Outside Cadiz, Raleigh in the *Warspite* was dispatched with his squadron to prevent ships from escaping along the coast. When he rejoined the fleet next morning he found that on the Lord Admiral's urging it had been decided not to risk the Queen's ships in an attack on the Spanish fleet in the harbour. Instead Essex was putting his men into boats for a landing, although the sea was too rough and they were being drowned. Immediately, with the consent of Essex, Raleigh went off to the *Ark* in his skiff to persuade Howard that the landing should be cancelled and they should enter the harbour with their ships. He came back and shouted up to Essex: '*Intramus!* [In we go!]' and Essex flung his hat into the sea with joy.

By the time the men were re-embarked and the anchors weighed it was near dusk and Raleigh recommended that the attack should be made next morning. It was to be led by Lord Thomas Howard in the *Nonparilla*, but Raleigh was out of bed earlier.

Raleigh, 'A relation of Cadiz action':
Having taken the leading, I was first saluted by the fort called Philip, afterward by the ordnance of the curtain, and lastly by all the galleys in good order. To show scorn to all which, I only answered first the fort and afterward the galleys, to each piece a blur with a trumpet; disdaining to shoot one piece at any one or all of those esteemed dreadful monsters.

The ships that followed beat upon the galleys so thick that they soon betook them to their oars, and got up to join with the galleons in the strait, as aforesaid: and then, as they were driven to come near me, and enforced to range their sides towards me, I bestowed a benediction amongst them.

But *St Philip*, the great and famous admiral of Spain, was the mark I shot at; esteeming those galleys but as wasps in respect of the powerfulness of the other; and being resolved to be revenged for the *Revenge*, or to second her with mine own life, I came to anchor by the galleons; of which the *Philip* and *Andrew* were two that boarded the *Revenge* . . .

. . . Now after we had beaten, as two butts, one upon another almost three hours (assuring your Honour that the volleys of cannon and culverin came as thick as if it had been a skirmish of musketeers) and finding myself in danger to be sunk in the place, I went to my Lord General [Essex] in my skiff, to desire him that he would enforce the promised fly-boats to come up, that I might board; for as I rid, I could not endure so great a battery any long time.

My Lord General was then coming up himself; to whom I declared that if the fly-boats came not, I would board with the Queen's ships; for it was the same loss to burn or sink, for I must endure the one. The Earl finding that it was not in his power to command fear, told me that whatsoever I did, he would second me in person upon his honour. My Lord Admiral, having also a disposition to come up at first, but the river was so choked as he could not pass with the *Ark*, came up in person into the *Nonparilla*, with my Lord Thomas.

While I was thus speaking with the Earl, the Marshal [Vere], who thought it some touch to his great esteemed valour, to ride behind me so many hours, got up ahead my ship; which my Lord Thomas perceiving, headed him again, myself being but a quarter of an hour absent. At my return, finding myself from being the first to be but the third, I presently let slip anchor, and thrust in between my Lord Thomas and the Marshal, and went further ahead than all them before, and thrust myself athwart the channel, so as I was sure none should outstart me again that day.

My Lord General Essex, thinking his ship's sides stronger than the rest, thrust the *Dreadnought* aside, and came next the *Warspite* on the left hand, ahead of all that rank but my Lord Thomas. The Marshal, while we had no leisure to look behind us, secretly fastened a rope to my ship's side towards him, to draw himself up equally with me; but some of my company advertising me thereof, I caused it to be cut off, and so he fell back into his place; whom I guarded, all but his prow, from the sight of the enemy.

Now if it please you to remember, that having no hope of my fly-boats to board, and that the Earl and my Lord Thomas both promised to second me, I laid out a warp by the side of the *Philip* to shake hands with her (for with the wind we could not get aboard), which when she and the rest perceived, finding also that the *Repulse* (seeing mine) began to do the like, and the Rear-Admiral my Lord Thomas, they all let slip and came aground, tumbling into the sea heaps of soldiers, so thick as if coals had been poured out of a sack in many ports at once, some drowned and some sticking in the mud.

The *Philip* and the *St Thomas* burned themselves; the *St Matthew* and the *St Andrew* were recovered by our boats ere they could get out to fire them.

The spectacle was very lamentable on their side; for many drowned themselves; many, half burnt, leaped into the water; very many hanging by the ropes' ends by the ships' sides, under the water even to the lips; many swimming with grievous wounds, strucken under water, and put out of their pain; and withal so huge a fire, and such tearing of the ordnance in the great *Philip*, and the rest, when the fire came to them, as, if any man had a desire to see hell itself, it was there most lively figured.

Raleigh, with a thigh wound, had himself carried ashore, to watch Cadiz taken with dash by the land forces under Essex and Vere (it was defended by few troops and half-broken walls) and to try to get a reasonable share of the loot; but he returned because his wound pained him, and there was in any case no one left in command of the ships, Howard having landed with a force of mariners to second Essex and bring him powder. The Generals had promised to look after Raleigh's interests.

He very soon sent off to the Generals for permission to secure a fleet of ships, fully laden for the West Indies and worth some millions of ducats, which were moored in the harbour and about which nothing had been done. But the Generals were busy sacking the town, and then, without taking possession of the ships first, entered protracted negotiations for their ransom. The Spaniards meanwhile unloaded what they could, and then burned the ships and the remaining cargoes.

The English, after a month in Cadiz, looting and holding people and houses to ransom (with a moderation in rape and bloodshed which astonished both the Spaniards and themselves) made their way home. Sixty-six gentlemen had been made knights, five 'other ranks' had been lost to the enemy: four Irishmen who wanted to join the Spanish army, and a Devonshire student thumbing his way to a Spanish university. Little was done about other Spanish shipping and nothing at all about the Indian fleets expected at the Azores; according to the Essex group this was the fault of Raleigh and Howard, according to Vere victuals were too short for anything but a direct return home.

A friend of Arthur Throgmorton's reached Court first and elaborated on the glorious deeds done by the sea forces, especially by Raleigh.[1] And a follower of Essex wrote to Burghley: 'Sir Walter Raleigh did (in my judgment) no man better, and his artillery most effect. I never knew the gentleman till this time; and I am sorry for it, for there are in him excellent things beside his valour.' [2] This was Anthony Standen, who at Plymouth had said that Raleigh behaved to Essex 'with the cunningest respect'.

Cadiz was generally regarded as a greater victory than that of 1588 which had been defensive and won largely by the wind. The Venetians said of Elizabeth: 'What a woman! if only she were a Christian!'

Recrimination about loot was internecine: the landsmen had too much, the seamen too little, the Queen none at all – 'much to her Majesty's misliking'. Raleigh got 'nought but poverty and pain', £1,500 or so, which barely covered expenses.

He found that Keymis had arrived back from Guiana, after noting the rivers south of the Orinoco (re-christened Raleiana) and having heard of a gold mine up the Raleiana twenty miles nearer than the Caroni. And he had news of young Sparrow, who had traded a half-penny knife for six women and then been captured by Spaniards; and of young Godwin said to have been eaten by a tiger. But he brought no gold.

Berrio, he said, was at the very mouth of the Caroni, but scarcely able to move from his fort for Indian hostility. Topiawari was dead. The Indians had expected not Keymis but Raleigh, and a force greater than a handful of men from a single ship.

Spain was sending out 10,000 settlers, men, women and children. All Raleigh could do was send Captain Berrie with a further ship, the *Wat* (little Wat was now two years old); he could get no official support.

However he was more at peace both with himself and the world. In condoling with Cecil on the death of his wife he used 'God' as something more than a figure of speech: 'The mind of man is that part of God which is in us, which, by how much it is subject to passion, by so much it is farther from him that gave it us. Sorrows draw not the dead to life, but the living to death.' [1]

His behaviour at Cadiz had greatly improved his relations with Essex, if not with the Essex faction, and also his general reputation. It even seemed that the Queen might regard his penance as at last, after five years, accomplished.

Newsletter, Whyte to Sidney, 2 June 1597:[2]
Yesterday my Lord of Essex rid to Chatham; in his absence Sir Walter Raleigh was brought to the Queen by Mr Secretary, who used him very graciously and gave him full authority to execute his place as Captain of the Guard, which immediately he undertook, and swore many men into the places void.

Aubrey:[3]
There came a country gentleman (or sufficient yeoman) up to town,

who had several sons, but one an extraordinarily proper handsome fellow, whom he did hope to have professed to be a Yeoman of the Guard. The father (a goodly man himself) comes to Sir Walter Raleigh, a stranger to him, and told him that he had brought up a boy that he would desire (having many children) should be one of her Majesty's Guard.

Quoth Sir Walter: 'Had you spake for yourself I should readily have granted your desire, for your person deserves it, but I put in no boys.'

Said the father: 'Boy, come in.'

The son enters, about eighteen or nineteen, but such a goodly proper young fellow as Sir Walter had not seen the like. He was the tallest of the Guard. Sir Walter swears him immediately; and ordered him to carry up the first dish at dinner, where the Queen beheld him with admiration, as if a beautiful young giant had stalked in with the service.

Newsletter, Whyte to Sidney, 2 June (continued):
In the evening [Sir Walter] rid abroad with the Queen and had private conference with her; and now he comes boldly to the Privy Chamber as he was wont.

13

The sack of Cadiz had stimulated, not discouraged, Philip. He was already preparing another armada. In reply, musters had been drilled in the coastal counties since the spring, and the returns – on printed forms – made in triplicate.

Raleigh was responsible as usual for the land forces of Cornwall and the Stannaries, and threw himself into preparations for another great preventive expedition. He had contracted to supply victuals for three months for six thousand men at 9*d* per man per day, and protested that he would be a loser by it but was not believed.

The Queen had objected to the expense of the expedition and said she believed in defence, not attack, but preparations went forward.

Raleigh's victualling was said to be well done, and he gave Essex as well as respect and careful obedience a rake-off.

He was to be third-in-command, Rear-Admiral, in the *Warspite*. Essex was in command, Lord Thomas Howard Vice-Admiral. Vere had a land command and at Essex's request shook hands with Raleigh, 'which we both did the willinger', wrote Vere, 'because there had nothing passed betwixt us that might blemish reputation'.

The first objective was to destroy the Spanish fleet on the Spanish coast without too much risk to the Queen's ships, or to chase it if it had already left for the shores of England or Ireland, and then go to the Azores, perhaps take an island as a base, and certainly to capture some treasure ships or carracks.

Essex and Raleigh rode to London for orders. With Cecil they appear to have seen *Richard II*,[1] and then returned to the west and at last set sail.

But appalling storms dispersed the fleet, and some of the gentlemen died of the tossing; a high proportion of the remainder decided to have no more of it. Back in port, Raleigh sent to Cecil glowing letters about Essex, and Essex received from Cecil little jokes about Raleigh: '. . . good Mr Raleigh, who wonders at his diligence, because diligence and he are not familiars'; 'The next [storm that] catches you at sea will not be appeased by praying till Jonah be thrown into the sea, which will be the captain of the *Warspite*.' The expedition was cut down in size and intention; the new plan was to make straight for the Azores.

Raleigh had Arthur Gorges as captain of his ship, and his master was John Davis who had looked three times for a north-west passage and had been his master at Cadiz. Another of his captains was Berrie, who had returned from Guiana in the *Wat*, having explored some of the rivers noted by Keymis and traded for tobacco. The 10,000 Spanish settlers had arrived at the Caroni with banners and best clothes, and despaired, fled and perished.

Essex was to go to Fayal, the most westerly of the Azores; Raleigh, according to Vere, was to go to another island but 'whether of set purpose or by mistake I leave others to judge' hurried to Fayal. He reached there the day after parting from Essex, and waited four days, and then, flouted by the island garrison, and his followers whispering of timidity, the forty-three-year-old family man, Rear-Admiral Raleigh, ordered a landing. He landed with only the mariners because Essex would regard the soldiers as his and might be touchy if they were mauled; and he made for the best defended point of the coast so that the watching soldiers should not think ill of his mariners.

Sir Arthur Gorges:[1]

As we made onwards with our boats, the shot played so thick upon us as that in truth the mariners would scarce come forwards, having the lesser liking to the business the nearer they came to it. And in like sort did I see some there stagger, and stand blank, that before made great shows, and would gladly be taken for valiant leaders; and some of these our Rear-Admiral did not spare to call upon openly, and rebuke aloud with disgraceful words, seeing their baseness.

And withal finding a general amazement amongst the mariners, and as it were a stay amongst all the boats . . . with a loud voice [he] commanded his watermen to row in full upon the rocks, and bade as many as were not afraid to follow him.

Once the landing had been made and the enemy troops had withdrawn to the town and one of the two forts, he invited the troops to join the mariners, and they made for this fort.

Gorges:

Our Rear-Admiral accompanied with divers other gentlemen of the best sort, to the number of forty, in the head of all the troops, with his leading staff, and no other armour than his collar (a bravery in a chief commander not to be commended) led on the company with soft march, full in face of the fort, descending down a little hill, whilst with their great ordnance and musketry we were very shrewdly pelted.

But he with this little vanguard was no sooner passed and entered under the covert of their trenches and barricadoes that were at the foot of this steep hill, but the main body of our little army, that a while marched in good order, began presently to break their ranks, and from marching fell to flat running in straggling manner . . . Our Rear-Admiral and we all cried out on them for this shameful disorder.

The next task was to send out scouts to explore ways up to the town, but it was exposed country and no one wanted to go.

Gorges:
Our Rear-Admiral seeing all men to make much scrupulosity of this business . . . thereunto answered that he would not offer that to any which he would himself refuse to undertake if need required . . . and therefore called for his corslet and casque, and said that he would both go and view the way for them, which they had made so nice of, and also the passages and ascents unto the hill-top, and as well as he could take view of the strength and fortifications thereof, for our better direction against the next morning that we should attempt it.

Captain Berrie thereupon very willingly offered himself to go, and did earnestly desire me to divert our Rear-Admiral from undertaking it . . . Notwithstanding he was obstinate therein, as well in scorn to them that had refused, as also indeed out of a desire to be the better informed of the strength and fortification of the high fort.

Wherein when I saw him resolved, I told him that I would out of love of a kinsman, in particular, and also out of an honest regard, take such part as he did . . . He thanked me for my offer, but yet wished me not to go if it were against my mind. Notwithstanding I accompanied him, and so did some eight or ten more of our servants and followers. But I say truly, and so afterwards it was much spoken of, that there was not any one more of quality that did accompany him in that business.

In this sort, and in this manner did he himself go to discover the passages, and also was careful and diligent to observe and search out the strength and ascents of the hill. In which doing, we were shrewdly troubled with the great artillery, which did beat upon the old walls alongst the which we were to pass, and therewithal much endangered and harmed us. For besides some that were hurt, two of our train had their heads stricken clean from their shoulders; myself was then shot through the left leg with a musket bullet, but missed the bone being but a flesh wound, but the bullet did burn both my silk stocking and buskin, as if it had been singed with an hot iron.

I was then hard by the Rear-Admiral, who also was shot through the breeches and doublet sleeves in two or three places.

[149]

And still they plied us so fast with small shot as that (I well remember) he wished me to put off a large red scarf which I then wore, being (as he said) a very fair mark for them.

But I was not willing to do the Spaniards so much honour at that time, albeit I could have wished it had not been on me, and therefore told the Rear-Admiral again that his white scarf was as eminent as my red, and therefore I now would follow his example.

Next day they took the town, and then Essex's ships came in. The Essex entourage immediately showed their disapproval.

Gorges:
And so had they inveighed the General against us all, as that all the forenoon was spent in reprehending and displacing all the land captains and officers that accompanied the Rear-Admiral in that action; who, being sent for to answer before the General aboard his ship, was before the messenger came for him gone in his barge to see the General and to guide him to the land, not so much as suspecting that anything had been ill taken in that matter, but rather looking for great thanks at the General his hands.

But so soon as he entered the General's ship he found all men's countenances estranged as he passed through them. And when he was entered into the General's cabin, after a faint welcome the General began to challenge him of breach of order and articles. To whom the Rear-Admiral answered that he knew not of any such breach.

My Lord replied that there was an article that none should land any of the troops without the General's presence or his order.

The Rear-Admiral desired the General to give him leave to defend himself by those laws which himself as well as others had desired, and his Lordship and the Council of War had authorised, and that then his Lordship should find that he had not committed any error at all.

There was talk of a court-martial and execution.

However, Raleigh was persuaded by Lord Thomas Howard, even if he was in the right, to admit error for the sake of peace, and Essex agreed to overlook the matter. He did not mention Raleigh's taking of Fayal in his dispatches.

[150]

The taking of Fayal was the only distinguished action of a muddled expedition, which was an economic loss and had left England without naval defence. When the fleet reached home an unopposed armada of a hundred Spanish ships was already off the Cornish coast. Raleigh hurried to his command of the Cornish land defences, and Essex put to sea again with the fleet; but once more it was the wind that beat the Spaniards.

Elizabeth wept with relief when a letter from Raleigh told her that Essex was safe, and was then furious at the latter's crass leadership and the danger to which he had exposed England. Perhaps to chasten Essex she had just made the Lord Admiral Earl of Nottingham and consequently precedent over him, but when Essex came to Court he fought her with indignation, threats, charm and by going sick.

Raleigh advised how to compose the trouble. Essex was made Earl-Marshal of England, and therefore precedent over the Lord Admiral.

Whereupon the Lord Admiral went sick.

And Raleigh retired to Sherborne for a month, and was ill himself.

14

The tone of life changed, Raleigh's own, England's, Europe's.

After three successive years of Guiana, Cadiz and the Azores, Raleigh went more quietly. He attended Court but had no conspicuously close relations with the Queen. He would have liked to be a Councillor but had still not become one in spite of Cecil's sworn support. He would have liked the vacant post of Vice-Chamberlain, but withdrew in favour of Essex's candidate, Sir Robert Sidney – from whom Elizabeth withheld it. He was unwilling to go to Ireland as Lord Deputy to deal with new disturbances. Although he planned for a dozen ships to go to Guiana (a map showing gold mines had reached him from Francis Sparrow, now in prison in Spain), Sir John Gilbert was to lead them. Neither Queen nor country was interested, being occupied with war and privateering, but the future

Charles IX of Sweden said he would provide a further dozen ships. However, the plan came to nothing.

The only progress he made – objectionable to neither Cecil nor Essex, costing the Queen nothing, and acquiesced in happily by a new Bishop-elect of Salisbury – was the acquisition of Sherborne as his absolute property.[1]

He was said to be discontented, but the only piece of Court foolishness in which he was involved[2] showed him a middle-aged obeyer of the sovereign's rules beside Essex's friend, Southampton.

Newsletter, Whyte to Sidney, 21 January 1598:[3]

[My Lord Southampton] with Sir Walter Raleigh and Mr Parker, being at primero in the Presence Chamber, the Queen was gone to bed; and [Ambrose Willoughby] being there as Squire for the Body desired them to give over.

Soon after, he spake to them again, that if they did not leave he would call in the Guard to pull down the board, which Sir Walter Raleigh seeing put up his money and went his ways.

But my Lord Southampton took exception at Willoughby, and told him he would remember it; and so finding him between the Tennis Court wall and the Garden struck him, and Willoughby pulled off some of his locks.

Abroad, the old national enemy, Philip II, with gout and stinking sores, died at seventy-two. Patriotic and religious and ambitious and over-administering to the last, he left Spain short of men, money, cattle, industry and merchant ships, and burdened with commitments three worlds wide.

The Low Countries, richer than when the fight began against their overlords, were now virtually a sovereign state and fought on. Their trading ships were everywhere.

In France Henry IV, with a mass, had brought unity and an end of civil war. He made his peace with Spain, and France began to rebuild its strength and prosperity.

In Ireland, the unarmoured dart-throwing kern who could be beaten at odds by the English were replaced now, in Tyrone's Ulster forces, by men well-armed and well-trained. In Munster the peasantry had wiped out, with much burning and de-gutting, the litigation-ridden English settlements, including Raleigh's and Spenser's.

On the sea, privateering and border-line piracy still flourished but were more and more thought to interfere with regular trade: when Sir John Gilbert took for Raleigh a Venetian prize worth £30,000, the Venetians seized in port eight English merchant ships. Besides, the Spaniards privateered as well as the English.

England was tired of subsidies for the war, of musters which cost more than the subsidies, of high rents which had risen in the prosperous years and never come down again, of high prices. The merchant and professional classes were still passionately loyal, but began to question arbitrariness of government: by what authority had money been demanded of the City for Cadiz, and when would it be paid back? The Queen had consented to forty-three Bills passed by the last Parliament, but what about the other forty-eight? By what authority were men who spoke up for the people – even those who requested, loyally, that she should nominate a successor – imprisoned without trial? And monopolies were still being granted; why? But Parliament continued to vote supplies before discussing grievances, and realised that England would have to fight until the Low Countries and Ireland were safe.

The old order was passing. Burghley, working and in pain almost to the last, was buried in the Abbey, leaving as the two most important men around the old Queen Essex and Cecil, both in their early thirties. Essex's followers were numerous and noisy; Cecil's were few, apart from the untrusted Raleigh, but he continued to draw into his hand virtually all the strings of government, all the preferment of the Crown.

15

For some while Raleigh had had three notable friends: the Earl of Northumberland with whom he played cards[1] and who had taken over the services of Hariot; the young Lord Cobham, who was Lord Warden of the Cinque Ports; and Cecil, whose dead wife had been Cobham's sister.

He became closer to them all, and especially to Cecil, as Essex became wilder in his hostility. Essex having gone gloriously to Ireland, blamed on Raleigh, Cecil and Cobham Elizabeth's contempt for his flaccid campaign; having returned against orders, he blamed on them his confinement in York House.

Raleigh cemented his friendship with Cecil by having at Sherborne Cecil's son, William, as a companion for his own handful, Wat.

Will Cecil to Raleigh:[1]
Sir Walter, we must all exclaim and cry out because you will not come down. You being absent, we are like soldiers that when their captain is absent they know not what to do. You are so busy about idle matters.

Raleigh to Cecil, from Sherborne, 27 March 1600:[2]
Whereas I wrote in my last he was a little troubled with a looseness, I thank God he is now freed thereof; and, I assure you, better in health and strength than ever I knew him . . . He is also better kept to his book than anywhere else.

Raleigh to Wat:
> Three things there be that prosper up apace
> And flourish, while they grow asunder far;
> But on a day, they meet all in a place,
> And when they meet they one another mar.
>
> And they be these: the Wood, the Weed, the Wag.
> The Wood is that which makes the gallow tree;
> The Weed is that which strings the hangman's bag;
> The Wag, my pretty knave, betokeneth thee.
>
> Mark well, dear boy, whilst these assemble not,
> Green springs the tree, hemp grows, the wag is wild;
> But when they meet, it makes the timber rot,
> It frets the halter, and it chokes the child.

Then bless thee, and beware, and let us pray,
We part not with thee at this meeting day.

Raleigh was an ally who must sometimes have made Cecil tremble. In a scheme to have Tyrone assassinated he signed a passport for the assassin instead of getting someone else to sign it. When he gave Cecil the sensible advice to see that Essex did not recover power, he put it in writing. Raleigh could put his own head on the block, and the head of an associate.

To a professional administrator his goodwill was irresponsibility. He had to negotiate with the Cornish tinners a guaranteed price at which the Duchy should buy all their tin. Having agreed a price he told them it was less than his permitted maximum; for which, of course, they then petitioned, and he supported their petition. And he pledged them his personal faith that the government's promises would be performed although it was not in his power to see that they were.

Nevertheless he was needed by Cecil. He was sopped for being kept out of the Council with the governorship of Jersey – which gave him extra responsibilities at the periphery and no extra power at the centre – and with the betrothal to Wat of a ward of Cobham's worth £3,000 a year, Cecil as Master of the Court of Wards consenting.

Essex was released. But his monopoly of sweet wines, which provided his basic income, was not renewed, so that anxiety and discontent wholly controlled the use to which he put his freedom. One Sunday morning he issued from Essex House (the old Leicester House near St Clement Danes, where Essex Street is now) and with nobles and gentlemen entered the City, crying that Raleigh and Cobham were about to murder him and that the Queen must be saved from evil advisers, and hoping that discontented merchants and Puritans would join him.

A few hours earlier Raleigh had gone to meet on the river a cousin, Sir Ferdinando Gorges, who had sent him a message from Essex House. Raleigh was alone. Gorges was with two gentlemen and followed by four shot in another boat; he had been told to kill Raleigh.[1] Instead, according to Raleigh's evidence at Essex's trial,

Gorges asked him to warn the Court. There was time to raise a few guards, and for Cecil to write a proclamation which made it clear to the City that the affair was treason. Essex and his followers returned to Essex House, and when the Lord Admiral trained cannon on it, surrendered.

At his execution on Tower Green, on 25 February 1601, Essex received the ministrations of three clergymen, confessed perhaps excessively his sins, and declared that Raleigh was a true servant of the Queen. When his henchman, Sir Christopher Blount, was on the scaffold three weeks later Raleigh prevented the Sheriff from cutting short his death speech. Blount then said that neither he nor Essex had really believed that Raleigh and Cobham meant to harm Essex.[1] However, in songs at Court and in the streets Essex was still idolised, and there were rhymes for Raleigh and Cecil.

Anon:[2]

> Little Cecil trips up and down,
> He rules both Court and Crown . . .
> He swore he saved the Town.
> Is it not likely?
>
> Raleigh doth time bestride,
> He sits 'twixt wind and tide,
> Yet uphill he cannot ride,
> For all his bloody pride.
>
> He seeks taxes in the tin,
> He polls the poor to the skin,
> Yet he vows 'tis no sin,
> Lord for thy pity!

16

For Raleigh the summer of 1601 had a number of irritations. In Ireland his wood-stave industry had been got going again, but he and his co-venturers were being monstrously swindled by the manager, Pyne.

At Sherborne his bailiff, Meers, refused to give place to a new one, Dolberry, and there was petty violence and public squabbling. Meers called Adrian Gilbert, whom Raleigh had made Constable of Sherborne Castle, a 'gorbellied rascal'; Mrs Meers said out of her window 'undecent words concerning Lady Raleigh'. Raleigh's servants sang ribald songs near Meers's house when Meers was in bed, and Raleigh personally put Meers in the stocks in Sherborne market place and walked off with the key.[1] Meers, lawyer as well as coin-clipper and forger, had powerful backing and appealed to the Star Chamber.

Raleigh in his letters to Cecil sandwiched moans for help against Meers (who was finally jailed) between items of news from his captains about the movements and intentions of the Spaniards.

An unsleeping monger of news, emotions and ideas is found tiresome by responsible officials; found dangerous if in addition his actions are not sufficiently regulated by convention and self-interest. Now that Essex was dead, Cecil could begin to dissociate himself from Raleigh. He showed coolness.

But in spite of Cecil's coolness, and of sickness, and of the troubles with Pyne in Ireland and Meers at Sherborne, Raleigh's letters took on a tone of rural and domestic contentment. He took to quoting his wife, with affection.

Raleigh to Cobham, August 1601:[2]
I hope your Lordship will be here tomorrow or a' Saturday, or else my wife says her oysters will be all spoilt and her partridge stale . . .
PS: Bess remembers herself to your Lordship, and says your breach of promise shall make you fare accordingly.

Raleigh to Cecil, 13 August:[3]
I pray believe that when all hearts are open and all desires tried, that I am your poorest and your faithfullest friend, to do you service.
Bess returns you her best wishes, notwithstanding all quarrels.

Raleigh to Cecil, 19 September:[4]
I have by this bearer sent you the gloves [from Bess], but it is

indented that if they serve not your own hands, you must of your grace return them again.

Raleigh to Cecil, October:[1]
My wife says that you came hither in an unseasonable time, and had no leisure to look abroad, and that every day this place amends, and London, to her, grows worse and worse.

The following month he was in London for Parliament, where he proposed a fourfold subsidy to pay for the Irish war – the Spaniards had landed on the coast of Munster with 4,000 men, and 1,600 saddles for horses which the Irish did not supply. The malaise which had entered his relations with Cecil showed itself in debate.

D'Ewes – Saturday 7 November 1601, at the committee in the House touching the Subsidy, after Raleigh had spoken:
Sir Edward Hoby: We cannot hear you speak out. You should speak standing that so the House might the better hear you.
So Sir Walter said that being a Committee he might speak either sitting or standing, and so repeated over again the former speech.
Mr Secretary Cecil: Because it is an argument of more reverence I choose to speak standing . . .

The following Monday:
Cecil (summing up Saturday's discussion):
And this I know, that neither pot nor pan, nor dish nor spoon should be spared when danger is at our elbow . . . By no means would I have the three-pound men exempted, because I do wish the King of Spain might know how willing we are to sell all in defence of God's religion, our Prince and country . . .
Raleigh: I like not that the Spaniards, our enemies, should know of our selling our pots and pans to pay subsidies; well may you call it policy, as an Honourable Person alleged, but I am sure it argues poverty in the State.

He also spoke against the export of iron ordnance, which went to arm England's enemies, and against a bill for 'more diligent coming

[158]

to church', and in favour of the repeal of bills which made compulsory the growing of hemp (for ships' cordage) and corn.

D'Ewes – 9 December, the Statute of Tillage – whether it should be repealed:
Raleigh: I think this law fit to be repealed; for many poor men are not able to find seed to sow so much as they are bound to plough, which they must do or incur the penalty of the law.

Besides, all nations abound with corn. France offered the Queen to serve Ireland with corn for sixteen shillings a quarter, which is but two shillings the bushel; if we should sell it here, the ploughman would be beggared. The Low Country man and the Hollander, which never soweth corn, hath by his industry such plenty that they will serve other nations . . .

And therefore I think the best course is to set at liberty, and leave every man free, which is the desire of a true Englishman.
Mr Secretary Cecil: I do not dwell in the country, I am not acquainted with the plough, but I think that whosoever doth not maintain the plough destroys the kingdom . . . My motion therefore shall be that this law may not be repealed.

The Commons made no difficulty about voting the subsidy. However, they went on to debate monopolies, which were given under the Queen's prerogative. Member after member rose to complain that his constituents were squeezed by the agents of the 'monopolitans' or of those to whom they had sold their rights. There were monopolies for salt, starch, vinegar, oil, fish, cards ('here Sir Walter Raleigh blushed'), wines, tin. Only one monopolitan spoke.

D'Ewes – 20 November 1601, an Act for the explanation of the Common Law in certain cases of Letters Patent:
Raleigh: I am urged to speak in two respects: the one because I find myself touched in particular; the other, in that I take some imputation of slander offered unto her Majesty, I mean by the gentleman that first mentioned tin: for that being one of the principal commodities of this kingdom, and being in Cornwall, it hath ever, so long as there were any, belonged to the Dukes of Cornwall, and they

had special patents of privilege. It pleased her Majesty freely to bestow upon me that privilege; and that patent being word for word the very same the Duke's is, and because by reason of mine office of Lord Warden of the Stannaries I can sufficiently inform this House of the state thereof, I will make bold to deliver it unto you.

When the tin is taken out of the mine, and melted and refined, then is every piece containing one hundred weight sealed with the Duke's seal. Now I will tell you, that before the granting of my patent, whether tin were but of 17/- and so upward to 50/- a hundred, yet the poor workman never had above 2/- the week, finding themselves. But since my patent whosoever will work may; and buy tin at what price soever, they have 4/- a week truly paid. There is no poor that will work there but may, and have that wages.

Notwithstanding, if all others may be repealed, I will give my consent as freely to the cancelling of this as any member of this House.

His speech was followed by a long silence. The next speaker congratulated the House on having given it a fair hearing, but wondered if everyone's memory and estimate of the facts were the same.

The House was anxious about the Queen's reaction to their discussion, so close to her prerogative. They need not have worried. She realised she must ease them, so she did it as of her own prerogative and not by their demand. A dozen or so monopolies had been abolished since the 1597-8 Parliament; now she abolished some more, and announced that others would be subject to trial at common law. Then she summoned the Commons to her, and made them the last of her speeches, putting the blame on her principal officers, praising the Commons, praising herself, gracious and magnificent.

D'Ewes – 30 November, in the Great Chamber before the Council Chamber at Whitehall, to the Speaker and seven score Members, the Queen said:
... Mr Speaker, you give me thanks, but I doubt me, I have more cause to thank you all than you me; and I charge you to thank them of the House of Commons from me, for had I not received a knowledge from you, I might have fallen into the lap of an error only for lack of a true information ...

[160]

Since I was Queen, yet did I never put my pen to any grant but that upon pretext and semblance made unto me that it was both good and beneficial to the subjects in general, though a private profit to some of my ancient servants who had deserved well . . . That my grants should be grievous to my people, and oppressions to be privileged under colour of our patents, our kingly dignity shall not suffer it; yea, when I heard it I could give no rest to my thoughts until I had reformed it . . .

I know the title of a king is a glorious title, but assure yourself that the shining glory of princely authority hath not so dazzled the eyes of our understanding but that we well know and remember that we also are to yield an account of our actions before the great Judge . . . For myself, I was never so much enticed with the glorious name of a king, or royal authority of a queen, as delighted that God hath made me his instrument to maintain his truth and glory, and to defend this kingdom . . . from peril, dishonour, tyranny and oppression. There will never queen sit in my seat with more zeal to my country, care to my subjects, and that will sooner with willingness yield and venture her life for your good and safety than myself. And though you have had and may have princes more mighty and wise sitting in this seat, yet you never had or shall have any that will be more careful and loving.

17

The next prince who would be sitting in that seat was likely to be James VI of Scotland. James, now thirty-five, had been governing Scotland all his adult life. Although of little virility he had succeeded by shifts in converting feudal Scotland into a centralised Tudor state, and in asserting the power of the Crown over the stiff-necked Kirk. He sent two emissaries to London early in 1601 to confer with Essex, his chief supporter, but they found him dead.

Essex had told James that Cecil, Cobham and Raleigh supported a rival claimant, the Infanta of Spain, descended from John of Gaunt.

And there were other possible claimants, Arabella Stuart and Edward Seymour, Lord Beauchamp. Cecil now quickly convinced the emissaries of his own fidelity to James, and then, by tactful and firm correspondence, convinced James himself.

The queen did not like her subjects to owe even fractional or supposititious loyalty elsewhere, so paying court to James had to be secret. Raleigh knew the necessity of courting him and it was probably he who sent Sir Arthur Gorges to Scotland;[1] but he was stiff in his loyalty to his reigning sovereign, and his intrigue havered and was uncertain. He half-confided in Cecil, listened to Cecil's advice to do nothing, and did almost nothing.

Cecil meanwhile was trying to discipline his future king into relying in English matters wholly upon himself and Lord Henry Howard, a man who had recently been re-admitted to Court after a life-time spent equivocally on the edge of Catholic plots.

Howard assisted Cecil by drawing, in a succession of letters to Scotland, a picture of 'the diabolical triplicity, that is, Cobham, Raleigh and Northumberland, that meet every day at Durham House'.[2] Raleigh was clever and evil, Cobham rash and with no brains, Northumberland ridiculous. 'Cecil sware to me this day that . . . he and they would never live under one apple tree.'

Cecil to James, February 1602:[3]
I do profess . . . that if I did not sometimes cast a stone into the mouth of these gaping crabs . . . they would not stick to confess daily how contrary it is to their nature to resolve to be under your sovereignty; though they confess – Raleigh especially – that . . . natural policy forceth them to keep on foot such a trade against the great day of mart.

Would God I were . . . free from offence towards God in seeking, for private affection, to support a person whom most religious men do hold anathema.

Howard also suggested to Cecil ways of getting rid of Raleigh and Cobham without waiting for the Queen to die.[4] She should be told of 'the rage of their discontent' at not being given higher offices, and of Bess's fury at not being re-admitted to Court; she should be told every day of some 'pageant' of theirs which would make her angry; if possible, she should be told of some deception practised on her for their own benefit.

The next step was to embark Cobham 'in some course the Spanish way'. He was in favour of peace with Spain and so could be put in touch with Spanish ministers suspected of organising plots against the Queen. 'I account it unpossible for him to scape the snares which wit may set.'

Raleigh was against a peace with Spain and had to be caught another way. If 'the springs of bounty' were stopped, he might 'shuffle the Stoic' and in some rash action fall into a trap which normally he would avoid.

Raleigh was forty-eight now. He had not for some while been absorbed in new schemes or the duties of great temporary posts of command. He was disgruntled at the way his petitions and projects were blocked, but happy in his important friendships and, in relaxed security, was fairly prosperous, fairly busy.

He had made no more attempts on El Dorado because of the Spaniards, who were both on the Orinoco and always threatening invasion at home (and perhaps because his own health had deteriorated), but he was sending a ship to Guiana every year or so.

There was still no settlement in Virginia, but he was developing a trade in Virginian sassafras which gave him a profit of 800 or 1,000 per cent as long as there was no competition, and in due course, he was sure, something more would be built up: 'I shall yet live to see it an English nation.'[1]

Of his Irish colony he had given up hope. He sold his rights and properties for £1,000.

His privateering ventures were still profitable. Cecil entered them with eagerness but asked for his name to be suppressed, 'though, I thank God, I have no other meaning than becometh an honest man in any of my actions'.

Secretary Cecil was trying at this time to detach from the unreliable Raleigh the reliable Sir George Carew. 'Cousin George' had been distinguishing himself as Lord President of Munster. With Lord Deputy Mountjoy he had defeated utterly Tyrone's Irish when they came south to join up with the Spanish invaders. Cecil was supplying

him with tobacco and with regular letters which mixed an armhold-
ing affection for Carew with sorrowful aspersions against Raleigh.[1]

There was now a new anxiety about the Spaniards. They had left
Ireland disgusted with the Irish, but were once more believed to be
about to invade England. Raleigh was sent to Jersey to see to its
defences and get information about Spanish movements.

Raleigh to Cecil, from Jersey, 20 July 1602:[2]
You will, I hope, give me leave to salute my Lord Cobham and you,
both in a letter. I can send no news from hence. I hear not from any
part of the world as yet. I cannot send away a bark for Spain, the
wind blowing continually at west and northwest. From France I
have heard nothing . . .

I beseech you bestow a line on me, that live in desolation. And, if
you find no cause to stay me here, I would willingly return . . .

I shall ever rest to do you service with all I have, and my life to
boot.
PS: Bess will convey me your letters, if you send any.

During the week he wrote this letter he instituted a public register
of land which has been a benefit to Jersey ever since. It had been
recommended for forty years but officials had not wanted the bother
of it.[3]

On his return he reported at Court, but his relations with the
Queen seem to have become loose. Earlier in the year she had complained that he made himself 'singular': such were 'not to be employed by princes of sound policy'.[4] He went to Bath and wrote to
Cecil: 'I am at this instant in pain and cannot write much'.

Northumberland was now writing to James, and gave his estimate
of Raleigh: 'I must needs affirm Raleigh's ever allowance of your
right, and although I know him insolent, extremely heated, a man
that desires to seem to be able to sway all men's courses, and a man
that out of himself, when your time shall come, will never be able to
do you much good nor harm, yet must I needs confess what I know,
that there is excellent good parts of nature in him . . .'[5]

In the New Year Elizabeth was melancholy. In March she was
refusing to go to bed for fear she would never get up again, was

refusing medicines and food, could not sleep, and was pensive and silent. On about the 20th she was got to bed.

Dr John Manningham, Diary:[1]
24 March 1603. This morning about three at clock her Majesty departed this life, mildly like a lamb, easily like a ripe apple from the tree . . . and I doubt not but she is amongst the royal saints in Heaven in eternal joys.

About ten o'clock the Council and divers noblemen having been awhile in consultation, proclaimed James the Six, King of Scots, the King of England, France and Ireland, beginning at Whitehall gates; where Sir Robert Cecil read the proclamation which he carries in his hand, and after read again in Cheapside. Many noblemen, lords spiritual and temporal, knights, five trumpets, many heralds . . . The proclamation was heard with great expectation and silent joy, no great shouting. I think the sorrow for her Majesty's departure was so deep in many hearts they could not suddenly show any great joy, though it could not be less than exceeding great for the succession of so worthy a king.

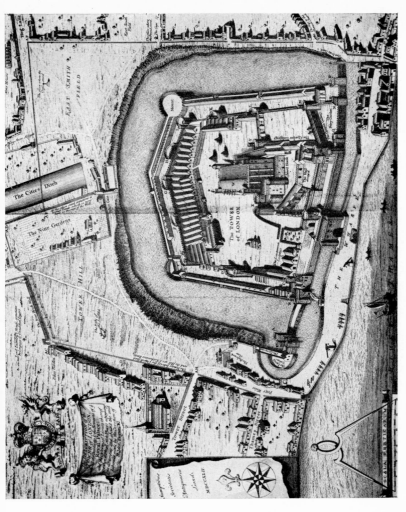

7. The Tower of London by William Hayward and J. Gascoyne, 1597

8. Sir Walter Raleigh, aged by sickness and his Cadiz leg wound, and wearing the arm sash of a commander, painted in 1597 by an unknown artist

Part Five 1603

I

James – handsome, kindly, witty, religious, learned, with light brown hair, blue eyes, a ruddy face, a curved clear-cut nose, a scattery beard trimmed square, neither tall nor short, neither fat nor thin – left his impoverished Kirk-ridden Scotland joyfully and crossed the Border to the inheritance which he believed his wisdom and good intentions would greatly benefit. Attended by young Scotsmen and Lord Henry Howard, and clustered round by English gentry and nobility, he feasted, freed prisoners, felt that at last he was rightly valued.

At Durham he liked the humour and sermons of the Bishop (Toby Matthew, Raleigh's Oxford contemporary). Certainly the See of Durham should have back Durham House in the Strand. Notice of eviction was sent off to Raleigh.

Raleigh had been in the west when Elizabeth died. There was a rumour that he was preparing some coup, and a pleasurable hurry to display a hostile attitude towards him.[1] Sir Amyas Preston sent him a challenge. Sir Ferdinando Gorges loudly talked his detestation. The Council said the King would need a new Captain of the Guard.

He decided to go to the Midlands to pay court to James before he reached the south, although the Council had forbidden such journeys. He took to Northamptonshire some draft letters connected with the Duchy of Cornwall, ostensibly for James's urgent signature.

Aubrey:[2]
When Sir Walter Raleigh's name was told, said the King: 'O my soul, mon, I have heard rawly of thee.'

Thomas Lake (sent by the Council to act as secretary to James) to Cecil, 25 April 1603:[3]
Upon the offering of these letters [the King] said that this was all

that Raleigh had to allege for excuse of his coming, and that he promised to write those letters, and willed me they might be speedily delivered that he were gone again, and to my seeming he hath taken no great root here.

Three days later he was back in London for Elizabeth's funeral. In the procession to the Abbey the Guard were at the rear, in ranks of five, halberds held downward.

James reached Theobalds, Cecil's house in Hertfordshire, having made more jokes and knights to the English mile than any monarch before or since, hunted more stags, listened to more sermons, given away more offices and lands. The Council were presented to him, and also the officers of Elizabeth's household, including Raleigh for the second time, and many others.

Aubrey:[1]
It was a most stately sight, the glory of that reception of his Majesty . . . and the company was so exceeding numerous that their obedience carried a secret dread with it.

King James did not inwardly like it, and, with an inward envy, said that he doubted not but that he should have been able on his own strength (should the English have kept him out) to have dealt with them, and get his right.

Said Sir Walter Raleigh to him: 'Would to God that had been put to the trial!'

'Why do you wish that?' said the King.

'Because,' said Sir Walter, 'that then you would have known your friends from your foes.'

But that reason of Sir Walter was never forgotten nor forgiven.

It was at Theobalds, in the room of the Scot, Sir Thomas Erskine, that some English ladies found some lice, and commented that there was already Scottish innovation at Court.

And at Theobalds a new Council was appointed. Proclamations began to issue. One of them inhibited the use of monopolies until they had been individually approved as in the public interest. Raleigh's income from wine, tin and cloth ceased immediately.

The following day he was summoned before the Council and told that the King wished Sir Thomas Erskine to be Captain of the Guard.

In a few days he was to receive one benefit. At Greenwich, where ten or twelve thousand noblemen and gentlemen crowded, begging successfully for offices, lands and pensions, he was released from an annual payment of £300 he had to make the Crown from his revenue as Governor of Jersey.

Ambassadors came to congratulate James, among them the Count of Aremberg from the Spanish Netherlands, who, reluctant to drag his gout upstairs, asked for his audience to be in the garden. It was with Aremberg that Cobham was having demi-official dealings for a peace, having been embarked 'in some course the Spanish way'.

England was still officially at war with Spain, of which James had approved while the Spanish Infanta had been a rival for the succession. The rivalry was over and he could be Jacobus Pacificus. In accordance with his peace policy he ordered that privateering was to stop forthwith.

Raleigh's 'springs of bounty' were now almost all dried up, and his only office at Court taken away – in the course of general policy, Cecil would have said, in which nothing was aimed against him personally.

He received from the law officers an order to leave Durham House within a fortnight. He had been there twenty years, spent £2,000 on the place, laid in stores for forty people and twenty horses.

Raleigh to the Lord Keeper of the Seal, the Lord Chief Justice and the Attorney General, June 1603:[1]
I am of the opinion that if the King's Majesty had recovered this house, or the like, from the meanest gentleman and servant he had in England, that his Majesty would have given six months' time for the avoidance, and I do not know but that the poorest artificer in London hath a quarter's warning given him by his landlord.

But in faith and without discretion he continued to present James with his thoughts as if they were welcome gifts from a trusted subject. He knew that the making of peace with Spain was James's dearest wish, but he offered to take an army against Spain at his own expense.[1]

Within a month of this violent offer, a conspiracy was discovered against James himself, who abominated conspiracies: he had had so many in Scotland that he wore a padded doublet. It was not three months since he had been welcomed to England with blessed and unexpected unanimity; not a month since he had been joined by his frivolity-starved Queen, Anne of Denmark; it was on the very day when he was investing with the Garter his grave nine-year-old son, Prince Henry. Fortunately the plot was detected by his English but invaluable Cecil.

The first suspect to be taken was one Copley, a Catholic.

The next, George Brooke, Cobham's brother.

Then Cobham.

Then Cobham's friend.

2

He was held first in Sir Thomas Bodley's house. After a day or two he was in the Tower.

He denied that he knew anything of a Catholic plot by Copley, Brooke, two priests (Clark and Watson), and others to 'surprise' the King and force him to grant toleration. Nor did he know anything of plots between Cobham and Aremberg, of which Brooke had spoken when questioned. But after he had been examined he sent a note to Cecil that he thought Cobham had been calling on a Flemish merchant named Laurencie, who was known to be an agent for Aremberg.

An extract from this note was shown Cobham who had denied either plotting or knowing of a plot, and had refused as a peer to sign the report of his examination. Now Cobham blurted that indeed he had been plotting with Aremberg, and that Raleigh was the cause of it all.

The Lieutenant of the Tower, Sir John Peyton, to Cecil, 23 July 1603: [2]
I never saw so strange a dejected mind as is in Sir Walter Raleigh.

[170]

I am exceedingly cumbered with him; five or six times a day he sendeth for me in such passions as I see his fortitude is impotent to support his grief.

He asked his keeper to buy him a long narrow knife to stir his wine, but the man refused. On 27 July, a week after Cobham's accusation, he stabbed himself with a Tower table-knife.[1]

He could handle weapons, he knew some anatomy, he had always acted effectively in the face of death – nevertheless the knife hit a rib. He was prevented from trying again.

After further examining, and much confronting of each suspected conspirator with parts of statements made by others, admissions about the 'surprising' treason were got from Copley, Brooke, Sir Griffin Markham, the two priests, and the young Puritan Lord Grey, son of the former Lord Deputy. As well, out of their memories of one another's grumbles, wishes, wild schemes, guesses, came one or two memories of statements that Cobham and Raleigh were involved in something bigger. This was labelled by the Crown's Commissioners the Main Plot, the other the Bye Plot.

Raleigh's governorship of Jersey was given to the Lieutenant of the Tower, and his Lieutenancy of Cornwall was held to be void. Keymis, as his gentleman-employee, was examined and kept a close prisoner, but gave no damaging evidence. Sir Arthur Gorges had been arrested early in the proceedings but released.

Meanwhile James had been crowned, on a wet St James's day, the Bishop of Winchester preaching on the text 'The powers that are, are ordained by God'.

The Court ran from London, where there was plague, and carried infection to Windsor, then to Hampton Court, Woodstock, Winchester and Wilton. In London there were a thousand deaths in a week, then two thousand, then three. Those who could not escape to the country with the doctors and J.P.s took to prayer or drink or both. Bells tolled without restriction, burials were attended by crowds in spite of the regulations, infected bedding and straw cluttered the streets. There were three plague deaths in the Tower.

The Courts were to meet in Winchester instead of Westminster, and on 10 November Raleigh and other prisoners set out from the Tower, guarded by fifty light horse.

Sir William Wade to Cecil, from Winchester Castle, 13 November 1603:[1]
It was hab or nab whether Sir Walter Raleigh should have been brought alive through such multitudes of unruly people as did exclaim against him. He that had seen it would not think there had been any sickness in London.

Anon:[2]

> Now you may see the sudden fall
>   Of him that thought to climb full high,
> A man well known unto you all,
>   Whose state you see doth stand Rawly.

Anon:[3]

> For thy skance and pride,
> Thy bloody mind beside,
> And thy mouth gaping wide,
>   Mischievous Machiavel!

> Essex for vengeance cries,
> His blood upon thee lies,
> Mounting above the skies,
>   Damnable fiend of hell,
>   Mischievous Machiavel!

3

There were to be four professional judges led by the Lord Chief Justice, Sir John Popham, and with them the seven Commissioners who had been examining the prisoners. These included Lord Thomas Howard, who was now Earl of Suffolk; Mountjoy, of Essex's faction before he became a successful Lord Deputy, now Earl of Devonshire; Cecil and Lord Henry Howard; and Sir William Wade, who had been an energetic examiner.

For the prosecution there were the Attorney General, Sir Edward Coke, handsome, clean, a bludgeoning prosecutor for the Crown, but later a stickler for the law against James; together with Serjeants Hele and Philips. Hele had acted for Raleigh in his case against his bailiff, Meers. The law allowed no counsel for the defence.

It was a strong court; it contained only one man, Wade, who was neither at the head of the legal profession nor a member of the Privy Council. It was virtually the government of England, anxious to preserve the peacefulness of the succession, and to show their zeal for their new, foreign king.

The lower-ranking conspirators were all found guilty and condemned, with the exception of one, Sir Edward Parham, who through the good offices of the Foreman of the Jury, supported by Cecil, was acquitted. He was the first man for forty-five years to be acquitted of a charge of treason.

Raleigh was to be tried before the two noblemen, Cobham and Grey. His trial took the whole of 17 November.

4

At the King's Bench Bar, Winchester, 17 November 1603:[1]
After that Sir Walter Raleigh was brought to the bar, he sat upon a stool within a place made of purpose for the prisoner to be in, and expected the coming of the Lords; during which time he saluted divers of his acquaintance with a very steadfast and cheerful countenance.

When the Commissioners were all assembled, having stood up a while, he desired the Marshal of the Court to ask leave of the Lords that he might sit, which was presently granted.

First, the commission of Oyer and Terminer was read by the Clerk of the Crown Office; and the prisoner bid to hold up his hand.

And presently the indictment, which was in effect as followeth: That he did conspire, and go about to deprive the King of his government; to raise up sedition within the realm; to alter religion, to bring in the Roman super-stition, and to procure foreign enemies to invade the kingdom.

To the indictment Sir Walter Raleigh pleaded not guilty, and put him-self on the country.

Sir Walter Raleigh, prisoner, was asked whether he would take exception to any of the jury.

Raleigh: I know none of them; they are all Christians, and honest gentlemen; I except against none.

Only this I desire. Sickness hath of late weakened me, and my memory was always bad. The points of the indictment be many, and in the evidence perhaps more will be urged. I beseech you, my Lords, let me answer every point severally, for I shall not carry all to the end.

But Mr Attorney pressed the Lords that 'the King's evidence ought not to be broken or dismembered, whereby it might lose much of its grace and vigour'.

Notwithstanding it was yielded, when Mr Attorney came to his proof Sir Walter Raleigh should have leave to answer his several points as they were objected.

5

Master Serjeant Hele opened the matter, and delivered the effect of the indictment; in whose speech this was observed, that he charged Sir Walter to have intended the entitling of the Lady Arabella Stuart to the Crown; who he said, had no more title thereunto than he had himself, and further said, after a little pause, that he for his part did disclaim and renounce all title hereunto, whereat Sir Walter Raleigh smiled.

The Serjeant concluding, Mr Attorney Coke began.

Att. Gen.: The Lord Grey, Brooke, Markham and the rest intended by force in the night to surprise the King's Court . . . They intended to take him that is a sovereign, to make him subject to their power, purposing to open the doors with muskets and calivers. They would extort a pardon from the King, and toleration for the Roman superstition, and make Watson Lord Chancellor, and Brooke Lord Treasurer, Markham Secretary, Grey Earl Marshal. Then they were going to send the Lord Mayor and Aldermen to the Tower.

Raleigh: You gentlemen of the Jury, I pray remember, I am not charged with the Bye, being the treason of the priests.

Att. Gen.: You are not; but their Lordships will see that all these treasons, though they consisted of several parts, closed in together like Samson's foxes, which were joined in their tails, though the heads were severed.

Attorney General Coke then went into some historical cases: the murder of Edward II, the treasons of Perkin Warbeck and Edmund de la Pole against Henry VII, etc.

But this case exceedeth in wickedness all that ever went before, in two things: *in determinatio finis* [in determination of end], and *in electione mediorum* [in choice of means]. For it was said (by these traitors) that there would be 'no safety in England until the fox and his cubs were taken away', meaning, until the King and all his royal issue should be destroyed.

Therefore in this treason the mischief exceeds the punishment and the terms of law; for this is not only *crimen laesae majestatis* [the crime of injuring majesty], but *extirpatae majestatis et totius progeniei suae* [of destroying majesty and all the progeny of majesty], for not only the King but all his posterity were to be cut off.

I shall not need, my Lords, to speak anything concerning the King, nor of the bounty and sweetness of his nature, whose thoughts are innocent, whose words are full of wisdom and learning, and whose works are full of honour . . . But to whom, Sir Walter, do you bear malice? To the royal children?

Raleigh: Master Attorney, I pray to whom, or to what end, speak you all this? I protest I do not understand what a word of this means, except it be to tell me news. The treason of Markham and the priests, what is that to me?

Att. Gen.: I will then come close to you. You indeed are upon the 'Main', but you followed them of the 'Bye' in imitation. I will prove you the notoriest traitor that ever came to the bar.

[175]

Raleigh: Prove one of these things wherewith you have charged me, and I will confess the whole indictment, and that I am the horriblest traitor that ever lived, and worthy to be crucified with a thousand thousand torments.

Att. Gen.: Nay, I will prove all. Thou art a monster. Thou hast an English face, but a Spanish heart. You would have stirred England and Scotland both.

Now, you must have money. Aremberg was no sooner in England – I charge thee, Raleigh – but you incited Cobham to go to him. The night he went you supped with the Lord Cobham, and he brought you to Durham House, and the same night by a back way he went with Laurencie to Count Aremberg to get a promise of the money.

Raleigh: Let me answer for myself.

Att. Gen.: Thou shalt not.

Raleigh: It concerneth my life.

Att. Gen.: Oh! do I touch you?

Ld Ch. Justice: Sir Walter Raleigh, Mr Attorney is yet but in the general; but when the King's Counsel hath given the evidence wholly you shall answer every particular.

Cecil: Mr Attorney, when you have done with this general charge do you not mean to let him answer every particular?

Att. Gen.: Yes, when we deliver the proofs to be read.

Raleigh: All this while you tell me news.

Att. Gen.: Oh, sir! I am the more large because I know with whom I deal, for we have to deal today with a man of wit.

Aremberg answered, the money should be performed, but knew not to whom it should be distributed. Then Cobham and Laurencie came back to Durham House, where they found Raleigh. Cobham and Raleigh went up, and left Laurencie below, where they had secret conference in a gallery; and after, Cobham and Laurencie departed from Raleigh.

Your jargon was Peace. What is that? Spanish invasion, Scottish subversion.

Then Cobham must go to Spain, and return by Jersey, where you were captain; and then, because Cobham had not so much policy, or at least wickedness, as you, he must have your advice for the distribution of the money.

[176]

I think you meant to make Arabella a titular Queen, of whose title I speak nothing; but sure, you meant to make her a stale. Ah! good lady, you could mean her no good.

Raleigh: Did I ever speak with this lady? I pray you to your proofs, and if you prove against me any one thing of those many that you have spoken of, I will ease you and here confess all the indictment.

Att. Gen.: Nay, you fall out with yourself for I say nothing to you yet. If you provoke me I will not spare you, and I have warrant for it.

I will only add one or two circumstances, and then come to my proofs.

My Lords, you know my Lord Cobham: he was never politician nor sword man. To the invention of these treasonable schemes belonged a politician; to the execution of them a sword man. Sir Walter Raleigh was both, united in cause with the Lord Cobham for both were discontented, and cause of his destruction.

And Raleigh in his Macchiavellian policy must make a sanctuary for treason. He must talk with none but Cobham, because, saith he, one witness can never condemn me.

Since his first examination he wrote to the Lord Cobham thus: 'I have been examined of you and confessed nothing.' Further you sent him by your trusty Keymis that one witness could not condemn, and therefore bade his Lordship be of good courage.

Notwithstanding this, the Lord Cobham did charge Raleigh.

And now you shall see the most horrible practices that ever came out of the bottomless pit of the lowest hell; for after Raleigh had gotten understanding in the Tower that Cobham had accused him, which he heard by young Sir John Peyton [son of the Lieutenant of the Tower] – who had not purposed to tell it him, but to the error of his youth I impute it –

Raleigh: I knew from the Lords who examined me that Cobham had accused me. Otherwise I had not been sent to the Tower.

Att. Gen.: After Raleigh understood that he was accused by my Lord Cobham, it was contrived that the Lord Cobham should retract his accusation.

Coke went on to describe an attempt by Cobham to make his proposed journey into Spain seem innocent by faking a back-dated correspondence with Sir Thomas Fane, Lieutenant Governor of Dover Castle.

Came this out of Cobham's quiver? No, but out of Raleigh's devilish and Macchiavellian policy. You shall hear that it was after Cobham had had intelligence with this viper in the Tower that he devised this false artifice. But Sir Thomas Fane would be no party in such a business, and sent the letter to the Council.

Raleigh: What is that to me? I do not hear yet that you have spoken one word against me. Here is no treason of mine done. If my Lord Cobham be a traitor, what is that to me?

Att. Gen.: All that he did was by thy instigation, thou viper, for I thou thee, thou traitor! I will prove thee the rankest traitor in all England.

Raleigh: No, no, Master Attorney, I am no traitor. Whether I live or die, I shall stand as true a subject as ever the King hath. You may call me a traitor at your pleasure; yet it becomes not a man of quality or virtue to do so.

But I take comfort in it. It is all that you can do; for I do not yet hear that you charge me with any treason.

Att. Gen.: Have I angered you?

Raleigh: I am in no case to be angry.

Ld Ch. Justice: Sir Walter Raleigh, Mr Attorney speaketh out of the zeal of his duty, for the service of the King, and you for your life. Be patient, on both sides.

Att. Gen.: I charge Sir Walter Raleigh with contriving and conspiring all this that I have recited. And now I will read my proofs.

6

The Clerk of the Crown Office read Cobham's examination of 20 July. In this examination Cobham confessed he had a passport for Spain, where he intended 'to deal with the King for 600,000 crowns, and to return by Jersey, and that nothing should be done until he had spoken with Sir Walter Raleigh for distribution of the money to them which were discontented in England'.

It was then stated in this examination that, when a note 'under Raleigh's hand' had been shown the examinate, 'he brake forth into the exclama-

tion "Traitor! villain! I will now tell you all the truth" ", *and proceeded to depose that he had* 'never entered into these courses but by Raleigh's instigation; and that he would never let him alone'.

Here Mr Attorney willed the Clerk of the Crown Office to read over these last words again: 'He would never let him alone'.

Besides, Raleigh spoke of plots and invasions, the particulars whereof they must not look from this examinate. He was so confounded with them as he did not remember them. And he feared Sir Walter Raleigh, when he had him in Jersey, would send him to the King.

Raleigh: Let me see the accusation! This is absolutely all the evidence can be brought against me. Poor shifts!

You gentlemen of the Jury, I pray you understand this. This is that which must either condemn me, or give me life; which must free me, or send my wife and child to beg their bread about the streets. This is that must prove me a notorious traitor or a true subject of the King.

Let me see my accusation that I may make my answer.

He looked at it.

Raleigh: At my first examination at Windsor, my Lords asked me what I knew of Cobham's practice with Aremberg. I answered negatively. And as concerning Arabella I protest before God I never heard one word of it. If that be proved let me be guilty of ten thousand treasons. It is a strange thing you will impute that to me, when I never heard so much as the name of Arabella Stuart, but only the name Arabella.

It is true I suspected that the Lord Cobham kept intelligence with Aremberg. For I knew that long since – in the late Queen's time – he held that course with him in the Low Countries, as was well known to my Lord Treasurer and to my Lord Cecil.

After being examined I told my Lord Cecil that I thought my Lord Cobham had conference with Aremberg. I suspected his visiting of him, for after he departed from me at Durham House, I saw him pass by his own stairs, and passed over to St Mary Saviour's where I knew Laurencie, a merchant and follower of Aremberg, lay, and therefore likely to go unto him. But I was willed by my Lord

[179]

Cecil not to speak of this, because the King, at the first coming of Aremberg, would not give him occasion of suspicion . . .

This letter of mine, being showed to the Lord Cobham, he presently entered into a rage against me, and in his fury he accused me. Yet ere he came to the stairs' foot he repented him, and, as I heard, acknowledged that he had done me wrong.

Master Attorney, whether to favour or to disable my Lord Cobham you speak as you will of him, yet he is not such a babe as you make him. He hath dispositions of such violence which his best friends could never temper.

But it is strange for me at this time to devise with the Lord Cobham that he should go to Spain to persuade the King to disburse so much money, he being a man that hath neither love nor following, and myself having resigned my room of chiefest command in an office I had in Cornwall.

I was not so bare of sense but I saw that, if ever this State was strong, it was now that we have the kingdom of Scotland united, whence we were wont to fear all our troubles; Ireland quieted, where our forces were wont to be dispersed; Denmark assured, which before was suspected. And instead of a lady whom Time had surprised, we had now an active King, a lawful successor, who would himself be present in all his affairs.

For me at this time to make myself a Robin Hood, a Wat Tyler, a Kett, or a Jack Cade! I was not so mad.

The state of Spain was not unknown to me. I knew his weakness, his poorness, his humbleness at this time.

I knew that six times we had repulsed his forces: thrice in Ireland, thrice at sea – once upon our own coast, twice upon his own. Thrice had I served against him myself at sea, wherein for my country's sake I had expended of my own property forty thousand marks.

I knew where beforetime he was wont to have forty great sail at the least in his ports, now he hath not past six or seven. And for sending to his Indies, he was driven to have strange vessels – a thing contrary to the institutions of his ancestors, who straitly forbade that, even in case of necessity, they should make their case known to strangers.

I knew of twenty-five millions which he had from his Indies he had scarce one left. Nay, I knew his poorness to be such at this time as the Jesuits, his imps, begged at his church doors.

I knew the King of Spain to be the proudest prince in Christendom, but now he cometh creeping to the King my master for peace.

Whoso knew what great assurances he stood upon with other states, for smaller sums, would not think he would so freely disburse to my Lord Cobham six hundred thousand crowns!

And if I had minded to set my Lord Cobham awork in such a case, I would have given him some instructions how to persuade the King. For I knew Cobham no such minion that could persuade a King that was in want to disburse so great a sum, without great reason and some assurance of his money.

Was it ever read or heard that any prince should disburse so much money without a sufficient pawn? I knew the Queen of England lent not her money to the States without she had Flushing, Brill and other towns in assurance for it. She lent not money to the King of France without she had Newhaven [Le Havre] for it. Nay, her own subjects, the merchants of London, did not lend her money without they had her lands in pawn for it.

And to show I am not Spanish – as you term me – at this time I had writ a treatise to the King's Majesty of the present state of Spain, and reasons against the peace.

For my inwardness with the Lord Cobham, it was only in matters of private estate, wherein, he communicating often with me, I lent him my best advice. At this time I was to deal with the Duke [of Lennox] for him, to procure a fee-farm from the King, for which purpose I had about me in my bosom when I was first examined £4,000 worth of his jewels.

He being a baron of this realm, upon whom all the honours of his house rested, his possessions great, having goodly houses worth at least £5,000 a year revenue, his plate and furniture as rich as any man's of his rank, is it likely I could easily incite such a man of these fortunes to enter into so gross treasons? . . .

As for my knowing that he had conspired all these things with Spain, for Arabella and against the King, I protest before Almighty God I am as clear as whosoever here is freest.

Sir Thomas Fowler, Foreman of the Jury: I desire to understand of the Court the time of Sir Walter Raleigh's first letter, and of the Lord Cobham's accusation.

Cecil: I am in great dispute with myself to speak in the case of this gentleman. A former dearness between me and him, tied upon the knot of his virtues, now slacked by a discovery of his imperfections, I cannot but acknowledge, and the most of you know it. I protest, did I serve a King that I knew would be displeased with me for speaking in this case, I would speak, whatever came of it. But seeing he is compacted of piety and justice, and one that will not mislike any man for speaking the truth, I will answer your question.

Sir Walter was stayed by me at Windsor, upon the first news of Copley that the King's person should be surprised by my Lord Grey and Mr George Brooke. When I found Brooke was in, I suspected Cobham. Then I doubted Raleigh to be a partaker.

I speak not this that it should be thought I had a greater judgment than the rest of my Lords in making this haste to have them examined.

Raleigh following to Windsor, I met with him upon the terrace, and willed him as from the King to stay, saying the Lords had something to say to him. Then he was examined, but not concerning my Lord Cobham, but of the 'surprising' treason.

My Lord Grey was apprehended, and likewise Brooke. By Brooke we found that he had given notice to Cobham of the 'surprising' treason, as he delivered it to us, but with as much sparingness of a brother as he might.

We sent for my Lord Cobham to Richmond. At first he stood much upon denial, yet afterward set down a confession but said he was not bound to subscribe, wherewith we made the King acquainted. Cobham said, if my Lord Chief Justice would say it were a contempt, he would subscribe; whereof being resolved, he subscribed.

For Sir Walter Raleigh, I must say that there was a light given by him that Laurencie had dealt betwixt Count Aremberg and the Lord Cobham. But that Sir Walter Raleigh at that time knew that the Lord Cobham was examined, I cannot say.

Att. Gen.: Sir Walter, you say the Lord Cobham's accusing you was upon heat and passion. I answer three ways.

First, after that the Lord Cobham had twice called for the letter, and twice paused a good while upon it, when he did see that Count Aremberg was touched, then he thought himself discovered and cried out: 'Oh, traitor! Oh, villain! now will I confess the whole truth.'

Second, as to probability, is it probable that my Lord Cobham would turn the weapon against his own bosom and overthrow himself in estate, in honour and posterity, out of malice to accuse you?

Third, could this be out of passion? Mark the manner of it. Cobham had told this at least two months before to his brother: 'You are but fools. You come upon the Bye. Raleigh and I are upon the Main. We mean to take away the King and his cubs.' This he delivered two months before.

Raleigh: Hath Cobham confessed this?

Ld Ch. Justice: This is spoken by Mr Attorney to prove that Cobham's speech came not out of passion.

Raleigh: Let it be proved that Cobham said so.

Att. Gen.: You affirm that you did not so much as suspect any confederacy. Cobham saith, he was a long time doubtful of Raleigh, that he would send him and the money to the King. Did Cobham fear lest you would betray him in Jersey? Then of necessity there must be trust between you. No man can betray a man but he that is trusted, to my understanding. This is the greatest argument to prove that he was acquainted with Cobham's proceedings.

And whereas he saith that our King is not only more wealthy and potent than his predecessors, but also more politic and wise, so that he could have no hope to prevail, I answer: there is no king so potent, wise and active, but he may be overtaken by treason.

Whereas you say Spain is so poor, discoursing so largely thereof, it had been better for you to have kept in Guiana than to have been so well acquainted with the state of Spain.

For his six overthrows, I answer, he hath the more malice, because repulses breed desire of revenge.

Then you say you never talked with Cobham but about leases, and letting lands, and ordering his house. I never knew you Clerk of the Kitchen, etc.

If you had fallen on your knees at first and confessed the treason, it had been better for you. But you seek to wash away all that is said by affirming the evidence against you to be but a bare accusation, without circumstances or reason to confirm it. That I will fully satisfy, for, as my Lord Cobham's confession stands upon many circumstances and concerns many others, I will by other means prove every circumstance thereof to be true.

7

Raleigh: My Lords, I claim to have my accuser brought here to speak face to face.

Though I know not how to make my best defence by law, yet since I was prisoner I have learned that by the law and statutes of this realm in case of treason a man ought to be convicted by the testimony of two witnesses if they be living.

I will not take upon me to defend the matter upon the statute of the 25th of Edward III, though that requires an overt act. But remember, I beseech your Lordships, the statute of the 1st of Edward VI, which saith: 'No man shall be condemned of treason unless he be accused by two lawful accusers.' And by the statute of the 5th and 6th of Edward VI, those accusers 'must be brought in person before the party accused, at his arraignment, if they be living'.

Remember also, my Lords, the statute of the 1st and 2nd of Philip and Mary, which says that 'at the arraignment of any man for treason every person who shall declare, confess or depose anything against him shall, if living and within the realm, be brought forth in person before the party arraigned, if he require it, and object and say openly in his hearing what he can against him; unless the party arraigned shall willingly confess the same'.

Whether at this day these laws be in force, I know not. But such was the wisdom of former times that any man accused must have, at the least, two lawful witnesses to be brought forth at the time of his arraignment.

If, Master Attorney, the wisdom of former times, the assemblies of all the three Estates in several Parliaments, thought it just to have the accusers produced, surely you will not withhold my accuser? If you proceed to condemn me by bare inference – without oath – without subscription – without witnesses – upon a paper accusation, you try me by Spanish Inquisition.

If my accuser were dead, or abroad, it were something; but he liveth, and is in this very house.

Consider, my Lords, it is no rare case for a man to be falsely accused; aye, and falsely condemned too. My Lords the Judges, remember, I beseech you, what one of yourselves said in times past: I mean Fortescue, a reverend Chief Justice of this kingdom.

He tells of a judge, in his time, who condemned a woman at Salisbury for murdering her husband, upon presumption and the testimony of one man; and after she was burned, a servant of the man that was slain, being executed for another crime, confessed that he slew his master himself, and that the woman was innocent.

What said this judge to Fortescue, touching the remorse of his conscience, for proceeding upon such slender proof? He told him that so long as he lived he should never purge his conscience of that deed.

And, my Lords, for the matter I desire remember too the story of Susannah. She was falsely accused, and Daniel called the judges fools because 'without examination of the truth, they had condemned a daughter of Israel', and he discovered the false witnesses by asking them questions.

I may be told that the statutes I before named be repealed, for I know the diversity of religion in the princes of those days caused many changes. Yet the equity and reason of those laws still remains. They are still kept to illustrate how the Common Law was then taken and ought to be expounded.

But howsoever that may be, the law of God saith: 'At the mouth of two or three witnesses shall he that is worthy of death be put to death; but at the mouth of one witness he shall not be put to death.' And, again: 'One witness shall not rise up against a man for any iniquity or sin that he sinneth. At the mouth of two or three witnesses shall the matter be established.'

Divers other places of the Old Testament are to like purpose, and

[185]

the same is confirmed by our Saviour, by Saint Paul, and by the whole consent of the Scriptures.

By the law of God, therefore, the life of man is of such price and value that no person, whatever his offence is, ought to die, unless he be condemned on the testimony of two or three witnesses.

If then by the Statute Law, by the Civil Law, and by God's word it be required that there be two witnesses, at the least, bear with me if I desire one.

Prove me guilty of these things by one witness only, and I will confess the indictment.

I stand not upon niceties of the law. If I have done these things, I deserve not to live, whether they be treasons by the law or no. I beseech you then, my Lords, let Cobham be sent for. Let him be charged upon his soul, upon his allegiance to the King, and if he will then maintain his accusation to my face, I will confess myself guilty.

Cecil: Sir Walter Raleigh presseth that my Lord Cobham should be brought face to face. If he ask things of favour and grace, they must only come from him that gives them. If we sit here as Commissioners, how shall we be satisfied whether he ought to be brought, unless we hear the Judges speak?

Ld Ch. Justice: There must not be such a gulf opened for the destruction of the King, which would be if we should grant this. You plead hard for yourself, but the laws plead as hard for the safety of the King.

I did never hear that course to be taken in case of treason, to write one to another, or speak one to another. There hath been intelligence between you and Cobham; and what underhand practices there may be, I know not.

If the circumstances agree not with the evidence, we will not condemn you.

Justice Gawdy: Sir Walter Raleigh, for the statutes you have mentioned, none of them help you. The statutes you speak of in cases of treason were found to be inconvenient, and were taken away by another law.

Those of Edward VI are general, but were repealed by the 1st and 2nd of Philip and Mary, which you have mentioned, which statute goes only to the treasons there comprised, and also appoints the trial of treasons to be as before it was, at the Common Law. Now the 25th of Edward III makes declaration what the Common Law was.

All is now therefore put to the Common Law. And by the Common Law, one witness is sufficient, and the accusation of confederates or the confession of others is full proof.

Neither is subscription of the party so material to the confession, if it be otherwise testified by credible persons.

And of all other proofs, the accusation of one who by his confession first accuseth himself is the strongest.

Justice Warburton: I marvel, Sir Walter, that you, being of such experience and wit, should stand on this point. For many horse-stealers should escape if they may not be condemned without witnesses.

By law, a man may be condemned upon presumption and circumstances, without any witness to the main fact. As, if the King – whom God defend – should be slain in his chamber, and one be shown to have come forth of the chamber, with his sword drawn and bloody. Were not this evidence, both in law and opinion, without further inquisition?

Raleigh: Yet by your favour, my Lord, the trial of fact at the Common Law is by jury and witnesses.

Ld Ch. Justice: No, the trial at the Common Law is by examination. If three conspire a treason, and they all confess it, there is never a witness; and yet they may all be condemned of treason.

Raleigh: I know not, my Lord, how you conceive the law. But if you affirm it, it must be a law to all posterity.

Ld Ch. Justice: Nay, we do not conceive the law. We know the law.

Raleigh: Notwithstanding, my Lords, let me have thus much for my life. Though the law may be as your Lordships have stated it, yet it is a strict and rigorous interpretation of the law.

Now the King of England, at his coronation, swears to observe the equity and not the rigour of the law. And if ever we had a just and good King, it is his Majesty; and such doth he wish his ministers and judges to be. Though, therefore, by the rigour and severity of the law, this may be sufficient evidence, without producing the witness, yet your Lordships, as ministers of the King, are bound to administer the law in equity.

Ld. Ch. Justice: Equity must proceed from the King. You can only have justice from us.

Cecil: Now that Sir Walter is resolved by my Lords the Judges that the accusation is sufficient, I pray you, Master Attorney, go on with the proofs.

8

Extracts were now read of statements by Cobham, Copley, Watson, Brooke and Laurencie.

Cobham had said, of an interview with Aremberg: 'The last letter I wrote him was that he would procure me a pass for my safe going to Spain; and that his master was at great charge, but if he should be advised to deliver 400,000 or 500,000 crowns, as I would direct, it should save his master millions. To this letter the Count of Aremberg returned the answer that money should be procured; but how it should be distributed – that was the difficulty, and prayed my direction.'

Copley, Watson and Brooke had heard that Cobham and Raleigh 'stood for the Spanish faction'.

Laurencie had deposed that Raleigh had supped with Cobham in the evening of the day on which Cobham had written to Aremberg; and that when a messenger from Aremberg brought one of his letters to Cobham, Raleigh was standing in the hall, and afterwards went upstairs.

And Raleigh's own statement was read: 'Lord Cobham offered me 10,000 crowns of the money, for the furthering the peace between England and Spain; and he said that I should have it within three days. I told him: "When I see the money, I will make an answer." For I thought it one of his ordinary idle conceits, and therefore made no account thereof. But this was, as I think, before Count Aremberg's coming over.'

Att. Gen.: Raleigh must have his part of this money; therefore now he is a traitor.

The crown shall never stand one year upon the head of the King, my master, if a traitor may not be condemned by circumstance.

For if A tell B, and B tell C, and C tell D, etc., you shall never prove treason by two witnesses.

You have read the letter of the law, but understand it not. This dilemma of yours about two witnesses led you into treason for you thought with yourself, 'Either Cobham must accuse me or not accuse me; if he accuse me, yet he is but one witness; if he accuse me not, then I am clear.'

But to fortify the Lord Cobham's accusation against you, I will prove, by circumstances, that many points therein are true; and this by your own confessions, and by the testimony of others.

Now to prove it by circumstances. Cobham says that he was to have a passport to go to Spain and to return by Jersey, there to confer with you. As to this, you say yourself, Sir Walter, that you promised to meet him at Jersey, though it was but to make merry with you and your wife.

Again, Cobham says that money was to be raised for discontented persons. You do not deny that money was to be raised, but you say it was to be for furtherance of the peace.

Raleigh: Master Attorney, you have seemed to say much, but in truth nothing that applies to me.

You conclude that I must know of the plots, because I was to have part of the money. But all you have said concerning this I make void, by distinguishing the time when it was spoken. It is true my Lord Cobham had speech with me about the money, and made me an offer. But how? And when?

Voluntarily, one day at dinner, some time before Count Aremberg's coming over. For he and I, being at his own board, arguing and speaking violently – he for the peace, I against the peace – the Lord Cobham told me that when Count Aremberg came he would yield such strong arguments for the peace as would satisfy any man. And withal he told – as his fashion is to utter things easily – what great sums of money would be given to some Councillors for making the peace; and named my Lord Cecil and the Earl of Mar.

I answering bade him make no such offer unto them, for they would hate him if he did offer it.

Now if, after this, my Lord Cobham changed his mind as to the use to be made of the money, and joining with the Lord Grey and others, has any such treasonable intent as is alleged, what is that to me? They must answer it, not I.

The offer of the money to me is nothing, for it was made me before Count Aremberg's coming. The offer made to the others was afterwards.

Serjeant Philips: Raleigh confesseth the matter, but avoids it by distinguishing of times.

You said it was offered you before the coming of Aremberg, which is false. For you, being examined whether you should have such money of Cobham, or not, you said: 'Yea', and that you should have it within three days.

Ld Henry Howard: Allege me any grounds of cause why you gave ear to my Lord Cobham, as receiving of pensions, in matters you had not to deal in.

Raleigh: Could I stop my Lord Cobham's mouth?

Att. Gen.: You are an odious man, for Cobham thinks his cause the worse that you are in it.

Now you shall hear of some stirs to be raised in Scotland.

9

From an examination of Copley these words were read: 'Also Watson told me that a special person told him that Aremberg offered to him a thousand crowns to be in that action, and that Brooke said the stirs in Scotland came out of Raleigh's head.'

Raleigh: Brooke hath been taught his lesson.

Ld Henry Howard: This examination was taken before me. Did I teach him his lesson?

Raleigh: I protest, before God, that I meant it not by any Privy Councillor.

Att. Gen.: Because money is scant, he will juggle on both sides.

Then from Raleigh's examination these words were read: 'The way to invade England were to begin with stirs in Scotland.'

Raleigh: I think so still. I have spoken it often to divers of the Lords of the Council, by way of discourse and my opinion.

Att. Gen.: Now let us come to those words of 'destroying the King and his cubs'.

Raleigh: Oh, barbarous! If they, like unnatural villains, spake such words, shall I be charged with them? I will not hear it!

I was never false to the crown of England. I have spent £40,000 of mine own against the Spanish faction, for the good of my country. Do you bring the words of these hellish spiders, Clark, Watson and others, against me?

Att. Gen.: Thou hast a Spanish heart, and thyself art a spider of hell, for thou confessest the King to be a most sweet and gracious prince and yet hast conspired against him.

Then extracts from other examinations were read:

From an examination of Watson: 'He said that George Brooke told him twice that his brother, the Lord Cobham, said to him: "You are but on the Bye, but Raleigh and I are on the Main." '

From an examination of Brooke: 'Being asked what was meant by this jargon, the Bye and the Main, he said that the Lord Cobham told him that Grey and others were on the Bye, he and Raleigh on the Main . . . by the Main was meant the taking away of the King and his issue; and thinks on his conscience it was infused into his brother's head by Raleigh.'

Raleigh: In all this I find not myself touched, scarce named. And the course of proof is strange. Witnesses speak by relation of one another. All the proof of my Lord Cobham's accusing me is Copley, Watson and Brooke, men with whom I never had to do.

If this may be, you will have any man's life in a week.

A further passage from one of Cobham's examinations was read: 'Keymis brought him a letter from Raleigh, and that part which was concerning the Lords of the Council was rent – that he was examined and cleared him of all; and that the Lord Henry Howard had made a syllogism against him: "Because you were discontented, therefore you were likely to enter an action of treason." And, further, that Keymis said to him, from Raleigh, that he should "be of good comfort, for one witness could not condemn for treason".'

Raleigh: This poor man hath been close prisoner these eighteen weeks. He was offered the rack, to make him confess. I never sent any such message by him.

[191]

I only did write to Cobham, to tell him what I had done with Mr Attorney; I having of his at that time the great pearl and a diamond.

Ld Henry Howard: No circumstance moveth me more than this. Keymis was never at the rack: the King gave charge that no rigour should be used.

The other Commissioners: We protest, before God, there was no such matter, to our knowledge.

Raleigh to Sir William Wade: Was not the keeper of the rack sent for, and he threatened with it?

Wade: When Mr Solicitor and myself came to examine Keymis, we told him he 'deserved the rack', but did not threaten him with it.

The other Commissioners: It was more than we knew.

10

Another extract was read from one of Cobham's examinations: 'He saith he had a book written against the title of the King, which he had of Raleigh, and that he gave it to his brother. And Raleigh said it was foolishly written.'

Att. Gen.: After the King came within twelve miles of London, Cobham never came to see him, and intended to travel without seeing the Queen and the Prince. Now in this discontentment you gave him the book, and he gave it to his brother.

Raleigh: I never gave it him: he took it off my table. For I remember, a little before that time, I received a challenge from Sir Amyas Preston, and for that I did intend to answer it, I resolved to leave my estate settled; therefore I laid out all my loose papers, amongst which was this book.

Ld Henry Howard: I remember well that, I being sent to take the Lord Cobham's confession, I pressed him about this book. He suddenly broke out into a great passion and said: 'A man is unhappy that must accuse his friend. I had the book of Sir Walter Raleigh. He made no account of it, but said it was against the King's title.'

When, Sir Walter Raleigh, you being questioned what it contained, said it concerned only the justifying of the late Queen's criminal proceedings against the late Queen of Scots, and nothing against the King's title, and you never gave it my Lord Cobham but, it lying upon your table, my Lord Cobham might take it.

Hereupon my Lord Cobham being afterwards examined, retracted what before he had said, and now said that it contained nothing against the King's title, and that he had it not from Sir Walter Raleigh but took it off from his table when he was sleeping.

Att. Gen.: I observe there was intelligence between you and Cobham in the Tower. For after he had said it was against the King's title, he denied it again.

Wade: First, my Lord Cobham confesseth it, and, after he had subscribed it, he revoked it again. To me he always said that the drift of it was against the King's title.

Ld Ch. Justice: Brooke, which was a learned man, said it was against the King's title.

Raleigh: I protest, before God and his works, I gave him not the book.

Ld Henry Howard: Where had you this book?

Raleigh: Here is much ado about this book. I will tell your Lordships how I came to it, and what little account I made of it.

I had it out of a Councillor's library long since. It was written, above twenty-six years past, by a lawyer and dedicated to a stranger.

Sir Walter Raleigh, being pressed from what Councillor he had it, confessed.

Raleigh: In the old Lord Treasurer's study, after his death.

Cecil: Did you ever show or make known the book to me?

Raleigh: No, my Lord.

Cecil: Was it one of the books which was left to me or my brother?

Raleigh: I took it out of the study in my Lord Treasurer's house in the Strand.

Cecil: After my father's death, Sir Walter Raleigh desired to search for some cosmographical description of the Indies, which he thought were in his study, and were not to be had in print. Which I granted, and would have trusted Sir Walter Raleigh as soon as any man; though since, for some infirmities, the bands of my affection to him have been broken; and yet, reserving my duty to the King, my master, which I can by no means dispense with, by God I love him and have a great conflict within myself.

But I must needs say, Sir Walter used me a little unkindly to take the book away without my knowledge.

Nevertheless, I need make no apology in behalf of my father, considering how useful and necessary it is for Privy Councillors and those in his place to intercept and keep such kind of writings; for whosoever should then search his study may in all likelihood find all the notorious libels that were writ against the late Queen, and whosoever should rummage my study, or at least my cabinet, may find several against the King, our sovereign Lord, since his accession to the throne.

Raleigh: There was no purpose in taking that book. But amongst other books and maps it seems it was cast in. Upon sorting of the papers afterwards, it came to my hand.

It was a manuscript, written upon by my Lord Treasurer: 'This book I had of Robert Snagge.' The scope of the book is to justify the late Queen's proceedings against the Queen of Scots.

But I marvel it should be now urged as a matter so treasonable in me to have such books; when it is well known that there came out nothing in those times but I had them, and might as freely have them as another.

And I do own, as my Lord Cecil has said, that I believe they may also find in my house almost all the libels that have been writ against the late Queen.

Att. Gen.: You were not a Privy Councillor, and I hope never shall be.

Cecil: He was not a sworn Councillor of State, but he has been called to consultations.

Raleigh: I think it a very severe interpretation of the law to bring me within the compass of treason for this book, writ so long ago, of which nobody has read any more than the heads of the chapters, and which was burnt by George Brooke without my privity . . .

Ld Ch. Justice: Wherefore should this book be burnt?

Raleigh: I burned it not.

Serj. Philips: You presented your friend with it when he was discontented. If it had been before the Queen's death it had been a less matter, but you gave it him presently when he came from the King, which was the time of his discontentment.

Raleigh: Here is a book supposed to be treasonable. I never read it, nor commended it, nor delivered it, nor urged it.

Att. Gen.: Why, this is cunning.

Raleigh: Everything that doth make for me is cunning, and everything that maketh against me is probable.

II

Att. Gen.: Now that Raleigh hath had conference in all these treasons it is manifest. The Jury hath heard out the matter.

Now, there is one Dyer, a pilot, that being in Lisbon met with a Portugal gentleman, which asked him if the King of England were crowned yet. To whom he answered: 'I think not yet, but he shall be shortly.' 'Nay,' saith the Portugal, 'that shall he never be; for his throat will be cut by Don Raleigh and Don Cobham, before he be crowned.'

Hereupon Dyer was called. He deposed upon oath to the hearing of those words in a conversation at Lisbon.

Raleigh: What infer you upon that?

Att. Gen.: That your treason hath wings.

12

Raleigh (the final speech for the defence): I am accused concerning Arabella, and concerning money out of Spain. My Lord Chief Justice saith that a man may be condemned without witness.

Cobham is guilty of many things . . . he hath accused himself. What can he hope for? My Lords – vouchsafe me but this grace – let him be brought, being alive and in the house hard by, let him avow any of these speeches; and I will confess the whole indictment, and renounce the King's mercy –

[195]

Cecil: Arabella Stuart is kinswoman to the King. Let us not scandal the innocent by confusion of speeches. She is as innocent of all these things as I, or any man here.

The Earl of Nottingham (Lord Charles Howard), 'being in a standing with the Lady Arabella': The lady doth here protest, upon her salvation, that she never dealt in any of these things.

Att. Gen.: For Arabella, I said she was never acquainted with matters.

Raleigh: The Lord Cobham hath accused me: you see in what manner he hath forsworn it. Were it not for his accusations, all this were nothing. Let him be asked if I knew of the letters which Laurencie brought to him from Aremberg.

Here the Attorney General sought again to interrupt Raleigh in his defence.

Raleigh: Let me speak for my life.

Cecil: This is his last discourse. Give him leave, Master Attorney.

Raleigh: It can be no hurt for him to be brought. He dareth not excuse me. If you grant me not this favour, I am strangely used. Campion was not denied to have his accusers face to face.

Ld Ch. Justice: Though the Lord Cobham must needs have justice, the acquitting of his old friend may move him to speak otherwise than the truth.

Raleigh: I have been 'the infuser of these treasons into him'. You, gentlemen of the Jury, mark this. He said I have been the cause of all his miseries and the destruction of his house; and that all the evil hath happened to him by my wicked counsel. If this be truth, whom hath he cause to accuse and to be revenged on, but on me? And I know him to be as revengeful as any man on earth.

Att. Gen.: He is a party, and may not come. The law is against it.

Raleigh: It is a toy to tell me of law. I defy law, I stand on the facts.

Consider, you Gentlemen of the Jury. There is no cause so weak, nor title so bad, but these men, by wit or learning, can maintain it for good; and that against men of their own profession. I beseech you, therefore, consider their ability and my disability, who never studied law till I came into the Tower of London.

They prove nothing against me. Only they bring the accusation of my Lord Cobham, which he hath lamented and repented, as heartily

[196]

as if it had been a horrible murder. For he knew that all this sorrow which should come to me is by his means.

Presumptions must proceed from precedent or subsequent facts. I have spent £40,000 against the Spaniard. I have not purchased £40 a year land. If I had died in Guiana, I had not left three hundred marks a year to my wife and son. I that have always condemned the Spaniard faction – methinks it is a strange thing that now I should affect it.

Remember what St Austin saith: '*Sic judicatis tanquam ab alio mox judicandi* [judge as you would be judged]'. Now if you would be content, on presumptions, to be delivered to the slaughter; to have your wives and children turned into the streets to beg their bread; if you would be contented to be so judged, judge so of me.

Cecil: I am afraid my often speech, whom am inferior to my Lords here in presence, will make the world think I delight to hear myself talk.

My affection to you, Sir Walter Raleigh, was not extinguished but slacked, in regard of your defects. You know the reason – to which your mind doth not contest – that my Lord Cobham cannot be brought.

Raleigh: He may be, my Lord.

Cecil: But dare you challenge it?

Raleigh: Now.

Att. Gen.: You say that my Lord Cobham, your main accuser, must come to accuse you. You say that he hath retracted. What the validity of all this is, is merely left to the Jury.

Let me only ask you this. If my Lord Cobham will say you are the only instigator of him to proceed in the treasons, dare you put yourself on this?

Raleigh: If he will speak it, before God and the King, that ever I knew of Arabella's matter for the money out of Spain, or of the 'surprising' treason, I put myself on it. God's will and the King's be done with me.

Ld Henry Howard: How if he speak things equivalent to that you have said?

Raleigh: Yes, in a main point.

Cecil: If he say you have been the instigator of him to deal with the Spanish King, had not the Council cause to draw you hither?

[197]

Raleigh: I put myself on it.

Cecil: Then call to God, Sir Walter, and prepare yourself, for I do verily believe my Lord will prove this.

Excepting your fault, I am your friend. The great passion in you, and the Attorney's zeal for the King's service, make me speak thus.

13

Serj. Philips (winding up for the prosecution): I hope to make this so clear as that the wit of man shall have no colour to answer it.

The matter is treason in the highest degree; the end, to deprive the King of his crown.

The particular treasons are these: first, to raise up rebellion and – to effect that – to procure money to raise up tumults in Scotland, by divulging a treasonable book against the King's right to the crown.

The purpose: to take the life of his Majesty and his issue.

Sir Walter Raleigh confesseth my Lord Cobham guilty of all these treasons. The question is, whether he is guilty, as joining with him or instigating him?

The course to prove this was my Lord Cobham's accusation. If that be true, he is guilty. If not, he is clear. So, whether Cobham say true, or Raleigh, that is the question.

Raleigh hath no answer. Of as much wit as the wit of man can devise, he useth his bare denial.

A denial of the defendant must not move the Jury. In the Star Chamber or in the Chancery, for matter of title, if a defendant be called in question, his denial on his oath is no evidence to the court to clear him. He doth it *in propria causa* [in his own cause]. Therefore much less in matter of treason.

But when one, accusing another, excuses not himself, but condemns himself, his testimony is as violent as the verdict of twelve men.

Raleigh: If truth be constant, and constancy be in truth, why hath he forsworn what he hath said?

You have not proved any one thing by direct proofs, but all by circumstances.

[198]

Att. Gen.: Have you done? The King must have the last.

Raleigh: Nay, Master Attorney, he which speaketh for his life must speak last. False repetitions and mistakings must not mar my cause. You should speak *secundum allegatum et probatum* [according to what has been alleged and has been proved].

I appeal to God and the King on this point, whether Cobham's accusation be sufficient to condemn me.

Att. Gen.: The King's safety and your clearing cannot agree. I protest I never knew a clearer treason. Go to! I will lay thee upon thy back for the confidentest traitor that ever came to a bar!

Why should you take 8,000 crowns?

Cecil: Be not so impatient, good Master Attorney. Give him leave to speak.

Att. Gen.: If I may not be patiently heard, you will encourage traitors and discourage us. I am the King's sworn servant, and must speak.

If he be guilty, he is an odious traitor. If not, deliver him.

Here the Attorney General sat down, and would speak no more, till the Commissioners urged and entreated him to go on.

Att. Gen.: Now see what it hath pleased God to work in the heart of my Lord Cobham – even since his coming to Winchester – which we knew not of.

The Lord Cobham hath confessed that, about four days before his coming from the Tower, there passed intelligence between him and Raleigh. Raleigh had an apple, and pinned a letter to it, and threw it into my Lord Cobham's window.

The content whereof was this: 'It is doubtful whether we shall be proceeded with or no. Perhaps now you shall not be tried.' That was to get a retraction. It was Adam's apple, whereby the Devil did deceive him.

Further he wrote this: 'Do not, as my Lord Essex did, take heed of a preacher. By his persuasion he confessed, and made himself guilty.'

O damnable atheist! He counsels him not to be led by the counsels of preachers, as Essex was – he died the child of God. God honoured him at his death. Thou wast by. *Et lupus et turpes instant morientibus ursae* [Both the wolf and the foul she-bears close in on the dying].

I doubt not but this day God shall have as great a conquest by this traitor, and the Son of God shall be as much glorified, as when it was said, '*Vicisti, Galilaeus* [You have conquered, Galilaean]' – you know my meaning.

Though Cobham retracted, yet he could not rest nor sleep till he had confirmed.

Yet again, if this be not enough to prove him a traitor, the King my master shall not live three years to an end.

Cobham's letter was then read:

I have thought it fit in duty to my Sovereign, and in discharge of my conscience, to set this down to your Lordships, wherein I protest, upon my soul, to write nothing but what is true. For I am not ignorant of my present condition, and now to dissemble with God is no time.

Sir Walter Raleigh, four nights before my coming from the Tower, writ to me desiring me to set it down under my hand – and send to him an acknowledgement under my hand, that I had wronged him; and that I should herein renounce what I had formerly accused him of.

I since have thought how he went about only to clear himself by betraying of me. Whereupon I have resolved to set down the truth, and under my hand to retract what he cunningly got from me; craving humble pardon of his Majesty and your Lordships for my double dealing . . .

With the like truth, I will proceed and tell you my dealings towards Count Aremberg to get him a pension of £1,500 per annum for intelligence; and he would always tell and advertise what was intended against Spain; for the Low Countries; or with France. And coming from Greenwich one night, he acquainted me what was agreed betwixt the King and the Low Countries, that I should impart it to Count Aremberg.

Att. Gen.: Ah! Is not this a Spanish heart in an English body?

Cobham's letter: But upon this motion for £1,500 per annum for intelligence, I never dealt with Count Aremberg.

Now, as by this may appear to your Lordships, he hath been the original cause of my ruin. For, but by his instigation, I had never dealt with Count Aremberg. And so hath he been the only cause of my discontentment: I never coming from the Court but still he filled and possessed me with new causes of discontentments . . .

Att. Gen.: What say you now to the letter?

Raleigh: Whereas I am accused to be a traitor, I will prove myself to the end, and in the end, a true subject and an honest man, and that Cobham is a base, poor, silly, perjured soul.

Att. Gen.: Is my Lord poor?

Raleigh: Yea, in spirit.

Att. Gen.: Is he base? I return it into thy throat, on his behalf. But for thee he had been a good subject.

Ld Ch. Justice: I perceive you are not so clear a man as you have protested all this while, for you should have discovered these matters to the King.

14

Sir Walter Raleigh was much amazed by the letter, but by and by he seemed to gather his spirits again, and spoke thus:

Raleigh: I pray you hear me in a word, and you shall see how many souls this Cobham hath. And the King shall judge, by our deaths, which of us is the perfidious man.

Before my Lord Cobham's coming from the Tower, I was advised by some of my friends to get a confession from him. Therefore, I wrote to him, thus: 'You or I must go to trial. If I first, then your accusation is the only evidence against me.'

It was not ill of me to beg him to say truth.

But his first letter was not to my contenting. I writ a second, and then he writ me a very good letter.

But I sent him word I feared Mr Lieutenant of the Tower might be blamed, if it were discovered that letters passed. Though, I protest, Sir George Harvey [who had succeeded Sir John Peyton] is not to blame for what passed. No keeper in the world could so provide but it might happen.

So I sent him the letter again, with this: 'It is likely now that you shall be first tried.' But the Lord Cobham sent to me again: 'It is not unfit you had such a letter.'

Which letter I have in my hand indeed. I beseech your Lordships that it may be read. It was all my hope, I confess.

Cecil, who knew Cobham's hand, was about to read the letter.

Att. Gen.: My Lord Cecil, mar not a good cause.

Cecil: Master Attorney, you are more peremptory than honest. You must not come here to show me what to do.

Cecil then read aloud Cobham's letter:

Now that the arraignment draws near; not knowing which should be first, I or you; to clear my conscience, satisfy the world, and free myself from the cry of your blood, I protest upon my soul, and before God and his angels, I never had conference with you in any treason; nor was ever moved by you to the things I heretofore accused you of. And, for anything I know, you are as innocent and as clear from any treasons against the King, as is any subject living.

Therefore I wash my hands and pronounce: '*Purus sum a sanguine hujus* [I am innocent of the blood of this man.]'

And so God deal with me and have mercy on my soul as this is true.

Att. Gen.: He hath learned some text of Scripture to serve his own purpose, but falsely alleged.

Raleigh: Now, my masters, you have heard both. That showed against me is but a voluntary confession. This is under oath, and the deepest protestations a Christian man can make. Therefore believe which of these hath most force.

Here was much ado. Mr Attorney alleged that this last letter was politicly and cunningly urged from the Lord Cobham, and that the first was simply the truth; and that lest it should seem doubtful that the first letter was drawn from my Lord Cobham by promise of mercy or hope of favour, the Lord Chief Justice willed that the Jury might thereon be satisfied. Whereupon the Earl of Devonshire [Mountjoy] delivered that the same was mere voluntary, and not extracted from the Lord Cobham upon any hopes or promise of pardon.

This was the last evidence. Whereupon a marshal was sworn to keep the Jury private. The Jury departed, and stayed not a quarter of an hour, but returned, and gave their verdict, Guilty.

Serjeant Hele demanded judgment against the prisoner.

Clerk of the Crown: Sir Walter Raleigh, thou hast been indicted, arraigned, and pleaded Not Guilty for all these several treasons, and for trial thereof hast put thyself upon thy country, which country are these who have found thee Guilty.

What canst thou say for thyself why judgment and execution of death should not pass against thee?

Raleigh: My lord, the Jury have found me Guilty. They must do as they are directed. I can say nothing why judgment should not proceed. You see whereof Cobham hath accused me. You remember his protestations that I was never guilty. I desire the King should know of the wrongs done unto me since I came hither.

Ld Ch. Justice: You have had no wrong, Sir Walter.

Raleigh: Yes, of Mr Attorney.

I desire my Lords to remember three things to the King. I was accused to be a practitioner with Spain – I never knew that my Lord Cobham meant to go thither, nor of his practice with Aremberg. Secondly, I never knew of the practices with Arabella. Thirdly, I never knew of the 'surprising' treason . . .

I submit myself to the King's mercy. I know his mercy is greater than my offence. I recommend my wife and son of tender years, unbrought up, to his compassion.

Ld Ch. Justice: I thought I should never see this day, to have stood in this place to give sentence of death against you, because I thought it impossible that one of so great parts should have fallen so grievously . . .

You might have lived well with £3,000 a year, for so I have heard your revenues to be. I know nothing might move you to be discontented . . . I never heard that the King took anything from you but the Captainship of the Guard, which he did with very good reason, to have one of his own knowledge, whom he might trust, in that place.

You have been taken for a wise man, and so have showed wit enough this day.

Again, for monopolies for wine, etc., if the King had said: 'It is a matter that offends my people; should I burden them for your private good?', I think you could not well take it hardly that his subjects were eased, though by your private hindrance.

Two vices have lodged chiefly in you: one is an eager ambition, the other corrupt covetousness . . .

Your case being thus, let it not grieve you if I speak a little out of zeal and love to your good. You have been taxed by the world with the defence of the most heathenish and blasphemous opinions, which I list not to repeat because Christian ears cannot endure to hear them . . . You shall do well, before you go out of the world, to give satisfaction therein, and not to die with these imputations on you.

In the first accusation of my Lord Cobham I have observed his manner of speaking; I protest before the living God, I am persuaded he spoke nothing but the truth.

You wrote that he should not in any case confess anything to a preacher . . . You have showed a fearful sign of denying God in advising a man not to confess the truth.

It now comes in my mind why you may not have your accuser come face to face, for such an one is easily brought to retract, when he seeth there is no hope of his own life . . .

Now it resteth to pronounce the judgment which I wish you had not been this day to have received of me . . . But since you have been found guilty of these horrible treasons, the judgment of the Court is this:

That you shall be had from hence to the place whence you came, there to remain until the day of execution; and from thence you shall be drawn upon a hurdle through the open streets to the place of execution, there to be hanged and cut down alive, and your body shall be opened, your heart and bowels plucked out, and your privy members cut off and thrown into the fire before your eyes; then your head shall be stricken off from your body, and your body shall be divided into four quarters, to be disposed of at the King's pleasure. And God have mercy upon your soul!

Sir Walter Raleigh besought the Earl of Devonshire, and the Lords, to be suitors on his behalf to the King, that in regard of the places of estimation he did bear in her Majesty's time, the rigour of his judgment might be qualified, and his death be honourable and not ignominious.

Wherein after the Lords promised to do their uttermost endeavour, the Court rose, and the prisoner went back with the Sheriff to the prison, with admirable erection, yet in such sort as a condemned man should do.

James's first reports of the trial were from an Englishman and a Scotsman. The Englishman said that 'never any man spoke so well in times past nor would do in the world to come'. The Scotsman said that, before, he would have gone a hundred miles to see Raleigh hanged; after, he would have gone a thousand to save his life.

James may have decided already that he was not to die, but it was nearly a month before Raleigh knew it. He begged Cecil for compassion, the Queen for intercession, the Lords Commissioners for time, the King for life. Bess busied herself trying to save him; so did Lady Pembroke, Philip Sidney's sister[1]; so did the Queen.

James delighted to ask all and sundry whether he should exercise justice or mercy, and to argue on both sides.

The two priests were hanged, drawn and quartered, and on Monday 6 December Brooke was beheaded in the Castle-yard. Raleigh, whose window overlooked the yard, was visited afterwards by the Bishop of Winchester, who had been instructed to prepare him for death and obtain a confession which would reconcile his story with Cobham's. The Bishop found him 'settled and resolved to die a Christian and a good Protestant', but he would confess nothing, except that the Spanish pension had been mentioned once but not proceeded with. Cobham was similarly visited by the Bishop of Chichester; he declared he would die repeating what he had said against Raleigh.

Cobham, Grey and Markham were to die in the yard on the Friday, Raleigh on the following Monday.

The Friday was wet. Markham was brought to the scaffold, but as he was about to lie down to the block he was taken away again. Grey was brought out and, after his praying had kept the spectators half an hour in the rain, he too was taken away. Cobham came, expressed sorrow for his offence, and, 'for Sir Walter Raleigh, he took it, upon the hope of his soul's resurrection, that what he had said of him was true'. As he was about to lie down Grey and Markham were brought out, and they were all three told that the King had given them their lives.

Raleigh wrote to the Lords begging to be spared also, but the scaffold remained in position for use on the Monday.

16

Raleigh to Bess:[1]

You shall receive, dear Bess, my last words in these my last lines. My love I send you, that you may keep it when I am dead; and my counsel, that you may remember it when I am no more. I would not, with my last will, present you with sorrows, dear Bess. Let them go to the grave with me, and be buried in the dust. And, seeing it is not the will of God that ever I shall see you in this life, bear my destruction gently and with a heart like yourself.

First, I send you all the thanks my heart can conceive, or my words express, for your many troubles and cares taken for me, which – though they have not taken effect as you wished – yet my debt is to you never the less; but pay it I never shall in this world.

Secondly, I beseech you, for the love you bare me living, that you do not hide yourself many days, but by your travail seek to help your miserable fortunes, and the right of your poor child. Your mourning cannot avail me that am but dust.

You shall understand that my lands were conveyed to my child, *bona fide*. The writings were drawn at midsummer was twelve months. My honest cousin Brett can testify so much, and Dolberry, too, can remember somewhat therein. And I trust my blood will quench their malice that desire my slaughter; and that they will not also seek to kill you and yours with extreme poverty.

To what friend to direct thee I know not, for all mine have left me in the true time of trial; and I plainly conceive that my death was determined from the first day.

Most sorry I am (as God knoweth) that, being surprised with death, I can leave you no better estate. I meant you all mine office of wines, or that I could purchase by selling it; half my stuff, and jewels, but some few, for my boy. But God hath prevented all my determinations; the great God that worketh all in all.

If you can live free from want, care for no more; for the rest is vanity. Love God, and begin betimes to repose yourself in him; therein shall you find true and lasting riches, and endless comfort. For the rest, when you have travailed and wearied your thoughts on all sorts of worldly cogitations, you shall sit down by sorrow in the end.

Teach your son also to serve and fear God, while he is young, that the fear of God may grow up in him. Then will God be a husband unto you, and a father unto him; a husband and a father which can never be taken from you.

Bailey oweth me £200, and Adrian £600. In Jersey also I have much owing me. The arrearages of the wines will pay my debts. And, howsoever, for my soul's health, I beseech you pay all poor men.

When I am gone, no doubt you shall be sought unto by many, for the world thinks that I was very rich; but take heed of the pretences of men and of their affections, for they last but in honest and worthy men. And no greater misery can befall you in this life than to become a prey, and after to be despised. I speak it (God knows) not to dissuade you from marriage – for that will be best for you – both in respect of God and the world. As for me I am no more yours, nor you mine. Death hath cut us asunder; and God hath divided me from the world, and you from me.

Remember your poor child for his father's sake, that comforted and loved you in his happiest times.

Get those letters (if it be possible) which I writ to the Lords, wherein I sued for my life, but God knoweth that it was for you and yours that I desired it, but it is true that I disdain myself for begging it. And know it (dear wife) that your son is the child of a true man, and who, in his own respect, despiseth Death, and all his misshapen and ugly forms.

I cannot write much. God knows how hardly I stole this time, when all sleep; and it is time to separate my thoughts from the world. Beg my dead body, which living was denied you; and either lay it at Sherborne if the land continue, or in Exeter church, by my father and mother.

I can write no more. Time and Death call me away.

The everlasting, infinite, powerful and inscrutable God, that Almighty God that is goodness itself, mercy itself, the true life and light, keep you and yours, and have mercy on me, and teach me to forgive my persecutors and false accusers; and send us to meet in his glorious kingdom.

My true wife, farewell. Bless my poor boy. Pray for me. My true God hold you both in his arms.

Written with the dying hand of sometimes thy husband, but now (alas!) overthrown.

Yours that was, but now not my own.

W. Raleigh.

Raleigh:

Give me my scallop-shell of quiet,
My staff of faith to walk upon,
My scrip of joy, immortal diet,
My bottle of salvation,
My gown of glory, hope's true gage;
And thus I'll take my pilgrimage.

Blood must be my body's balmer,
No other balm will there be given;
Whilst my soul, like a white palmer,
Travels to the land of Heaven,
Over the silver mountains,
Where spring the nectar fountains;
And there I'll kiss
The bowl of bliss,
And drink my eternal fill
On every milken hill.
My soul will be a-dry before,
But, after, it will thirst no more.

And by the happy blissful way
More peaceful pilgrims I shall see,
That have shook off their gowns of clay,
And go apparelled fresh like me.
I'll bring them first
To quench their thirst

And taste those nectar suckets
At the clear wells
Where sweetness dwells,
Drawn up by saints in crystal buckets.

And when our bottles and all we
Are filled with immortality,
Then the blessed paths we'll travel,
Strowed with rubies thick as gravel;
Ceilings of diamonds, sapphire floors,
High walls of coral and pearly bowers.
From thence to Heaven's bribeless Hall,
Where no corrupted voices brawl;
No conscience molten into gold;
No forged accusers bought and sold;
No cause deferred, no vain-spent journey;
For there Christ is the King's Attorney,
Who pleads for all without degrees,
And he hath angels, but no fees.
And when the grand twelve-million jury
Of our sins, with direful fury,
Against our souls black verdicts give,
Christ pleads his death, and then we live.

Be thou my speaker, taintless pleader,
Unblotted lawyer, true proceeder,
Thou movest salvation even for alms,
Not with a bribed lawyer's palms.
And this is mine eternal plea
To him that made Heaven, earth, and sea,
Seeing my flesh must die so soon,
And want a head to dine next noon,
Just at the stroke, when my veins start and spread,
Set on my soul an everlasting head.
Then am I ready, like a palmer fit,
To tread those blest paths which before I writ.

I

He was not executed. He was returned to the Tower.

He had two thick-walled tiny-windowed rooms on the second floor of the Bloody Tower; which is part of the inner wall and looks inwards over Tower Green to the chapel of St Peter ad Vincula and outwards on the back of St Thomas's Tower, which is part of the outer wall and looks on the river. In other towers were Cobham, Grey, two or three important Irishmen, and a priest.

Two of his own staff attended him: Dean, and Talbot, a schoolmaster. The bill he had to pay for the keep of the three of them was £4 a week; but his income had dropped, he told Cecil in letters of impotent and despondent beggary, from £3,000 a year to £300 a year, and he owed £3,000. Debts were owing to him but, legally dead, he could not recover them. 'My tenants refuse to pay my wife her rent . . . My woods are cut down; my grounds waste; my stock – which made up my rent – sold.' However Bess got from the King a promise that she could keep her own goods and chattels.

He was visited fairly freely by Bess and by Shelbury, his agent; and George Carew came to see him just before Christmas, and again in January. His waterman, Owen, brought him beer and ale. A visit from a servant of his successor as Lord Lieutenant of Cornwall gave him an occasion to re-assert himself. He refused to hand over the seal, for which the man had been sent: it had been received at the hands of Queen Elizabeth and should be returned to the Crown, not passed on in vulgar short-circuit.

He addressed the King once more. With a prayer that he would 'continue and perfect his mercies begun', and with a wit framed to appeal to James, he prostrated himself.

Raleigh to James, 21 January 1604:[1]
The life which I had, most mighty Prince, the law hath taken from

me, and I am now the same earth and dust out of which I was made
. . . Name, blood, gentility or estate, I have none; no, not so much as
a being; no, not so much as *vita plantae* [vegetable life]. I have only a
penitent soul, in a body of iron, which moveth towards the lodestone of Death, and cannot be withheld from touching it, unless
your Majesty's mercy turn the point towards it which repelleth . . .

This being the first letter which ever your Majesty received from a
dead man, I humbly submit myself to the will of my supreme Lord.

2

In March it was time for James to make his formal procession
through London. As an act of clemency prisoners from the Tower
were released, but not Raleigh, Cobham and Grey who were removed to the Fleet Prison, which was less comfortable. James and
Anne then entered the Tower from the river, and while the conduits
of Fleet Street, Cornhill and Cheapside ran with claret, they pro-
cessed through seven gates raised in the City. In a few days James
opened Parliament and told both Houses their duty to their King.

Raleigh, Cobham and Grey were returned to the Tower, and in a
cold spring, depressed and sick, Raleigh explored his freedoms. He
was allowed to have Bess and Wat live with him. He was allowed to
have a trunk of his books and papers, after Cecil had kept a few for
vetting. The door of his cell was open all day and he could walk on
the terrace at the top of the inner wall, now known as Raleigh's
walk, and in the Lieutenant's garden, which was surrounded only by
a fence and low broken-down walls over which he could see and be
seen by all who came to the Lieutenant's house. He was allowed to
turn a lath-and-plaster house in this garden, once occupied by Latimer and more recently by chickens, into a laboratory.

Although he was a dead man his fortunes were not as low as they
had seemed at first. His own goods and chattels, it was decided now,
could be kept in trust for him; and his offices of Ranger of Gilling-
ham Forest and Captain of Portland Castle had been passed on to
Carew Raleigh. He was still struggling to keep Sherborne, and

thanks largely to Bess's energetic begging it was promised, for the term of his life, to herself and her children (children in the plural – she was pregnant again).

But neither his health nor his spirits improved. By day he thought he was dying of paralysis, by night of suffocation. He had next door to him a woman with a running plague sore, whose child died of the plague. 'Now my wife and child, and others in whom I had comfort, have abandoned me.'

His state contrasted with Cecil's and Lord Henry Howard's. As reward for a peace treaty with Spain, Howard was made Earl of Northampton, and secretly given by Spain a pension of £1,000 a year; Cecil was made Viscount Cranborne, and by Spain was given £1,500 a year.

He had other troubles. The arrears due to him from wine licences, running into four figures, had been seized by the old Lord Admiral, who only after Bess's ruthless begging to Cecil (she said the Lord Admiral had already gained £3,000 a year and £6,000 by Raleigh's fall) gave them up.

And Bess was soon ruthlessly insisting with both Raleigh and Cecil that she and her (two) children must have a hold on Sherborne beyond her husband's death. He himself thought that it should not be forfeit to the King at all, because in 1602 he had conveyed it to Wat; but the conveyance, drawn up by an eminent lawyer, had accidentally omitted a phrase which was essential, and now the law officers were discussing whether or not it was void. He descended deeper into sickness and self-pity.

Raleigh to Cecil (now Earl of Salisbury):[1]
I lay before your Lordship the true cause of my importunities.

The one is (which I speak in the presence and fear of God) that I am every second or third night in danger either of sudden death or of the loss of my limbs and sense, being sometimes two hours without feeling or motion of my hand and whole arm. I complain not of it. I know it vain, for there is none that hath compassion thereof.

The other, that I shall be made more than weary of my life by her crying and bewailing who will return in post when she hears of your Lordship's departure, and nothing done. She hath already brought her eldest son in one hand and her sucking child in the other, crying out of her and their destruction; charging me with unnatural negligence, and that having provided for mine own life I am without sense and compassion of theirs.

Report by Raleigh's doctor, Dr Peter Turner:[1]
To speak like a physician, it were good for him if it might stand with your Honours' liking, that he were removed from the cold lodging where he lieth unto a warmer, that is to say, a little room which he hath built in the garden adjoining to his still-house.

3

On 5 November 1605 there were bells and bonfires in the City, and Catholic toleration receded centuries into the future. Guy Fawkes was brought to the Tower, tortured over many days and celled in 'Little Ease', and other Gunpowder Plotters were distributed. In a few days Northumberland, who had not hidden his disappointment that Catholics still suffered heavy penalties or his preference of Prince Henry to his father, was in the Martin Tower, suspected of complicity.

Raleigh, too, was suspected and examined by the Council: he was a friend of Northumberland's; and he had been visited in the Tower by a servant of Northumberland's at least once; and Lady Raleigh had gone down to Sherborne in September and had all the armour and weapons scoured.[2]

For a while his freedoms were cut down, but his health and energies improved. They may have been stimulated by Northumberland's irrepressible presence in the Tower. Northumberland asserted his right to be comfortable.[3] He had many servants, tipped the warders, and paid the Lieutenant £100 a year in order not to be fed by him. He put windows in his rooms, built himself a still-house and, in the garden used by him and Cobham, put gravel on the paths and built a bowling-alley with a canvas roof. To his quarters there was a continual flow of books of geography, history, astronomy and occultism, and he was helped in his enthusiastic but unsystematic studies by Hariot and others. Hariot, who probably made for him the sundial on the south wall of the Martin Tower, was working chiefly on optics at this time. He had just sent Kepler the angle of refraction for hock and other liquids, and a correct explanation of rainbows.

Raleigh's still-house activities were more serious than Northumberland's. They were partly with minerals, partly with medicines, and he cured tobacco, experimented with the turning of salt water to sweet, and noted recipes for the preserving of meat at sea. The wife of the French ambassador sent for some of his 'Balsam of Guiana'; and his 'Great Cordial',[1] a compound of pearl, musk, hart's horn (ammonia), bezoar stone (a concretion found in the intestines of ruminants), mint, borage, gentian, mace, aloes, sugar, sassafras, spirits of wine, etc., was still being written about and used by the physician to Charles II, grandson of the first royal user, James's Queen Anne,[2] and it was used by Robert Boyle.[3] His pills were taken by the Countess of Rutland (the gossips said she died of them),[4] and later he sent a plaster for the spleen to Sir Thomas Overbury when he was imprisoned in the Bloody Tower.[5]

Northumberland's still-house was occupied largely with the repeated distillation of stale beer and wine in order to make, after the addition of ambergris, musk, etc., a whiskey. Apart from Hariot being on both visiting lists, the only evidence of communication between the Martin Tower and the Bloody is an entry in Northumberland's accounts for a purchase from Raleigh of Greek wine.

Raleigh was reading vigorously – on English history, on the politics, military strategy, chronology and geography of the ancient world, and the moral lessons of the Bible. And he kept in touch with explorations and expeditions.

Since he entered the Tower there had been two or three voyages to Virginia, and in 1606 a group of adventurers, including a nephew of his and Richard Hakluyt, received a patent to plant colonies there. With the end of privateering and the coming of peace there was new interest in colonies and more money available for them. Raleigh asked permission to go with the expedition, and the Queen took his part.

And there was an alternative chance of freedom. Anne's brother,

Christian, the King of Denmark, paid James a visit. Christian, blonde like Anne, was a great drinker. He was feasted to the accompaniment of drums and trumpets, some of the ladies loyally vomiting and passing out. The two kings embraced, hunted the deer in St James's and Hyde Parks, tilted, were rowed up and down the Thames, and at the Tower looked at James's jewels and ordnance and lions. Christian asked if he could have Raleigh as his admiral.

But Christian returned to Denmark without Raleigh, and an expedition of 105 persons sailed off to Virginia and founded Jamestown and in due course a nation, but without Raleigh.

There was still Guiana.

4

In the first play at Court in the Christmas season of 1604-5 Desdemona was told by Othello about Raleigh's Ewaipanoma – 'the men whose heads do grow beneath their shoulders'.[1] Neither they nor El Dorado had yet been seen by Englishmen, but in the ten years since 'The Discovery of Guiana' regular trading to the Orinoco had been developed by the English and the Dutch.

A little further down the coast, on the Oyapoco, Raleigh's friends, the brothers Leigh, were trying to found a colony for trade, planting and gold-mining, which would soon disintegrate for lack of supplies, while a colony of 400 Frenchmen would soon be wiped out by Indians. Raleigh sent an Oyapoco tribe messages and some English woollens.

Suddenly those casks full of stone which he had brought back in 1595 gave him a hope. A refiner found that some stone of which Raleigh had taken little notice, contained gold.

Raleigh to Cecil (Earl of Salisbury): [2]
It is true that I promised him twenty pound if he could find gold or silver in the ore. Now, if he have dealt justly, or – in the hope of the money – falsely, it may be easily examined . . . I have reserved a little quantity of each to make a second trial.

I beseech your Lordship, then, to consider what I offer . . . I am content both to go and come as a private man; that both the charge of the ship be given to another – which I desire might be the bearer hereof – and that he have order that if I do but persuade a contrary course to cast me into the sea. Your Lordship may also appoint the master, and all other officers. Only, if God give us leave to arrive in safety, that upon the land they may be directed by me, or by any joint commissioners, if your Lordship shall so please.

The charge of the journey will amount to £5,000, of which if the Queen's Majesty (to whom I am bound for her compassion) and your Lordship will bear two parts, I and my friends will bear a third; or if her Majesty and your Lordship will not adventure, I will find means to bear all, and present her Majesty and your Lordship with the one half, so we may be assured to enjoy the rest . . .

We will break no peace; invade none of the Spanish towns. We will only trade with the Indians, and see none of that nation except they assail us.

Raleigh, from a notebook:[1]
I tried the ore of Guiana in this sort. I took of the ore beaten small 12 grains, of filed lead half an ounce, of sandiver a quarter of an ounce. I beat the sandiver small and then mixed all together and put it into a cruset, covering it with another cruset that had a little hole in the top and luted both together. Then I covered all with good coal, and with two pairs of ordinary bellows we blew to it till all was melted down. Then we put the lead upon a test under a muffle till the lead was consumed, and had of the 12 grains a quarter of a grain of gold.

Cecil listened to the scheme but then, Raleigh complained, retired into an *arrière-boutique*. There was no action. It was not a time for offending Spain.

In the Tower the regulations were revised and re-affirmed: doors of prisoners' quarters were not to be left open all day; at 5 p.m. when the bell rang, prisoners were to leave their gardens and go into their quarters and stay there; at night the watch, when they made their rounds, were to 'call upon' the prisoners; the wives of Northumberland and Raleigh were not to drive into the Tower in their coaches and treat the prisons as dwelling houses.

Raleigh sent Wat, aged fourteen all but two days, no longer betrothed to the rich heiress, to Corpus Christi College, Oxford, and warned one of his two tutors of Wat's addiction to violent exercise and 'strange company'. Wat, who had his father's pig-eye, was 'a handsome lusty stout fellow, very bold and apt to affront'.

James was also finding an elder son undocile. Prince Henry was thirteen. He loved all sports except hunting, his father's favourite; disliked the young Scot, Carr, whom his father pawed; was decorous and punctilious, the opposite of his father; had boxes for fines in his various houses, for the punishment of swearing – they would have ruined James; studied the art of war, James's anathema.

Henry, like his mother, had developed an admiration for Raleigh. He had on his staff Raleigh's cousin and friend, Sir Arthur Gorges, who published in 1607 an account of Raleigh's courage and correctness on the Azores expedition of 1597. And at about the same time, when Henry was planning to rebuild one of the King's ships, he received a note from Raleigh of points which he should watch.

Raleigh to Prince Henry:[1]
To make her strong consisteth in the care and truth of the workman.

To make her swift is to give her a large run or way forward, and so afterward – done by art and just proportion; and that in laying out of her bows before, and quarters behind, the shipwright be sure that she neither sink nor hang into the water, but lie clear and above it; wherein shipwrights do often fail, and then is the speed in sailing utterly spoiled.

That she be stout-sided, the same is provided by a long bearing-floor, and by shaving off from above waters to the lower edge of the ports; which done, then will she carry out her ordnance all weathers.

To make her to hull and to try well – which is called a good sea-ship – there are two things principally to be regarded: the one, that she have a good draught of water; the other, that she be not over-charged . . .

The extreme length of a ship makes her unapt to stay, especially if she be floaty, and want of sharpness of way, forward . . . and there-fore, an hundred foot by the keel, and thirty-five foot broad, is a good proportion for a great ship.

In 1608 work started on Henry's ship: it was to be called the *Prince Royal*. The old *Ark Raleigh* was also remade and renamed the *Anne Royal*.

Henry said: 'Who but my father would keep such a bird in a cage!' [1]

It was probably in 1608 that Raleigh, with his vitality recovered, and encouraged by the virtues of the young Prince who was worth the labour of teaching, and through whom once again he might be accepted as the servant of sovereignty, began to compose into a single articulated picture his experience and understanding of human existence. Gathering up his long meditation on 'the Lord's wonders in the deep', his long and diffidently held ambition to write 'the story of all ages past', and many years of reading, note-making and questioning, and restless with 'those inmost and soul-piercing wounds which are ever aching while uncured', he set to work on a 'History of the World' which would demonstrate for his future king the manner in which the divine Sovereign 'was and is pleased to make himself known by the work of the world: in the wonderful magnitude whereof (all which he embraceth, filleth, and sustaineth), we behold the image of that glory which cannot be measured, and withal, that one, and yet universal nature which cannot be defined'.

The Tower, which had been inconvenient for the shipping man, was admirable for the historian: 'Although the air which compasseth adversity be very obscure, yet therein we better discern God.'

6

Raleigh, The History of the World, Preface:
Certainly, as all the rivers in the world, though they have divers
risings and divers runnings, though they sometimes hide themselves
for a while underground, and seem to be lost in sea-like lakes, do at
last find, and fall into the great ocean; so, after all the searches that
human capacity hath, and after all philosophical contemplation and
curiosity, in the necessity of this infinite power, all the reason of man
ends and dissolves itself.

Knowledge of God came to us, he said, by two routes: through
God's word and through the visible world. The Bible was both a
record of God's word and the most ancient and reliable historical
record of the visible world. His *History of the World* was intended
to supplement the Bible by cutting through some of the learned
jungle which in the course of time had smothered it, and by telling
the remainder of history, as known, up to the end of the reign of
Henry VIII, displaying the manner in which God had stirred up
great spirits to establish and destroy in accordance with his purpose,
appraising military and political actions in the light of God's com-
mandments, tracing the consequences of virtue and sin, and binding
the whole of history into a single body. It would be necessary to
correlate biblical and pagan chronologies, and sometimes to clarify
ancient geography.

He had some qualifications not common in historians. He had
spent his life in political, military and commercial affairs, and was
still active in them or hoping to be active; and he had, by contemporary standards, great geographical and considerable scientific
knowledge. In addition he was a poet; and he had at times a Macchiavellian clarity of vision, and power, and magnanimity. He was
habitually accurate in detail.

One of his limitations was linguistic; he had Latin, Italian and
French but no Hebrew (Dr Robert Burhill is thought to have helped
him), and no great facility in Greek (he seems to have read Greek
authors in Latin translations). Another was the unusually narrow

range of good brains available for his picking (probably few other than Hariot on science and Ben Jonson on Rome). And he was limited by his own point in time.

His method of handling a jungle-grown section of the Bible is seen in his treatment of the Flood.

The Flood was crucial for settling the chronologies of all the re-peopled countries of the world, so he dealt with it at length. He showed that for the waters to cover the earth to above the top of the highest mountain (Teneriffe, he said, thirty miles high) there was no need for new matter to have been created as some thought (although the Bible made it clear that no matter was created after the Sixth Day), since some of the waters came from within the earth, where there could have been ample since the diameter of the world was 7,000 miles. There was no need to doubt that there was room in the ark for all the animals, since fewer animals had to be accommodated than were usually realised: for example, the north Virginian thrush, which had some black and carnation on its feathers, was really the same as the English thrush, and 'the dogfish of England is the shark of the south ocean', and so on.

The ark was built very close to where it finally rested, since without sails and probably without wind it would not have moved far; and it came to rest, not in Armenia where many scholars had placed Ararat, but further east, since afterwards Nimrod came west to build the tower of Babel, and since the Far East was repeopled before the Middle East – the Chinese had writing, printing and gunpowder very early, and India, when invaded by Semiramis, already had an enormous population.

He examined a number of other ancient floods, showing that none was as ancient as Noah's. In the course of this examination he made use of the fact that 'Galilaeus, a worthy astrologer now living' had observed with his 'perspective glass' the horns of Venus. Galileo had made his observations of Venus within a few months of starting to make telescopes in June 1609, and Hariot (who had taken 'perspective glasses' to Virginia in 1585) had been making telescopes and looking at the heavens a matter of weeks before or after Galileo. Yet Raleigh made no mention of either Hariot or himself having seen the horns of Venus. It is as if he were keeping astronomy at a safe distance.

When he came to the story of Joshua stopping the sun in mid-heaven, he did not mention the Copernican theory of a sun-centred universe (he owned a copy of Copernicus)[1]. He probably knew (as Hariot already did) that Galileo had seen Jupiter's satellites, which seemed to astronomers to confirm the theory, but Raleigh would allow nothing, certainly no bare hypothesis about nature, to tempt him, even momentarily or in supposition, from detailed reliance on the Bible, or to confuse or undermine his consciousness of God.

7

The object of history, he said, was 'to teach by examples of times past, such wisdom as may guide our desires and actions'. There was therefore another episode in Joshua's life on which he commented more fully.

Raleigh, The History of the World, Book II Chapter VI Section viii:
Out of the passage between Joshua and the Gibeonites, the doctrine of keeping faith is so plainly and excellently taught, as it taketh away all evasion, it admitteth no distinction, nor leaveth open any hole or outlet at all to that cunning perfidiousness, and horrible deceit of this latter age, called equivocation.[2]

For, notwithstanding that these Gibeonites were a people of the Hevites, expressly and by name, by the commandment of God, to be rooted out, and notwithstanding that they were liars, and deceivers, and counterfeits, and that they did overreach, and, as it were, deride Joshua and the princes of Israel, by feigning to be sent as ambassadors from a far country, in which travel their clothes were worn, their bread mouldy, which they avowed to have been warm for newness when they first set out; their barrels and bottles of wine broken, their shoes patched, and their sacks rent and ragged: yet Joshua having sworn unto them by the Lord God of Israel, he durst not, though urged by the murmur of the people to lay violent hands on them; but he spared both their lives and the cities of their inheritance.

Now if ever man had warrant to break faith, and to retract his promise made, Joshua had it . . . For he needed not in this case the help of equivocation or mental reservation: for what he sware, he sware in good faith; but he sware nothing, nor made any promise at all, to the Gibeonites. And yet, to the end that the faithless subtlety of man should borrow nothing in the future from his example, who knowing well that the promises he made in the name of God were made to the living God, and not to the dying man, he held them firm and inviolable, notwithstanding that they to whom he had sworn it were worshippers of the Devil.

For it is not, as faithless men take it, that he which sweareth to a man, to a society, to a state, or to a king, and sweareth by the name of the living Lord, and in his presence, that this promise (if it be broken) is broken to a man, to a society, to a state, or to a prince; but the promise in the name of God made, is broken to God.

Out of doubt, it is a fearful thing for a son to break the promise, will, or deed of the father; for a state or kingdom to break those contracts which have been made in former times, and confirmed by public faith. For though it were 400 years after Joshua, that Saul, even out of devotion, slaughtered some of those people descended out of the Gibeonites; yet God, who forgat not what the predecessors and forefathers of Saul and the Israelites had sworn in his name, afflicted the whole nation with a consuming famine, and could not be appeased, till seven of Saul's sons were delivered to the Gibeonites grieved, and by them hanged up.

He was never tired of repeating that the God who interpenetrated the universe with love and value was in judgment inexorable; that the God who punished sins in Israel and Judah was the same God who punished the same sins in England, France and Spain.

God forbade Samson's mother to drink alcohol while she was pregnant; it was a commandment too frequently forgotten in contemporary England.

God forbade stealing; in England there was too much pardoning of thieves, especially of first offenders.

God forbade killing: Archimedes, Raleigh was to say later in the *History*, was to be praised because the machines he devised for the defence of Syracuse against the Romans could not be used offensively, 'neither did he altogether publish the knowledge how to use them, but reserved so much to his own direction, that after his death more of the same kind were not made, nor those of his own making were employed by the Romans . . . For to enrich a mechanical trade, or teach the art of murdering men, it was beside his purpose.'

8

While Raleigh had been working on the *History* a colonising expedition set out for Virginia with at last truly wide backing: 56 City Companies, 21 peers, 96 knights, 110 merchants, and James himself. However, it met a hurricane which blew the flagship to haven in Bermuda – giving Shakespeare a setting for *The Tempest* and England a colony which for several years seemed more promising than Virginia.

Meanwhile James had acted with open-handedness over Sherborne. It had been ruled that it was definitely his since the conveyance to Wat was flawed, but he promised that Bess and her children should have it for as long as they lived. Then he wanted it for his favourite, Carr, and gave Bess £400 a year for the term of her life, and £8,000, to compensate for the lease he had promised. Then Prince Henry demanded it for himself, possibly in order to give it back in due course to Raleigh.[1] So James compensated Carr with £20,000.

Easy spending put James in need of money, but he was in deadlock with his Puritan and difficult Parliament. One of his own plans to raise funds, and at the same time cement the world peace of which he felt he could be the maker, was to make rich marriages for Prince Henry and Princess Elizabeth, if possible one Catholic and one Protestant. Raleigh dropped for a while the *History* to write for Henry two discourses analysing, with many historical parallels, the disadvantages of two of these proposed marriages, which after all were not proceeded with.

Other possible sources of income were explored by Cecil. Without Parliament he imposed new Customs duties; with Parliament he tried, unsuccessfully, to barter so-much reform for so-much money. He even tried Guiana. He had strengthened his hand against Spain by a treaty of mutual assistance with France, and so could safely connive in 1610 in an attempt by Sir Thomas Roe, an intelligent and discreet young man, to make a thorough-going search for Manoa, survey other Guiana possibilities, and convert the golden dream into terms fit for consideration in a Whitehall office. Raleigh invested £600 out of the £2,500 invested in Roe's expedition.

In mid-1611 Roe was back, reporting that Manoa appeared not to exist. On the other hand there were fifteen English, French and Dutch ships trading at Trinidad for tobacco; and Berrio's old settlement at San Tomé, up the Orinoco, now occupied by his son, Ferdinando Berrio, was rich and weak. The Spaniards said they were planning the conquest and plantation of Guiana, but Roe thought Ferdinando Berrio was content to let things stay as they, profitably, were. Nevertheless, to do no more than maintain English trade at the present level would involve armed clashes with the Spaniards.

Cecil would not risk Raleigh offending the Spaniards if there was no proof of easy-to-get gold. It was perhaps because of this that he and Raleigh had an angry quarrel one day soon after Roe's return, when the Council, visiting the Tower, found in Raleigh 'the same boldness, pride and passion that heretofore hath wrought more violently but never expressed itself in a stronger passion'. As a result he was kept under closer imprisonment. After some months of it he was complaining to Queen Anne of lack of exercise and shortness of breath.

9

The History of the World was by no means finished. The first two Books had centred on the Israelites, with occasional references to contemporaneous happenings elsewhere: 'In the same age together with Moses lived Prometheus'; 'about the eleventh year of Gideon was that famous expedition of the Argonauts'.

In the third to fifth Books he was concentrating on the dominant

[225]

empire of the time, Persian, Greek or Roman, and referring to other peoples and bringing their histories up to date, whenever they came in collision with the dominant empire. Prince Henry had asked for the Greeks and Romans to be dealt with more fully than Raleigh had intended, and these Books became out of proportion to the earlier. For the most part they consisted of very detailed telling of the historical story, with less moral commentary, more political and military, and with more modern parallels, than in the first two Books. Every now and again he broke off to consider a particular point for general discussion: the use of mercenaries, the abuse of duelling, the importance of sea-power, the varieties of tyranny, the quality of the common soldier in great conquering armies.

Raleigh, The History of the World, Book V Chapter I Section i:
If therefore it be demanded, whether the Macedonian or the Roman were the best warrior, I will answer, the English . . .

Now let us in general compare with the deeds done by these best of Roman soldiers [Caesar's] in their principal service [in Gaul], the things performed in the same country, by our common English soldier, levied in haste from following the cart, or sitting on the shop-stall: so shall we see the difference . . .

In Caesar's time, France was inhabited by the Gauls, a stout people, but inferior to the French by whom they were subdued . . . The country of Gaul was rent in sunder (as Caesar witnesseth) into many lordships . . . But when King Edward the Third began his war upon France, he found the whole country settled in obedience to one mighty king . . .

Caesar himself doth witness that the Gauls complained of their ignorance in the art of war, and that their own hardiness was over-mastered by the skill of their enemies. Poor men, they admired the Roman towers and engines of battery, raised and planted against their walls, as more than human works . . . What such help, or what other worldly help than the golden metal of their soldiers, had our English kings against the French? . . . Let us hear what a French writer saith of the inequality that was between the French and English when their King John was ready to give the onset upon the Black Prince at the battle of Poitiers. John had all the advantages over

Edward, both of number, force, show, country, and conceit (the which is commonly a consideration of no small importance in worldly affairs) and withal, the choice of all his horsemen (esteemed then the best in Europe) with the greatest and wisest captains of his whole realm . . . I think it would trouble a Roman antiquary to find the like example in their histories . . .

All that have read of Crécy and Agincourt will bear me witness that I do not allege the battle of Poitiers for lack of other, as good examples of the English virtue . . .

If any man impute these victories of ours to the long bow, as carrying further, piercing more strongly, and quicker of discharge than the French cross-bow, my answer is ready: that in all respects it is also (being drawn with a strong arm) superior to the musket; yet is the musket a weapon of more use. The gun, and the cross-bow, are of like force when discharged by a boy or woman as when by a strong man; weakness, or sickness, or a sore finger, makes the long bow unserviceable. More particularly, I say that it was the custom of our ancestors to shoot, for the most part, point blank . . . This takes away all objection: for when two armies are within the distance of a butt's length, one flight of arrows, or two at the most, can be delivered, before they close . . .

If any man ask, how then came it to pass that the English won so many battles, having no advantage to help him? I may, with best commendation of modesty, refer him to the French historian; who relating the victory of our men at Crevant, where they passed a bridge in face of the enemy, useth these words: 'The English comes with a conquering bravery, as he that was accustomed to gain everywhere, without any stay.'

10

In 1612 there were new prospects of release. In May Cecil died, of scurvy and dropsy, a much-aged forty-eight. The departure of the great and careful man was rejoiced in. The Council became less

cautious; some of its members did not care if Spain were offended in
Guiana or anywhere else.

Raleigh to the Lords of the Council:[1]
Your Lordships, as I remember, did offer to be at the charge to transport Keymis into Guiana with such a proportion of men in two ships
as should be able to defend him against the Spaniards inhabiting upon
Orinoco, if they offered to assail . . . [his] passage to the mine,
which is not above five miles from the navigable river, taking the
nearest way.

Now your Lordships do require of me that if Keymis live to arrive, and shall then fail to bring into England half a ton, or as much
more as he shall be able to take up, of that slate gold ore whereof I
gave a sample to Lord Knyvett, that then all the charge of the journey shall be laid upon me and by me be satisfied, whereto I willingly
consent. And though it be a difficult matter – of exceeding difficulty
– for any man to find the same acre of ground again in a country
desolate and overgrown, which he hath seen but once, and that sixteen years since (which were hard enough to do upon Salisbury
Plain), yet that your Lordships may be satisfied of the truth I am contented to adventure all I have, but my reputation, upon Keymis's
memory . . .

But that which your Lordships do promise is that half a ton of the
former ore being brought home, then I shall have my liberty, and in
the meanwhile my free pardon, under the Great Seal, to be left in his
Majesty's hands till the end of the journey.

Again, nothing came of the project. But there was a new chance.
Henry was pressing for his release.

Meanwhile, Henry and Queen Anne saw the *Prince Royal*
launched, and Wat went to Paris to complete the education of a
gentleman. At Oxford he had played off one tutor against the other,
with Bess opposing and Raleigh trying to support their bumbling
efforts to control 'his planetary and irregular motions'.[2] He visited
splendid Paris (inadequately gendarmed, hour-long traffic jams) in
the learned care of Ben Jonson.

William Drummond of Hawthornden (1585–1649): [1]
This youth being knavishly inclined, among other pastimes (as the setting of the favour of damsels on a codpiece), caused [Ben Jonson] to be drunken, and dead drunk, so that he knew not where he was, thereafter laid him on a car, which he made to be drawn by pioneers through the streets, at every corner showing his governor stretched out, and telling them, that was a more lively image of the Crucifixion than any they had; at which sport young Raleigh's mother delighted much (saying, his father young was so inclined), though the father abhorred it.

Then Prince Henry died of typhoid.

Newsletter, John Chamberlain to Dudley Carleton, 12 November 1612:[2]
The physicians are much blamed, though no doubt they did their best . . . They tried all manner of conclusions upon him, as letting his blood in the nose, and whatsoever else they could imagine, and at the last cast gave him a quintessence sent by Sir Walter Raleigh (which he says they should have applied sooner) that brought him to some show of sense and opening of his eyes, and (some will needs say) speech, but all failed again presently.

Among the rest he hath lost his greatest hope, and was grown into special confidence with him, insomuch that he had moved the King divers times for him, and had lastly a grant that he should be delivered out of the Tower before Christmas.

II

With his patron-pupil dead, and having in three-quarters of a million words tired out his first intuition, he gave up the *History*. He had reached Rome's conquest of Macedonia. He had intended to continue to the Roman conquest of Britain, and then to follow British history, relating to it all other histories.

However English history did not entirely escape him for he added a Preface. He stated his theme: 'The judgments of God are for ever unchangeable; neither is he wearied by the long process of time, and won to give his blessing in one age to that which he cursed in another'; and proceeded to examine 'what profit hath been gathered by our own kings, and their neighbour princes: who having beheld, both in divine and human letters, the success of infidelity, injustice, and cruelty, have (notwithstanding) planted after the same pattern'. He listed the sins of all the kings of England one by one, and their inevitable punishments, from William I to Elizabeth's father, Henry VIII. The characters of these former kings were in contrast, of course, to James's 'temperate, revengeless, and liberal disposition'.

And he added a few final words to the *History* itself.

Raleigh, The History of the World, Book V Chapter VI Section xii:
The kings and princes of the world have always laid before them the actions, but not the ends, of those great ones which preceded them. They are always transported with the glory of the one, but they never mind the misery of the other, till they find the experience in themselves. They neglect the advice of God while they enjoy life, or hope it; but they follow the counsel of Death upon his first approach. It is he that puts into man all the wisdom of the world, without speaking a word; which God with all the words of his law, promises, or threats, doth not infuse.

Death, which hateth and destroyeth man, is believed; God which hath made him and loves him, is always deferred . . .

It is therefore Death alone that can suddenly make man to know himself. He tells the proud and insolent that they are but abjects, and humbles them at the instant; makes them cry, complain, and repent, yea, even to hate their forepassed happiness. He takes the account of the rich, and proves him a beggar; a naked beggar, which hath interest in nothing but in the gravel that fills his mouth. He holds a glass before the eyes of the most beautiful, and makes them see therein their deformity and rottenness; and they acknowledge it.

O eloquent, just and mighty Death! whom none could advise, thou hast persuaded; what none hath dared, thou hast done; and whom all the world hath flattered, thou only hast cast out of the world and despised: thou hast drawn together all the far stretched greatness, all the pride, cruelty, and ambition of man, and covered it all over with these two narrow words, *Hic jacet*.

12

The History of the World was published on 29 March 1614, with an allegorical frontispiece and a title page with his name and portrait. In nine months there was official action.

Newsletter, Chamberlain to Carleton, 5 January 1615:[1]
Sir Walter Raleigh's book is called in, by the King's commandment, for divers exceptions, but especially for being too saucy in censuring princes. I hear he takes it much to heart, for he thought he had won his spurs and pleased the King extraordinarily.

He had censured individual kings but, describing the origin of kingship, he had never suggested, for he did not believe, that kings had to account to their subjects for their actions; and he had explicitly praised James for his putting down of Scottish feuds, and for his 'True Law of Free Monarchies'.

The book was soon released again for publication. There was no change, except the omission of the title page with Raleigh's name and portrait.

He had feared what the professional historians would say, but the professors praised it, and churchmen praised it. There were ten editions in its own century, as well as abridged versions. It was a book to be much loved by Milton, Hampden, Marvell and Cromwell.

Because he was victimised by a Stuart, and was a patriot, and an expositor of God's working in history, the coming generation of Parliamentarians hero-worshipped him; but he held different views of the rights of Parliament. He expressed these in a piece of unwanted advice which he sent James, *The Prerogative of Parliaments*. James was being pressed by courtiers not to call Parliament in order to raise the money he needed, for fear of what it would demand. Raleigh said he should call it. He showed with historical examples that

English Parliaments had often, like James's, tied in one parcel their gift of money and their demand for reforms. Kings had been compelled to promise reforms, but after they had the money they ignored their promises if they thought fit, 'for all binding of a king by law upon the advantage of his necessity makes the breach itself lawful in a king . . . The bonds of subjects to their kings should always be wrought out of iron, the bonds of kings unto subjects but with cobwebs.' James therefore should call Parliament, and he should allow it to consider and recommend the removal of grievances provided that his revenue was not affected. If he decided to carry out what the Commons asked, he should do so because the Commons was right, not because it had power.

James did not call Parliament, but his worries were sweetened by a new favourite, George Villiers. Villiers had been groomed and pushed forward by the anti-Spanish party, because Carr was allied with the pro-Spanish Howards and Gondomar, the new Spanish ambassador. The Spanish faction for a time was weakened: Lord Henry Howard died, Carr (now Somerset) fell from grace after the poisoning of Sir Thomas Overbury in the room below Raleigh's, and as Secretary there was anti-Spanish Ralph Winwood. Now it was the majority of the Council who did not object to a clash with Spain in Guiana; if it brought gold, so much the better.

In March, 1616, with Secretary Winwood's help, and a bribe of £1,500 to the brother of Villiers so that Villiers might persuade the King, Raleigh was given permission to prepare ships for Guiana, and meanwhile to stretch his old legs.

Part Seven 1616–1618

I

After thirteen years of prison he was still the same Raleigh: 'Water', 'Ocean'; captain rather than general; political commentator rather than politician; business-man efficient in short-term enterprise, inattentive in long; lover of projects which involved great distances; most fully himself when concerned with an absolute – virginity, truth, sovereignty, death – or a limited, clearly envisaged action; in impotence despairing, self-pitying, melodramatic; wanting to be loved, but singular, unclubbable, untrusted; truster of friends and servants beyond their honesty and strength; disdainer of self-protection, offended when hurt; a Bottom in his skills – as fighter, explorer, poet, assayer, economist, moralist, medicine-man, business-man, historian, ship-designer, empire-builder, mathematician, theologian, seaman, statesman. Still the same man, but with a greater reputation. The same, but grey, lame, malaria-ridden, and aged sixty-two.

He went straight, probably, to a house in Broad Street owned by Bess. In a few days he gave £500 on account to Phineas Pett, the royal shipbuilder, for a ship of 500 tons.

Newsletter, Chamberlain to Carleton, 27 March 1616:[1]
Sir Walter Raleigh was freed out of the Tower the last week, and goes up and down seeing sights and places built or bettered since his imprisonment.

London had had a dozen years of peace, and of prosperity for everyone but James. There had been rebuilding of timber and wattle-and-daub, and the New River had been cut to bring water to Islington and thence by pipes into London homes.

In the Strand, the Durham House frontage had been turned by Cecil into the New Exchange, the two-storeyed arcade of shops loved by Pepys fifty years later. Ivy Bridge Lane, the eastern boundary of Durham House grounds, had been moved by Cecil forty yards west (where it still is), so that he could build little Salisbury House by the side of his Great Salisbury House. West of Durham House, beyond York House, was the mansion which Lord Henry Howard had erected with his risen fortunes. There had been fresh building around St James's Park, in Tothill Fields, and the south side of Westminster Abbey. In the open country north of the Strand, building was going on in Long Acre, a narrow seven-acre field stretching from St Martin's Lane to the newly cobbled Drury Lane.

Country wagons, carrying goods and passengers higgledy-piggledy and drawn by seven or eight horses, and London carts, carrying beer, coal, wood, cluttered the streets even more than in 1603 and refused to give way for carriages, of which there were now many more.

The suburbs had grown, especially eastward. At Deptford where Phineas Pett was going to build him his ship, Drake's *Golden Hind* was still on show.

Now that privateering was forbidden Raleigh found it more difficult to raise money than thirty years before for the first Virginian expeditions. The City was not interested. It preferred, for a flutter, the Muscovy Company which had been doing well with whaling and spending some profits on sending out Hudson and Baffin to look for the North-West Passage; or the East India Company, which now had a factory on the Indian mainland and could reckon on bringing home a cargo worth £100,000 a time (for England a good sum, but only half the value of the Great Carrack's cargo in 1592). America was not a popular field of investment; France and Holland were being active there, but the new Virginian colony could raise money only by lotteries, no money could be raised for New England, and Bermuda had been dependent on a large piece of ambergris the colonists had found, as good as a small goldmine. Raleigh's friends invested in his company, but did not invest enough.

There was other difficulty. Gondomar, the Spanish ambassador, was bothering James to stop the expedition, if James really wanted a royal Spanish marriage for Prince Charles, the new heir, as he did –

to balance the marriage of Princess Elizabeth to a Protestant prince of Germany, and to bring a dowry of £600,000. Luckily there was a way for Raleigh to get the gold without, technically, fighting the Spanish settlement at San Tomé. He was negotiating for some French troops; they could act as a shield while the gold was being mined, and take the blame if there was fighting. In any case, if he brought gold James could say that the territory was not Spanish (the Peace of 1604 had left unsettled the question of Spanish and English rights in America); if he brought none James could disown him.

In July he received his commission. The King was to have his fifth of gold and silver; Raleigh with his associates was to enjoy quietly the remainder; and he was to have power of life and death over his company.

He sailed down to Dover, in a new pinnace, simply for pleasure, with Phineas Pett, Wat, now aged twenty-two, and Carew, who had been conceived and christened in the Tower, aged eleven. He enjoyed social life again. He was forbidden the Court, but he dined at Secretary Winwood's and other important houses.

Aubrey:[1]
Sir Walter Raleigh, being invited to dinner to some great person, where his son was to go with him, he said to his son:

'Thou art such a quarrelsome, affronting creature that I am ashamed to have such a bear in my company.'

Mr Wat humbled himself to his father, and promised he would behave himself mightily mannerly. So away they went . . .

He sat next to his father and was very demure at least half dinner time. Then said he:

'I this morning, not having the fear of God before my eyes, but by the instigation of the devil, went to a whore. I was very eager of her, kissed and embraced her, and went to enjoy her, but she thrust me from her and vowed I should not: "For your father lay with me but an hour ago."'

Sir Walter, being so strangely surprised and put out of his countenance at so great a table, gives his son a damned blow over the face. His son, as rude as he was, would not strike his father, but

[235]

strikes over the face of the gentleman that sat next to him, and said:
'Box about. 'Twill come to my father anon.'

Phineas Pett, Autobiography:[1]
1616. The 16th of December I launched the great ship of Sir Walter
Raleigh's called the *Destiny*, and had much ado to get her into the
water, but I delivered her to him on float in good order and fashion;
by which business I lost £700 and could never get recompense for it.

Raleigh was 'nothing appalled' by the report that Spanish sea
forces were going to intercept him, and was 'as confident of finding
the Guiana gold as . . . of not missing his way from his dining-room
to his bedchamber'.

2

Nevertheless he interested himself in an alternative. James had
momentarily composed a quarrel between Savoy and Milan by
counselling simultaneous disarmament: if either was attacked by the
other he would come to their help. Savoy was attacked by Milan,
and war broke out: Savoy and Venice on one side, Milan (which
included Genoa) and Naples on the other. The Savoy ambassador,
after a talk with Raleigh, suggested to James that he fulfil his promise by sending the Guiana expedition to sack Genoa. Venice was
advised: 'This knight . . . is excellently informed upon the situation
and the conditions of this place, and he feels sure he can take it by
surprise.'

But James required assurances that he would receive his share of the
booty. When he had them, he said that he would lend ships, but not
Raleigh, who he was determined should go to Guiana. Then he
lent no ships.

Raleigh's arrangements were in hand for ships and men from
France, and he was promised by the Lord Admiral of France a licence
to bring his own ships and goods back to a French port. From there
he could bargain with James if that proved necessary.

Gondomar continued to press James's Council to stop him from sailing. The Council replied that the King was set on his sailing, but if he overstepped his instructions his head would pay for it.

Newsletter, Chamberlain to Carleton, 29 March 1617:[1]
Sir Walter Raleigh took his leave yesternight of Mr Secretary . . . He makes away with all speed he can for fear of a countermand . . . I fear he doth but go (as children are wont to tell their tales) to seek his fortune.

It was generally believed that, in debt and unpardoned, he would turn pirate and never come back.

3

He assembled his fleet at Plymouth, whence he sent two Frenchmen, Faige and Belle, to get the licence he required from the French Admiral, and to bring the French ships to meet him at the Orinoco.

His captains were of mixed quality. Some under-victualled their ships. For one, Bess had to raise money in London. Another, Wollaston, was half a pirate. Another, Captain Bayley of the *Southampton*, had taken offence when in the Thames his anchor had fouled the *Destiny's* and his hawser had been cut on Raleigh's order; now, having in transit married a girl in the Isle of Wight, he said he would only sail if he could be the first messenger sent home.[2]

Others were reliable. Keymis, in his fifties, tall and still slim, with a cast in one eye, commanded the *Convertine*. Sir Warham St Leger, son of the former Provost-Marshal of Cork, commanded the *John and Francis*. Samuel King, who had served Raleigh many years, commanded a fly-boat. The *Destiny*, which carried Raleigh as General, together with 80 gentlemen, 100 sailors, 20 watermen, and servants and labourers, was commanded by Wat. The ships were heavily armed.

On 12 June he sailed.

News trickled back to London. He had been forced into Falmouth;

he set ashore there a considerable number of men who had been quarrelling and fighting. He had been forced into Cork. He had sailed again, after two months in Cork – with thirteen ships, a thousand men, and restored victuals. He had landed in the Canaries, and there had been a skirmish.

James was angry: he had instructed that there was to be no clash with subjects of Spain.

Captain Bayley arrived back in England; he said that Raleigh had turned pirate.

On 16 October Gondomar received assurances: 'His Majesty is very disposed and determined against Raleigh, and will join with the King of Spain in ruining him.'

Raleigh, Journal:[1]
The last of October at night, rising out of bed, being in a great sweat, by reason of a sudden gust and much clamour in the ship before they could get down the sails, I took a violent cold which cast me into a burning fever . . . For the first twenty days I never received any sustenance but now and then a stewed prune, but drank every hour day and night, and sweat so strongly as I changed my shirts thrice every day and thrice every night . . .

The 11 of November we made the North Cape of Oyapoco, the cape then bearing SW by W as they told me for I was not yet able to move out of my bed . . . I sent in my skiff to inquire for my old servant, Leonard the Indian, who been with me in England three or four years . . . but I could not hear of him . . . for he was removed 30 mile into the country, and because I had an ill road and five leagues off I durst not stay his sending for, but stood away for Caliana, where the cacique was also my servant and had lived with me in the Tower two years . . .

The 14th day we . . . passed by three or four islands . . . from whence we stood alongst into six fathom, and came to an anchor. Thence I sent my barge ashore to inquire for my servant, Harry the Indian, who [sent] his brother unto me with two other caciques, promising to come to me with provisions if I came not into the river within a day or two. These Indians stayed with me that night, offering their service and all they had. Mine own weakness which still continued, and the desire I had to be carried ashore to change the air, and out of the unsavoury ship, pestered with many sick men which being unable to move poisoned us with a most filthy stench, persuaded me to adventure my ship over a bar where never any vessel of burden had passed. In the road my barge found one Jansen of Flushing . . . who came to me where I rid without, offering me his service for the bringing in of my ship . . .

17 November. After I had stayed in Caliana a day or two my servant Harry came to me, who had almost forgotten his English, and brought me a great store of very good cassava bread, with which I fed my company some seven or eight days, and put up a hogshead full for store. He brought great plenty of roasted mullets which were very good meat, great store of plantains and pines with divers other sorts of fruits and pistachios, but as yet I durst not adventure to eat of the pine which tempted me exceedingly. But after a day or two being carried ashore and sitting under a tent, I began to eat of the pine, which greatly refreshed me. And after that I fed on the pork of the country, and of the armadillos and began to gather a little strength.

Here I also set all my sick men ashore, and made clean my ship and where they all recovered . . .

Captain Jansen whom we found a very honest man, departed from Caliana towards Flushing . . . and Captain Alley being still troubled with the vertigo desirous to return because unable to endure the rolling of the ship, I got passage for him with Jansen.

4

Nathaniel Brent to Carleton, 7 February 1618:[1]
On Tuesday last Captain Alley came hither from Sir Walter Raleigh, and hath brought news of his good success in Guiana . . . He is within the bowels of the golden mines, and hath the absolute possession of whatsoever he hoped for in those parts . . .
PS: I have opened this letter after since it was sealed to tell your Lordship what I heard from a gentleman who saw Sir Walter

Raleigh's letter to his wife: that he is in Guiana but not in the midst of the mines.

Raleigh to Bess, 'from Caliana in Guiana', 14 November 1617:[1]
Sweet Heart,

I can yet write unto you but with a weak hand, for I have suffered the most violent calenture, for fifteen days, that ever man did, and lived: but God that gave me a strong heart in all my adversities, hath also now strengthened it in the hell-fire of heat.

We have had two most grievous sicknesses in our ship, of which forty-two have died, and there are yet many sick; but having recovered the land of Guiana, this 12 November, I hope we shall recover them. We are yet two hundred men; and the rest of our fleet are reasonably strong – strong enough I hope to perform what we have undertaken, if the diligent care at London to make our strength known to the Spanish King by his ambassador, have not taught the Spanish King to fortify all the entrances against us . . .

In passage to the Canaries I stayed at Gomerah, where I took water in peace, because the country durst not deny it me. I received there, of a countess of an English race, a present of oranges, lemons, quinces, and pomegranates, without which I could not have lived. Those I preserved in fresh sands, and I have of them yet to my great refreshing. Your son had never so good health, having no distemper in all the heat under the line . . .

Remember my service to my Lord Carew and Mr Secretary Winwood. I wrote not to them for I can write of nought but miseries yet. Of men of sort, we have lost our Sergeant-Major, Captain Piggott [Raleigh's second-in-command]; and his lieutenant, Captain Edward Hastings – who would have died at home, for both his liver, spleen and brains were rotten; my son's lieutenant, Peyton; and my cousin, Mr Hughes; Mr Mordaunt; Mr Gardiner; Mr Hayward; Captain Jennings, the merchant; Keymis of London; and the Master Surgeon; Master Refiner; Mr Moore, the Governor of the Bermudas; our Provost Marshal, W. Steed; Lieutenant Vescie; but to my inestimable grief, Hammon and Talbot. By the next, I trust, you shall hear better of us; in God's hands we are, and in him we trust . . .

To tell you I might be here King of all the Indians were a vanity; but my name hath lived among them. Here they feed me with fresh meat, and all that the country yields; all offer to obey me. Commend me to poor Carew my son.

5

In his absence a new edition of the *History* had been published, this time with his name and portrait; his friend, Secretary Winwood, had died: and the Exchequer had failed to pay Bess her £400-a-year pension.

In an inquiry into Bayley's accusation of piracy, Bayley's men witnessed against Bayley. In Ireland Bayley had robbed a Scottish ship. He had quarrelled with Wat and fled his challenge. Off Cape St Vincent he had seized a shallop, for which Raleigh then paid the owner. It was true there had been a mild skirmish at Lancerota in the Canaries, but Raleigh had behaved correctly and his men had been attacked. However, James promised Gondomar that if the pirate returned, he would be sent to Spain for execution.

In Spain action had not been as vigorous as Raleigh feared. It was queried whether the information sent from England was reliable; it was not known when or where to send a fleet; and sending a fleet would be expensive. Instead a warning was dispatched to the governors in the West Indies, and they were told to reinforce one another.

In France the messengers, Faige and Belle, had gone on a trading trip instead of delivering Raleigh's letters. In Rome, Belle made confession to a Jesuit who told him to take the letters to the Spanish government in Madrid. So no French ships sailed to the Orinoco, and there was no licence to land in France.

On 13 May 1618 Gondomar, who had heard from Spain that Raleigh had destroyed San Tomé, hurried to the palace and asked for immediate audience. James was engaged but Gondomar wanted to say a single word. Admitted, he said: 'Pirates! Pirates! Pirates!'[1]

Ten days later two of Raleigh's ships came in with letters. One of his letters was to Winwood, who was dead, another to Bess.

[241]

I was loth to write because I know not how to comfort you. And God knows, I never knew what sorrow meant till now. All that I can say to you is, that you must obey the will and providence of God, and remember that the Queen's Majesty bare the loss of Prince Henry with a magnanimous heart . . . Comfort your heart (dear Bess), I shall sorrow for us both; and I shall sorrow the less because I have not long to sorrow, because not long to live. I refer you to Mr Secretary Winwood's letter who will give you a copy of it if you will send for it. Therein you shall know what hath past, which I have written by that letter, for my brains are broken, and 'tis a torment for me to write, and especially of misery. I have desired Mr Secretary to give my Lord Carew a copy of his letter. I have cleansed my ship of sick men and sent them home, and hope that God will send us somewhat ere we return. Commend me to all at Lothbury. You shall hear from me, if I live, from Newfoundland, where I mean to make clean my ship and to revictual; for I have tobacco to pay for it. The Lord bless you, and comfort you, that you may bear patiently the death of your valiant son.

Your

W. Raleigh.

PS: I protest before the majesty of God, that as Sir Francis Drake and Sir John Hawkins died heart-broken when they failed of their enterprise, I could willingly do the like, did I not contend against sorrow, in hope to provide somewhat for you to comfort and relieve you. If I live to return, resolve yourself that it is the care for you that hath strengthened my heart. It is true, that Keymis might have gone directly to the mine, and meant it. But, after my son's death, he made them to believe he knew not the way, and excused himself upon the want of water in the river, and, counterfeiting many impediments, left it unfound. When he came back I told him that he had undone me, and that my credit was lost for ever.

He answered, that when my son was lost and that he left me so weak that he resolved not to find me alive, he had no reason to enrich a company of rascals, who after my son's death made no account of him. He further told me that the English sent up into Guiana could hardly defend the Spanish town of St Thomas which they had taken, and therefore for them to pass through thick woods it was impossible; and more impossible to have victuals brought them into the mountains. And it is true that the Governor Diego Palumeque, and four other captains, being slain, of which my son Wat slew one; Plessington, Wat's sergeant, and John of Morocco, one of his men, slew other two. I say five of them slain in the entrance of the town, the rest went off in a whole body, and took more care to defend the passages to their mines (of which they had three within a league of the town, besides a mine that was about five miles off) than they did of the town itself.

Yet Keymis, at the first, was resolved to go to the mine; but when he came to the bank side to the land, he had two of his men slain outright from the bank, and six other hurt, and Captain Thornix shot in the head, of which wound and the accidents thereof he hath pined away these twelve weeks.

Now when Keymis came back, and gave me the former reasons which moved him not to open the mine – the one, the death of my son; the second, the weakness of the English, and their impossibilities to work and to be victualled; a third, that it was a folly to discover it for the Spaniards, and the last, both my weakness and my being unpardoned – and that I rejected all these arguments, and told him that I must leave him to himself to resolve it to the King and to the State, he shut up himself into his cabin, and shot himself with a pocket pistol, which brake one of his ribs; and finding that it had not prevailed, he thrust a long knife under his short ribs up to the handle, and died.

Thus much I have writ to Mr Secretary, to whose letters I refer you. But because I think my friends will rather hearken after you than any other to know the truth, I did after the sealing break open your letter again, to let you know in brief the state of that business, which I pray you impart to my Lord of Northumberland, and Sil. Skory and to Sir John Leigh.

For the rest, there was never poor man so exposed to the slaughter as I was; for being commanded upon my allegiance to set down, not only the country, but the very river by which I was to enter it, to name my ships, number my men and my artillery; this was sent by the Spanish ambassador to his master, the King of Spain. The King wrote his letters to all parts of the Indies, especially Palumeque of Guiana, El Dorado and Trinidad; of which the first letter bare date the 19 March 1617 at Madrid, when I had not yet left the Thames; which letter I have sent Mr Secretary . . . The King also sent a commission to levy 300 soldiers out of his garrison of Nuevo Regno de Granada or Puerto Rico, with ten pieces of brass ordnance to entertain us. He also prepared an armada by sea to set upon us.

It were too long to tell you how we were preserved. (If I live I shall make it known.) My brains are broken, and I cannot write much. I live yet, and I have told you why.

Whitney, for whom I sold my plate at Plymouth, and to whom I gave more credit and countenance than all the captains of my fleet, ran from me at the Granadas, and Wollaston with him; so as I am now but five ships, and one of those I have sent home – my fly-boat – and in her a rabble of idle rascals, which I know will not spare to wound me; but I care not. I am sure there is never a base slave in the fleet hath taken the pains and care that I have done; hath slept so little, and travailed so much. My friends will not believe them; and for the rest I care not. God in heaven bless you and strengthen your heart.

Your

W. Raleigh.

6

The day that his letters reached London he himself arrived in the *Destiny* at Kinsale in Munster, finding his three remaining ships already there. Morale and discipline had disappeared. It was three months since the muddled failure at San Tomé, six months since the leadership had been shattered by his own sickness and the death of his second-in-command and other senior officers.

The men and some of the captains thought they had been made fools of. Had Raleigh ever believed in the mine himself? – he had talked just as much of the £40,000 worth of tobacco which he said would be in San Tomé. Had he meant to privateer or had he not? –

he talked as if he had a French commission, but no one had seen it and he stopped them from privateering. What instructions, if any, had he given his land companies before they went up the river? Was it true that San Tomé had been moved from its earlier site, and that on the way up the river Keymis had said they would have to take it before they could work the mine? – which would have been contrary to the King's commission. Was it true that in the fight, when Wat left his pikemen and rushed into the fighting which was more forward, he shouted: 'Come on, my hearts, here's the mine that you must expect! They that look for any other mine are fools!' Afterwards Keymis had fumbled around for three weeks without taking them to any mine. When they arrived back at the ships Raleigh had blamed everything on Keymis, but if he had been betrayed by Keymis why did he still have him to dine in his cabin? He had talked of 'doing some good upon the Spaniard', but they were going home with nothing but a little tobacco. Did he trick them into coming home against their will, or did they force him to come home, against his? – there were different opinions even of that.

In mid-June the *Destiny* came alone into Plymouth. James had just issued a proclamation of his 'utter mislike and detestation' of the taking of San Tomé which was 'under the obedience of our dear brother the King of Spain', to whose daughter he was still trying to marry Prince Charles (negotiations were at a particularly tricky juncture). Spain, in reprisal for San Tomé, had seized English merchant ships, closed the courts to English merchants, and frozen their credits.

Raleigh moored his ship and sent his sails ashore. When he had settled his affairs he set out towards London to surrender to the King. He was met after twenty miles by Sir Lewis Stukeley, the Vice-Admiral of Devon, who had a verbal warrant for his arrest. They returned to Plymouth and for some days he was left alone by Stukeley.

He thought of escaping after all to France. One of his captains, Samuel King, chartered a bark. He took off towards it one night in a dinghy, but changed his mind and returned to shore.

In the Council George Carew and others had opposed James's plan to send Raleigh to Spain if Philip wanted, but all James would promise, when Carew made a personal appeal, was that Raleigh should have a hearing.[1]

In the last week of July an order from the Council reached Stukeley that he was to bring his prisoner to London forthwith. They set off: Raleigh, Bess, Captain King, Stukeley, a French doctor named Manourie, and some servants.

Once in London, he would be put in the Tower, unable to publish an account of his actions. He must write an 'Apology' before they reached London. To get the opportunity, at Salisbury he performed a jape.

'*A Declaration of the Demeanour and Carriage of Sir Walter Raleigh, knight . . .*' (*published by the Government after his execution, to show reason for it*):[2]

Sir Walter Raleigh addressed himself unto Manourie, and asked him if he had any of his vomits, or other medicines; which he telling him that he had, he prayed him to make one ready against the next morning, and to tell no one thereof . . .

The same evening, as soon as he arrived, he laid him down upon a bed, complaining much of his head . . . Notwithstanding he supped very well; but after supper he seemed to be surprised with a dimness of sight, by a swimming or giddiness in his head, and, holding his hand before his face, he rose from his bed; and, being led by the arm by Sir Lewis Stukeley, he staggered so, that he struck his head with some violence against a post of the gallery before his chamber . . .

The next day in the morning, he sent the lady his wife and most of the servants, to London, and also Captain King; and Cuthbert and Manourie and Sir Lewis Stukeley, being in Stukeley's chamber, a servant of Sir Walter, named Robin, came and told them that his master was out of his wits, and that he was naked in his shirt upon all fours, scratching and biting the rushes upon the planks; which greatly pitied Sir Lewis Stukeley, who, rising in haste, sent Manourie to him, who, when he came, found him gotten again to his bed . . .

Sir Walter asking him for his vomit, he gave it him, who made no bones but swallowed it down incontinently: at which time, Sir Lewis Stukeley coming in, Sir Walter began again to cry and rave; then . . . Sir Walter Raleigh began to draw up his legs and arms all in a heap, as it had been in a fit of convulsions and contractions of the sinews; and that with such vehemency, that Sir Lewis Stukeley had much ado with the help of others to pull out straight, sometimes an arm, sometimes a leg . . .

This feigned fit being thus passed, Sir Walter Raleigh called Manourie, and when he came, he prayed him to stay by him, and said he would take some rest. Manourie shut the door, and being alone with him Sir Walter Raleigh told him that his vomit had done nothing as yet, and said that he would take another more violent, but Manourie assuring him that without doubt it would work, he contented himself, and asked Manourie if he could invent anything that might make him look horrible and loathsome outwardly, without offending his principal parts, or making him sick inwardly . . . which at his entreaty he effected speedily . . .

Sir Lewis Stukeley perceiving the places where Manourie had put this composition to be all pimpled, his face full of great blisters of divers colours, having in the midst a little touch of yellow, and round about like a purple colour, and all the rest of his skin as it were inflamed with heat, he began to apprehend the danger of the disease, that it was contagious; and . . . brought unto Raleigh two physicians to see and visit him . . . There came also a third, a bachelor of physic, who all . . . gave their opinion and advice, that the patient could not be exposed to the air without manifest peril of his life . . .

Sir Walter Raleigh . . . was exceedingly contented thereat, especially that in the presence of the said physicians the vomit began to work both upwards and downwards. And, because he doubted that the physicians would ask to see his water, he asked Manourie to do something to make it seem troubled and bad; which to content him, giving him the urinal into his bed, Manourie rubbed the inside of the glass with a certain drug, which as soon as he had made urine therein, the urine, even in the hands of the physicians, turned all into an earthy humour, of a blackish colour, and made the water also to have an ill savour; which made the physicians judge the disease to be mortal, and without remedy but from heaven.

He made Manourie also to tie his arms about with black silk riband, which he took from his poniard, to try if it would distemper the pulse; but that succeeded not as he thought it would.

The day following he called Manourie and prayed him to make some more such blisters upon him, as upon his nose, his head, his thighs and his legs, which Manourie having done . . . he was very jocund and merry . . .

Manourie went to the 'White Hart' in Salisbury and bought him a leg of mutton and three loaves, which he ate in secret; and by this subtlety it was thought that he lived three days without eating, but not without drink. Thus he continued until Friday, the last of July, seeming always to be sick in the presence of company, and nevertheless, being alone, he writ his Declaration or Apology, and prayed Manourie to transcribe it, which was since presented to the King.

8

He decided again to escape to France. He petitioned that in view of his sickness he might stay in the house in Broad Street, and he told Captain King to hire a boat.

Unable not to trust, he told Manourie of his plans. Manourie told Stukeley, who tightened his guard.

When they reached Staines he decided that he could only escape if he took Stukeley into his confidence as well and made it worth his while to go with him. Through Manourie he offered a jewel and some money, and Stukeley agreed.

They reached Brentford on Friday, 7 August. A Frenchman, La Chesnay, came to the inn and on behalf of the French Agent offered him a bark in which to escape, and letters of recommendation to the Governor of Calais and others.

The next day they reached Broad Street. La Chesnay came to see him, and in the evening brought the French Agent. Raleigh said he would be glad to have the letters but refused the bark because King had already arranged with a man who had once been his boatswain for a ketch to be at Tilbury, 25 or 30 miles down the river (the arrangements had been betrayed instantly). King wanted him to escape that same night, but he would not go.

The next night, Sunday, in a false beard and with his page, Stukeley, and Stukeley's son, he met King at the Tower dock. King had two wherries for the party. There were delays and suspicions.

As they rowed down-river Raleigh frightened the watermen by asking whether they would row on or go back if anyone called on them to stop in the King's name.

They saw a wherry which looked as if it had been watching for them, and Raleigh became sure from words of the ex-boatswain that he had been betrayed.

At Galleon's Reach, near Plumstead, he ordered the wherries to return: he would try to get back to his house. After two hundred yards they met a boat which had been trailing them. Trailers and trailed went to a tavern for the night, and the next morning, Monday, 10 August, he entered the Tower.

He had been allowed almost to escape in the hope that his plots would be revealed. On his person there would be papers which would expose the intentions of his Guiana voyage, for which the mythical gold was only an excuse, and the treasons which he was plotting with the French.

He was searched and inventoried: £50 in gold; jewellery, including 'one ring with a diamond which he weareth on his finger, given him by the late Queen'; a gold whistle; a spleen stone; a lodestone in a red purse; a gold and copper image from Guiana; some assays of a silver mine and some maps of Panama and Guiana; a small lump or two of gold and a piece of Guiana ore.

9

Spain had decided that he was to die in England, so the law officers had to find just cause. It would be sufficient if he had deceived the State about the existence of the mine, or had had traitorous dealings with France. His company were examined, and in September a patient official, Sir Thomas Wilson, was sent to live with him in the Tower and extract evidence in the course of sympathetic conversation.

Wilson found him 'sick of a rupture and swollen on his left side', with sores, and 'ever and anon puling, pining and groaning', but talking like a fit man when conversation interested him. 'He hath not had the benefit of nature these twenty-two days but as it hath been forced by medicine.'

Bess, who was confined to Broad Street, wrote to him that the swelling of his side, due he thought to a swollen liver, was partly psychological and partly wind.

Complaining, one day, of his misery he told Wilson that some people held a man might kill himself and still die 'in God's favour'. Wilson and the Lieutenant of the Tower wondered whether to take away the vast array of chemical stuffs with which he experimented and dosed himself, but he said: 'Why, if you shall take away all those such means from me, yet if I had such a mind I could run my head against a post and kill myself.'

After some days he confessed that La Chesnay had offered him a French bark and brought the French Agent to see him;[1] but this in itself was not incriminating. He was harried for more details; and the King wanted to know more about events before his arrival in England. He obliged the King.

Raleigh to James, 24 September 1618:[2]
May it please your most excellent Majesty –
If in my journey outward bound, I had my men murdered at the Islands, and yet spared to take revenge; if I did discharge some Spanish barks taken without spoil; if I forbore all parts of the Spanish Indies, wherein I might have taken twenty of their towns on the sea

coasts and did only follow the enterprise I took for Guiana, where without any directions from me a Spanish village was burned which was new set up within three miles of the mine; by your Majesty's favour, I find no reason why the Spanish ambassador should complain.

If it were lawful for the Spaniards to murder thirty-six Englishmen, tying them back to back and then cutting their throats when they had traded with them a whole month and came to them on the land without so much as one sword, and that it may not be lawful for your Majesty's subjects, being charged first by them, to repel force by force, we may then justly say, O miserable English!

If Parker and Metham took Campeach and other places in the Honduras seated in the heart of the Spanish Indies, burned towns, and killed the Spaniards, and had nothing said unto them at their return; and myself forbore to look into the Indies, because I would not offend, I may as justly say, O miserable Sir Walter Raleigh!

If I have spent my poor estate, lost my son, suffered by sickness and otherwise a world of miseries; if I have resisted with my manifest hazard of my life the robberies and the spoils which my companions would have made; if when I was poor I could have made myself rich; if when I have gotten my liberty, which all men and nature itself doth much prize, I voluntarily lost it; if when I was sure of my life, I rendered it again; if I might elsewhere have sold my ship and goods and put five or six thousand pounds in my purse, and yet brought her into England – I beseech your Majesty to believe that all this I have done because it should not be said to your Majesty that your Majesty had given liberty and trust to a man, whose end was the recovery of his liberty, and who had betrayed your Majesty's trust.

My mutineers told me that if I returned for England I should be undone, but I believed in your Majesty's goodness more than in all their arguments. Sure I am that I am the first that being free and able to enrich myself, yet hath embraced poverty and peril. And as sure I am that my example shall make me the last.

Queen Anne to George Villiers, Marquis of Buckingham:[1]
My kind Dog,
   If I have any power or credit with you, I pray you let me have a

trial of it, at this time, in dealing sincerely and earnestly with the King that Sir Walter Raleigh's life may not be called in question.

He was examined no more, and after Wilson on 4 October asked to be relieved of his duties his thoughts were for a time allowed to find their own subject.

Raleigh to Bess, 4 October 1618:[1]
There is in the bottom of the cedar chest some paper books of mine. I pray make them up all together, and send them to me. The title of one of them is *The Art of War by Sea*. The rest are notes belonging unto it.

There is amongst the little glasses the powder of steel and pumex, for to stay the flux. If you can, find it now, for I have had a grievous looseness . . . Send some more bittony.

10

No new treason had been found, so the old would have to serve. There was no great difficulty about that, but it took a few weeks to settle a suitable routine. There must be no opportunity for him to make a public performance as in 1603.[2]

At the King's Bench Bar in Westminster Hall, 28 October 1618: [3]
Mr Attorney (Mr Henry Yelverton) spake in effect thus: My Lords, Sir Walter Raleigh, the prisoner at the bar, was fifteen years since convicted of high treason, by him committed against the person of his Majesty and the state of this kingdom, and then received the judgment of death, to be hanged, drawn, and quartered. His Majesty, of his abundant grace hath been pleased to show mercy upon him till now that justice calls unto him for execution. Sir Walter Raleigh hath been a statesman, and a man who in regard of his parts and quality is to be pitied. He hath been as a star at which the world gazed; but stars may fall, nay they must fall when they trouble the sphere wherein they abide. It is therefore his Majesty's pleasure now to

call for execution of the former judgment, and I now require order for the same.

Then Mr Fanshawe, Clerk of the Crown, read the record of the conviction and judgment, and called to the prisoner to hold up his hand, which he did. Then was the prisoner asked what he could say for himself why execution should not be awarded against him.

Raleigh: My Lords, my voice is grown weak by reason of my late sickness, and an ague which I now have, for I was now brought hither out of it.

Ld Ch. Justice (Sir Henry Montagu): Sir Walter, your voice is audible enough.

Raleigh: My Lord, all that I can say is this: that the judgment which I received to die so long since, I hope it cannot be strained to take away my life; for that since it was his Majesty's pleasure to grant me a commission to proceed in a voyage beyond the sea, wherein I had power, as marshal, on the life and death of others, so, under favour, I presume I am discharged of that judgment. For by that commission I departed the land and undertook a journey to honour my sovereign and enrich his kingdom with gold, of the ore whereof this hand hath found and taken in Guiana . . .

Being about to proceed, he was by the Lord Chief Justice interrupted.

Ld Ch. Justice: Sir Walter Raleigh, this which you now speak touching your voyage is not to the purpose, neither can your commission any way help you; by that you are not pardoned; for by words of a special nature, in case of treason, you must be pardoned, and not implicitly. There was no word tending to pardon in all your commission, and therefore you must say something else to the purpose, otherwise we must proceed to give execution.

Raleigh: If your opinion be so, my Lord, I am satisfied, and so put myself on the mercy of the King, who I know is gracious; and, under favour, I must say, I hope he will be pleased to take commiseration upon me. As concerning that judgment which is so long past, and which I think here are some could witness, nay his Majesty was of opinion, that I had hard measure therein . . .

Ld Ch. Justice: Sir Walter Raleigh, you must remember yourself; you had an honourable trial, and so were justly convicted . . .

I am here called to grant execution upon the judgment given you fifteen years since; all which time you have been as a dead man in the law, and might at any minute have been cut off, but the King in mercy spared you. You might think it heavy if this were done in cold blood, to call you to execution, but it is not so; for new offences have stirred up his Majesty's justice, to remember to revive what the law hath formerly cast upon you. I know you have been valiant and wise, and I doubt not but you retain both these virtues, for now you have occasion to use them. Your faith hath heretofore been questioned, but I am resolved you are a good Christian, for your book which is an admirable work, doth testify as much . . .

Execution is granted.

I I

The hearing had been in the morning. The execution was to be early next day in Old Palace Yard (between the east end of Henry VII's chapel and the entrance to today's House of Lords). Meanwhile he was taken to a room in the gatehouse of the old Westminster monastery, a little to the west of the Abbey (close to where today's Great Smith Street meets Broad Sanctuary).

On the scaffold he would have the traditional right to make his peace with the world, but he spent some of the day in writing a statement which could be published if his speech on the scaffold were cut short. By the evening he had also settled such affairs as he could, and was a free man.

Raleigh, 'on the snuff of a candle the night before he died':
> Cowards fear to die, but courage stout,
> Rather than live in snuff, will be put out.

The Dean of Westminster, Dr Robert Tounson, to Sir John Isham, 9 November 1618:[1]
When I began to encourage him against the fear of death, he seemed to make so light of it that I wondered at him; and when I told him that the dear servants of God, in better causes than his, had shrunk

back and trembled a little, he denied not, but yet gave God thanks he never feared death; and much less then, for it was but an opinion and imagination; and the manner of death though to others might seem grievous, yet he had rather die so than of a burning fever; with much more to that purpose, with such confidence and cheerfulness that I was fain to divert my speech another way, and wished him not to flatter himself, for this extraordinary boldness, I was afraid, came from some false ground . . . If it were out of an humour of vain glory or carelessness or contempt of death, or senselessness of his own estate, he were much to be lamented, etc. For I told him that heathen men had set as little by their lives as he could do, and seemed to die as bravely.

He answered that he was persuaded that no man that knew God and feared him could die with cheerfulness and courage except he were assured of the love and favour of God unto him; that other men might make shows outwardly, but they felt no joy within; with much more to that effect, very Christianly.

Newsletter, Chamberlain to Carleton, 7 November:[1]
His lady had leave to visit him that night, and told him she had obtained the disposing of his body. To which he answered smiling:
'It is as well, Bess, that thou mayest dispose of it dead, that hadst not always the disposing of it when it was alive.'
And so dismissed her anon after midnight, when he settled himself to sleep for three or four hours.

Raleigh, written this night in his Bible – the last stanza of a bachelor poem to Bess (p. 100), with two lines added:

> Even such is Time, which takes in trust
> Our youth, our joys, our all we have,
> And pays us but with earth and dust;
> Who in the dark and silent grave,
> When we have wandered all our ways,
> Shuts up the story of our days.

But from this earth, this grave, this dust,
My God shall raise me up, I trust.

John Pory to Carleton, 7 November:[1]
About 4 o'clock in the morning a cousin of his, Mr Charles Thynne, coming to see him, Sir Walter finding him sad began to be very pleasant with him. Whereupon Mr Thynne counselled him:

'Sir, take heed you go not too much upon the brave hand, for your enemies will take exception at that.'

'Good Charles,' quoth he, 'give me leave to be merry, for this is the last merriment that ever I shall have in this world. But when I come to the sad part, thou shalt see, I will look on it like a man.'

Dean Tounson to Sir John Isham, 9 November (continued):
After he had received the Communion in the morning, he was very cheerful and merry, and hoped to persuade the world that he died an innocent man, as he said.

Thereat I told him that he should do well to advise what he said; men in these days did not die in that sort innocent, and his pleading innocency was an oblique taxing of the Justice of the Realm upon him.

He confessed justice had been done, and by course of law he must die; but yet, I should give him leave, he said, to stand upon his innocency in the fact . . .

He was very cheerful that morning he died – ate his breakfast heartily, and took tobacco, and made no more of his death than if he had been to take a journey.

Chamberlain to Carleton, 7 November (continued):
The morning that he went to execution there was a cup of excellent good sack brought to him, and being asked how he liked it, 'As the fellow,' said he, 'that drinking at St Giles's bowl as he went to Tyburn said, it was good drink if a man might tarry by it.'

12

Collated from contemporary accounts: [1]
Sir Walter Raleigh was led up to the scaffold in the Old Palace Yard
by the two sheriffs of London, accompanied by Dr Tounson, Dean of
Westminster. Sir Hugh Beeston meeting them as they came near the
scaffold delivered his letter [for a good place], but the sheriff by
mishap had left his spectacles at home and put the letter in his pocket.
In the meantime Sir Hugh being thrust by, Sir Walter bade him
farewell and said:

'I know not what shift you will make, but I am sure of a place.'

The throng was great upon his coming, and he was much pressed
and crowded, so as he was breathless, and seemed fainting upon his
arrival on the scaffold. But after he had paused awhile his spirits
seemed very cheerful, and his countenance smiling, and he saluted
divers of the Lords and others who were in his sight. The principal
Lords were Arundel, Oxford, and Northampton, the Lord Viscount
Doncaster [James Hay, the Scot who had reported the 1603 trial to
James], the Lord Windsor, the Lord Sheffield who was on horseback, Sir Richard Sackville, General Cecil, and Sir Henry Rich.

His attire was a wrought night-cap, a ruff-band, an hair-coloured
satin doublet, with a black wrought waistcoat under it, a pair of
black cut taffeta breeches, a pair of ash-coloured silk stockings, and a
wrought black velvet gown.

After a proclamation of silence by an officer appointed, and putting off his hat, he addressed himself to speak in this manner:

'My honourable good Lords, and the rest of my good friends that
come to see me die, I desire to be borne withal, for I have had these
two days two fits of an ague. Yesterday I was notwithstanding taken
out of my bed in one of my fits; and whether I shall escape it this day
or no I cannot tell. If therefore you perceive any weakness in me, I
beseech you attribute it to my malady, for this is the hour I look for
it.

'I thank God of his infinite goodness that he hath vouchsafed me to
die in the light, in the sight of so honourable an assembly, and not in
darkness.'

[257]

But by reason the Lords that were in Sir Randal Crew's window were some distance from the scaffold that he perceived they could not well hear him, he said:

'I will strain my voice, for I would willingly have your Honours hear me.'

But my Lord Arundel said:

'Nay, we will rather come upon the scaffold.'

Whereupon the Earls of Arundel and Northampton and the Viscount Doncaster came up to the scaffold, and after several salutations he began again to speak:

'As I said, I thank God heartily that he hath brought me into the light to die, and hath not suffered me to die in the dark prison of the Tower, where I have suffered so much adversity and a long sickness. And I thank God that my fever hath not taken me at this time, as I prayed God it might not.

'There are two main points of suspicion wherein his Majesty, as I conceive, hath been informed against me, which I desire to clear and to resolve your Lordships of.

'One is, his Majesty hath been informed that I had some practice with France, and his Majesty had some reasons to induce him thereunto. One reason that his Majesty had so to believe was that when I came back from Guiana, being come to Plymouth, I had a desire in a small bark to pass to Rochelle, which was for that I would have made my peace, before I had come to England. Another reason was that upon my flight I did intend to fly into France, for saving of my life, having had some terror from above. A third reason was the French Agent's coming to my house here in London, and it was reported that I had a commission from the French King at my going forth.

'These are the reasons that his Majesty had, as I am informed, to suspect.

'But this I say, for a man to call God to witness to a falsehood at any time is a grievous sin, and what shall he hope for at the Tribunal Day of Judgment? But to call God to witness to a falsehood at the time of death is far more grievous and impious, and a man that so doth cannot have salvation, for he hath no time for repentance, and there is no hope for such an one. I do therefore call God to witness, as

I hope to see him in his kingdom, which I hope I shall within this quarter of this hour, or to have any benefit or comfort by the passion of my Saviour, I did never entertain any conspiracy, nor ever had any plot or intelligence with the French King, nor ever had any advice or practice with the French Agent, neither did I ever see the French hand or seal, as some have reported I had a commission from him at sea. Neither, as I have a soul to be saved, did I know of the French Agent's coming till I saw him in my gallery unlooked for. If I speak not true, O God, let me never come into thy kingdom.

'The second suspicion was, his Majesty hath been informed, that I should speak dishonourably and disloyally of him. But my accuser is a runagate Frenchman, who having run over the face of the earth hath no abiding place. This fellow because he had a merry wit, and some small skill in chemical medicines, I entertained rather for his taste than his judgment; one that I knew to be perfidious – he perjured himself at Winchester in my former troubles, revealing that, the next day, which he vowed to the contrary the day before to me.

'It is not for me to fear or to flatter kings. I am now the subject of Death, and the great God of Heaven is my sovereign before whose tribunal seat I am shortly to appear. And to speak falsely now, were it to gain the favour of the King, were vain. Therefore by the same protestation I have already made, I never did speak any disloyal, dishonourable, or dishonest words of the King, neither to this Frenchman nor to any other. If I did, the Lord blot me out of the Book of Life. Nay, I will protest further, I never in all my life thought any such evil of his Majesty in my heart. Therefore methinks it seemeth something strict that such a base fellow should receive credit against the protestation I make upon my salvation.

'And so much for this point. I have dealt truly, and I hope I shall be believed.

'I confess I did attempt to escape, I cannot deny it. I had advertisement from above that it would go hard with me. I desired to save my life.

'And I do likewise confess that I did dissemble and feign myself sick at Salisbury, but I hope it was no sin. David, a man after God's own heart, yet for the safety of his life did make himself a fool and did let the spittle fall upon his beard, and it was not imputed to him as sin. I intended no ill but to prolong time till his Majesty came, hoping for some commiseration from him.

'Touching Sir Lewis Stukeley, he is my countryman and kinsman, and I have this morning taken the sacrament of Master Dean and forgiven both Stukeley and the Frenchman. But that they are perfidious I think I am bound in charity to speak, that others may take warning how to trust such.

'Sir Lewis Stukeley hath justified against me before the Lords that I did tell him that my Lord Carew and my Lord Doncaster here sent me word to get me gone when first I landed. I protest upon my salvation neither did they send me any such word, neither did I tell Stukeley any such matter, for if I had I presume he would not have left me six, seven, eight, nine or ten days together, alone, to go whither I listed, whilst he rode himself about the country.

'Again he accused me that I should tell him that my Lord Carew and my Lord Doncaster would meet me in France, which was never my speech or thought.

'Thirdly, he accused me that I showed him a letter whereby I did signify unto him that I would give him ten thousand pounds for my escape; but God cast my soul into everlasting fire if I made any such proffer of £10,000 or £1,000. But indeed I showed him a letter that, if he would go with me, there should be order taken for his debts when he was gone. Neither had I £10,000 to give him, for if I had had so much I could have made my peace better with it other ways than in giving it to Stukeley.

'But Sir Lewis Stukeley did me a further injury, which I am very sensible of, howsoever it seem not much to concern me. In my going up to London we lodged at Sir Edward Parham's house, an ancient friend and follower of mine, whose lady is my cousin-germane. There he made it to be suggested to me, and he himself told me, that I had there received some dram of poison, when I answered that I feared no such thing, for I was well assured of them in that house, and therefore wished him to have no such thought. I know it grieves the gentleman there should such a conceit be held; and for the cook who was suspected, having been once my servant, I know he will go a thousand miles to do me good.'

Then he looked over his note of remembrance.

'Well,' said he, 'thus far have I gone. A little more, and a little more, I will have done by and by.

'It was told the King that I was brought perforce into England, and that I did not intend to come again, whereas Captain Charles Parker, Mr Tresham, Mr Leak, and divers others, that knew how I was dealt withal, shall witness for me. For the common soldiers, which were 150, mutinied against me, and fortified the gunroom against me, and kept me within my own cabin, and would not be satisfied except that I would take a corporal oath not to bring them into England till I had gotten their pardons, there being four of them unpardoned, or else they would cast me into the sea.

'Now after I had taken this oath, being forced to come to them with money, with clothes, and wine, such as I had, I drew some of the chiefest to desist from their purposes, and at length I persuaded them to go into Ireland, which they were willing unto; where they would have landed in the north parts, but I would not, and told them that they were Redshanks that inhabited there, and with much ado I persuaded them to come into the south, hoping from thence to write to his Majesty for their pardons. In the meantime I was forced to give them £125 at Kinsale, to bring them to several places in Devonshire and Cornwall to lie safe there till they had been pardoned, otherwise I had never got from them.

'I hear likewise there was a report that I meant not to go to Guiana at all, and that I knew not of any mine, nor intended any such matter but only to get my liberty, which I had not the wit to keep.

'But as I will answer it before the same God I am shortly to appear before, I endeavoured and hoped for gold, for gold for the benefit of his Majesty, and myself, and of those that ventured and went with me, with the rest of my countrymen. But Keymis, that knew the head of the mine, a wilful fellow, would not discover it when he saw that my son was slain, but made himself away.

'But I am glad that my Lord of Arundel is here, for his Lordship and divers others being with me in the gallery of my ship at my departure, I remember your Honour took me aside and desired me faithfully and freely to resolve him in one thing, which was whether I intended to return home or no, whatsoever fortune I had. I there told his Lordship and gave him my hand, that whatsoever succeeded, if I lived, I would return.'

'And so you did,' answered my Lord, 'it is true, I do very well remember it, they were the very last words I spake unto you.'

'Another slander was raised of me, that I would have gone away from them and left them at Guiana. But there were a great many of worthy men that accompanied me always, as my Sergeant Major George Raleigh, and divers others (*which he then named*) that knew my intent was nothing so.

'Another opinion was held of me that I carried to sea £16,000 in gold, and that was all the voyage I intended, only to get money into my hands. As I shall answer it before God, I had not in all the world either in my hands or others', to my use either directly or indirectly, above £100, whereof I gave my wife when I went £25. The error, I perceive, came in searching the scrivener's books: there was entered £20,000, and yet but £4,000 in the surveyor's book. Now I gave my bill for the other £16,000 for divers adventurers, but I protest I had not a penny of money more than £100, as I hope to be saved.

'Other reports are raised of me touching that voyage which I value not: as that I would not allow the sick persons water enough. Those that go such voyages know that things must be done in order and proportion; if it had been given out by gallons to some that were sick, all had perished. But these, and such like, I will pass by.

'Only I will borrow a little time of Mr Sheriff's to speak of one thing more, and that doth make my heart bleed to hear such an imputation laid upon me. It is said that I was a persecutor of my Lord of Essex, and that I stood in a window over against him when he suffered, and puffed out tobacco in disdain of him. God I take to witness, my eyes shed tears for him when he died, and as I hope to look in the face of God hereafter, my Lord of Essex did not see my face when he suffered. I was afar off in the Armoury, where I saw him, but he saw not me.

'I confess indeed I was of a contrary faction, but I knew my Lord of Essex was a noble gentleman, and that it would be worse with me when he was gone; for those that set me against him, afterwards set themselves against me, and were my greatest enemies, and my soul hath been many times grieved that I was not nearer unto him when

[262]

he died, because I understood that he asked for me at his death, to be reconciled unto me.

'And these be the material points I thought good to speak of. I am now at this instant to render up my account to God, and I protest as I shall appear before him, this that I have spoken is true, and I hope I shall be believed.

'And now I entreat you all to join with me in prayer, that the great God of Heaven, whom I have grievously offended, being a great sinner of a long time and in many kinds, my whole course a course of vanity, a seafaring man, a soldier, and a courtier – the temptations of the least of these were able to overthrow a good mind and a good man; that God, I say, will forgive me, and that he will receive me into everlasting life. So I take my leave of you all, making my peace with God.'

Then proclamation being made that all men should depart the scaffold, he prepared himself for death, giving away his hat and wrought night-cap, and some money to such as he knew that stood near him. And then taking his leave of the Lords, knights, gentlemen, the Dean of Westminster and the two Sheriffs, and amongst the rest taking his leave of my Lord of Arundel, he thanked him for his company, and entreated him to desire the King that no scandalous writing to defame him might be published after his death, saying further unto him:

'I have a long journey to go, and therefore I will take my leave.'

Then putting off his gown and doublet, he desired the headsman to show him the axe, which not being suddenly granted unto him, he said:

'I prithee, let me see it. Dost thou think that I am afraid of it?'

And having it in his hands, he felt along upon the edge of it, and smiling spake unto Mr Sheriff saying:

'This is a sharp medicine, but it is a physician that will cure all my diseases.'

Then he went first on the one side of the scaffold and requested them all that they would heartily pray to God to assist and strengthen him, and then turned to the other side and made the like request to them.

Then having ended his speech, the executioner kneeled down and asked his forgiveness, the which laying his hand upon his shoulder he forgave him.

The executioner threw down his own cloak because he would not spoil the prisoner's gown.

When he was laid down some found fault that his face was westward, and would have him turned. Whereupon rising he said:

'So the heart be right, it is no great matter which way the head lieth.'

So he laid his head on the block, his face being towards the east.

He had given order to the executioner that after some short meditation when he stretched forth his hands he should dispatch him. After once or twice putting forth his hands, the fellow out of timorousness (or what other cause) forbearing, he was fain bid him:

'Strike, man, strike!'

And so at two blows he took off the head, though he stirred not a whit after the first.

His head was showed on each side of the scaffold. The people were much affected at the sight, insomuch that one was heard to say:

'We have not such another head to cut off!'

It was then put into a red leather bag, and his wrought velvet cloak cast over his body, which was afterward conveyed away in a mourning coach of his lady's.

13

Bess to Sir Nicholas Carew:[1]
I desire, good brother, that you will be pleased to let me bury the worthy body of my noble husband, Sir Walter Raleigh, in your church at Beddington,* where I desire to be buried. The Lords have given me his dead body, though they denied me his life. This night he shall be brought you with two or three of my men. Let me hear presently. God hold me in my wits.

E. R.

* The body was buried after all in St Margaret's, Westminster.

Dean Tounson to Sir John Isham, 9 November (continued):
The last week was a busy week with me, and the week afore that was more. I would gladly have writ unto you but could find no time, yet I hope you had the relation of Sir Walter Raleigh's death . . . He left a great impression in the minds of those that beheld him . . .

This was the news a week since, but now it is blown over, and he almost forgotten . . .

The King and Prince, thanks be to God, are very well.

NOTES

PART ONE

page 1 1 *Brief Lives*, MS Aubrey 6 fol 77v.

2 A. M. C. Latham, 'A Birth-date for Sir Walter Raleigh', *Etudes Anglaises*, July/Sept. 1956.

2 1 Raphael Holinshed, *Chronicles of England, Scotland and Ireland*, ed. John Hooker, 1587, III 1016.

2 *Acts and Monuments*, 1583 ed, II 2051.

4 1 W. J. Harte, 'Some Evidence of Trade between Exeter and Newfoundland up to 1600', *Devon Ass. Trans.*, LXIV.

5 1 Deed in Sidmouth Parish Church.

7 1 *Annales . . . regnante Elizabethae*, ed. Hearne, Oxford 1717, I 198.

2 P. Lefranc points out in 'Un Inédit de Raleigh sur le Conduite de la Guerre 1597-8', *Etudes Anglaises* July/Sept. 1955, that Raleigh said: '. . . the Duke of Beaufort came over the Loire in my own time in France, and won La Charité, in spite of D'Aumale' (Spanish Alarum, *Works* VIII 676). This means that he was in France by May 1569, whereas Champernowne's troop did not leave England until September and join the French Protestant forces until 5 October.

3 Book V Ch II Sect 16.

8 1 *ibid.*

2 Hakluyt said in 1587, in his dedication to Raleigh of his translation of René de Laudonnière's history of four French voyages to Florida, that Raleigh had spent more years in France than he, that is to say, more than five. This may have been a joke and a juggle. Raleigh was certainly in France by May 1569; if he arrived there in March it would have been 1568 by the old reckoning, and 1568 to 1572 was five years inclusive.

9 1 *Apophthegms New and Old*, 1625, no. 269.

10 1 *Brief Lives*, MS Aubrey 6 fol 75v.

12 1 *ibid* 185.

16 1 Latham points out that he was described as such when he answered an interrogatory on 3.2.81 for a Chancery case, Humphrey Gilbert v W. Hawkins of Plymouth, PRO Town Bundles C 24/150.

17 1 This poem is headed in MS Harleian 7392 'A poem put into my Lady Layton's pocket by Sir Walter Raleigh'. According to Nichols, Elizabeth Knollys (daughter of Sir Francis Knollys and distant kinswoman of the Queen) was one of the Ladies in Waiting who gave a New Year's present to Elizabeth on 1 January 1576, 1578 and 1579; she was

[267]

Lady Layton (Thomas Layton was Captain of Guernsey) by July 1580 (on 1.7.80 'Lady Layton' was among those at Court 'troubled with a strange new sickness', Edmund Lodge, *Illustrations of British History*, 1791, II 174).

page 18 *1* SP Dom CXXVI 49.

19 *1* Holinshed, *Chronicles*, ed. Hooker, 1587, III 1369.

PART TWO

28 *1* *ibid*, II 170.

30 *1* *ibid*, II 171.

  2 *SP Spanish* III 57.

32 *1* Holinshed, II 173.

33 *1* *SP Ireland*, LXXX 82, reprinted Edwards II 11.

36 *1* *A View of the Present State of Ireland*, 1596, printed J. Ware, *The History of Ireland*, Dublin, 1633.

37 *1* Holinshed, II 174.

39 *1* MS Harleian fol 5.

PART THREE

41 *1* Bacon, *Apophthegms*, no. 31.

46 *1* *The History of the Worthies of England*, 1663 ed., 262.

47 *1* *Brief Lives*, MS Aubrey 6 fol 75, 75v.

48 *1* *Worthies*, 262.

49 *1* *Fragmenta Regalia*, 1653 ed., 60.

50 *1* MS Addl 15891 fol 30, reprinted Sir Harris Nicolas, *Memoirs of the Life and Times of Sir Christopher Hatton*, 1847, p. 297.

51 *1* T. N. Brushfield, *Devon Ass. Trans.*, XLI (1909).

  2 Nicolas Faunt to Anthony Bacon 6.5.83, quoted Thomas Birch, *Memoirs of the Reign of Queen Elizabeth*, 1754, I 34.

52 *1* ed. J. P. Halliwell, 1842.

  2 John Strype, *Annals of the Reformation*, Oxford 1824, IV 590, reprinted Edwards II 21.

  3 *Hatfield* XIII 228, Nichols I 228.

53 *1* MS Addl 4231 fol 85, quoted Edwards II 19.

55 *1* Hakluyt VIII 289; a collated version Quinn, *Roanoke Voyages*, I 82.

56 *1* *Brief Lives*, MS Aubrey 6 fol 76.

57 *1* MS Addl 6788 fol 469.

  2 *ibid* 490.

  3 Schedule of rents of manors of Sherborne, attached to Raleigh's letter to the Council 1604, *Hatfield* XVI 260, printed Edwards II 309.

page 58 1 Middlesex Cty Records, 5.10.84, quoted T. N. Brushfield, *Devon Ass. Trans.*, XXXV (1903).

2 Hieremias Drexelius, *Trismegistus Christianus*, 4th ed. Munich, 1629, p. 556.

60 1 V. von Klarwill, *Queen Elizabeth and some Foreigners*, 1928, p. 323.

61 1 *ibid* 336.

64 1 *Cat. of British seal-dies in BM*, 1952, no. 347.

2 Raleigh's three letters to the University are in the University Registry, quoted Edwards II 24, 27, 28.

65 1 Ld. Treas. Burghley (who was also Chancellor of the University) to the Vice-Chancellor of Camb. Univ., Strype, *Annals of the Reformation*, III (i) 498.

66 1 MS Addl 15891 fol 147, printed Nicolas, *Hatton*, 415.

68 1 John Harington, '*A Brief View of the State of the Church of England*' 1653, p. 111; Hist. MS Comm., *MS Dean and Chapter of Wells*, II 307–8.

69 1 *The Survey of Cornwall*, 1602, dedicated to Raleigh.

2 Raleigh to Devon Justices 15.2.92, Devon Cty Records 193, printed A. H. A. Hamilton, 'The Jurisdiction of the Lord Warden of the Stannaries in the time of Sir Walter Raleigh', *Devon Ass. Trans.*, VIII (1876).

3 *SP Dom* XXIX 126.

70 1 *Worthies*, 262.

72 1 MS Harleian 6994 fol 2, quoted Edwards II 33.

2 Walsingham to Leicester 1.4.86, MS Cotton, Galba C ix fol 157, quoted *Correspondence of Robt. Dudley, E. of Leicester*, ed. John Bruce, 1844, p. 205.

73 1 *Brief Lives*, MS Aubrey 6 fol 75, 76v.

2 *The Character of Queen Elizabeth*, 1693.

3 MS Addl 12049 fol 18.

74 1 *Epigrams both Pleasant and Serious*, 1615 ed.

77 1 Thomas Morgan to Mary, Queen of Scots 19.4.85, *Hatfield* III 96.

79 1 MS at Hardwick Hall, *Hist. MS Comm. Third Report*, 42.

80 1 Alfonso Ferrabosco, *Ayres*, 1609; Samuel Pepys, *Diary*, 12.2.67; Samuel Butler, *Hudibras*, I ii 1169.

2 *Spanish State Papers* 8.1.87; *Venetian SP* 13.2.87.

3 MS Addl 6697 fol 227–235.

4 Thomas Churchyard, *Churchyard's Challenge*, 1593, 7th page of introd.

81 1 MS Tanner 76 fol 84b–85a.

84 1 *SP Dom* CCVII 87.

85 1 *SP Suppl.* 9/55, quoted Quinn, *Roanoke Voyages*, II 559.

page 86 1 From a MS of Raleigh's quoted by P. Lefranc in *Etudes Anglaises*, 1955, p. 207.

2 *The History of the World*, Book V Ch I Sect 6.

87 1 *Report of the Truth of the Fight about the Isles of the Azores*, 1591, reprinted Hakluyt VII 39.

88 1 *Spanish SP* 12.1.89.

2 *Brief Lives*, MS Aubrey 6 fol 77.

90 1 Francis Allen to Anthony Bacon 17.8.89, quoted Birch I 56.

94 1 MS in possession of Philip and Lionel Robinson, facsimile in W. F. Oakeshott, *The Queen and the Poet*, 1960.

96 1 *The Faerie Queene*, Book III canto 5, Book IV canto 7.

2 Oakeshott suggests that one of his poems was the spearhead: 'Would I were changed into that golden shower That so divinely streamèd from the skies To fall in drops upon my dainty flower . . .' That Elizabeth was not averse to 'deep petting', whatever she felt about more Jovial love-making, is suggested, of course, by Jonsons's 'for her delight she tried many', and also by a concatenation of ambiguously genital images in lines 221–256 of the 'XIth and last book of the Ocean to Cynthia', where Raleigh is describing 'of women's love the careful charge'.

97 1 MS Tenison 605 fol 140, quoted Edwards II 41.

99 1 *The Times*, 20, 21 Sept 1958.

100 1 Arthur Throgmorton's diary, quoted A. L. Rowse, *Ralegh and the Throckmortons*, 1962, 160. Raleigh also had at some time a bastard daughter whom in the last years of the century he betrothed to a page of whom, as Governor of Jersey, he had the *garde noble*, MS journal of Elie Brevint, Ministre de Sercq (contemporary of Raleigh), vol 3 fol 358, quoted R. R. Lemprière, Messire Walter Raleigh, *Bulletin Société Jersiaise*, IX.

101 1 See page 126.

103 1 Raleigh to Burghley 16.10.91, MS Lansdowne LXIX fol 60v, printed Edwards II 43.

2 MS Stonyhurst, Anglia VI 117, quoted Philip Caraman, *The Other Face*, 1960.

104 1 *Complete Collection of State Trials*, ed. William Cobbett, 1809, I col 1308; Strype, *Life and Acts of John Whitgift*, Oxford 1821–1843, II 98–100.

105 1 'D. Andreas Philopater', *Elizabethae Angliae Reginae Haeresim Calvinianam Propugnantis, Saevissimum in Catholicos sui Regni edictum . . . cum Responsione*, Augsburg 1592, reprinted E. A. Strathmann, *Sir Walter Raleigh, a study in scepticism*, New York 1951, p. 26.

106 1 Raleigh to Cecil 25.8.94, *Cecil Papers* xxvii 101, quoted Edwards II 96.

page 107 *1* Raleigh to Cecil 10.3.92, W. Murdin, *Burghley Papers*, 663, quoted Edwards II 44.

    2 Arthur Throgmorton's diary, quoted A. L. Rowse, *Ralegh and the Throckmortons*, 1962, 160.

    3 W. Murdin, *Burghley Papers*, 663, quoted Edwards II 44.

    4 A. R. Wagner, *The Times*, 2 April 1962, suggests 'Damerel' but Rowse in *The Times*, 3 May 1962, prefers 'Damerei' as in Throgmorton. Incidentally in Book VI of *The Faerie Queene* Serena has a male baby and suffers acutely, while Calepine, who seems to represent one side of Timias-Raleigh, is unhelpful and unheroic.

    5 Throgmorton's diary, quoted Rowse, 161–162.

108 *1* MS Ashmole 1729 fol 177, quoted H. E. Sandison, 'Arthur Gorges, Spenser's Alcyon and Raleigh's Friend', *Proc. Mod. Langs. Ass.*, 1928.

109 *1* quoted Rowse, 162.

PART FOUR

111 *1* Clare Williams, *Thomas Platter's Travels in England 1599*, 1937, p. 159.

112 *1* Hist. MS Comm., *MS Allan George Finch*, I fol 33–34.

    2 *Hatfield* IV 220, quoted Edwards II 51.

113 *1* *SP Dom* CCXLII 131, quoted Edwards II 52.

114 *1* Strype, *Annals of the Reformation*, IV 180, reprinted Edwards II 67.

    2 Strype, *Annals of the Reformation*, IV 177, reprinted Edwards II 71.

    3 *SP Dom* CCXLIII 17.

116 *1* *The Journals of all the Parliaments during the reign of Queen Elizabeth*, 1682.

117 *1* *Historical Collections, or . . . the Four Last Parliaments of Queen Elizabeth*, 1680.

119 *1* MS Harleian 6848 fol 185–186, 190.

    2 MS Harleian 6849 fol 183–190, quoted *Willobie his Avisa*, ed. G. B. Harrison, 1926, App. III.

124 *1* Oakeshott and Rowse believe this was written in the Tower in 1592. but it was unlike Raleigh to write a long poem in prison without any prison imagery. Lines 221–227 seem to have sprung partly from his known diversion of a stream through the Sherborne grounds.

126 *1* Lady Raleigh to Cecil 8.2.94, *Hatfield* IV 485, quoted Edwards II 397.

    2 MS Harleian 6849 fol 183–190, quoted *Willobie his Avisa*, ed. G. B. Harrison, App. III.

127 *1* Henry Foley, *Records of the English Province of the Society of Jesus*, Roehampton 1875–1883, III 461–462.

    2 J. W. Shirley, 'Sir Walter Raleigh's Guiana Finances', *Huntingdon Library Qtly*, XIII.

128 *1* *Hatfield* VI 104, quoted Edwards II 398.

page 136   *1 Hatfield* V 457, quoted Edwards II 109.

    2 Rowland Whyte to Sir Robert Sidney, 15 October 1595, Hist. MS Comm., *MS Lord De l'Isle and Dudley*, II 173.

    3 John Britton, *Natural History of Wiltshire*, 1847, p. 64.

137   *1 De Guiana Carmen Epicum.*

    2 MS Sloane 1133 fol 45, quoted V. T. Harlow, *Discovery of Guiana*, 1928, App. C.

138   *1 Letters and Memorials of State*, ed. Arthur Collins, 1746, II 24.

139   *1 SP Dom* CCLVII 52.

140   *1 Hatfield* VI 169, quoted Edwards II 129.

    2 Hatfield VI 174.

    3 Hatfield VI 175, quoted Edwards II 381.

    4 Birch I 486.

    5 Charles Chester was the subject of a well-known story of Aubrey's:

'In [Sir Walter Raleigh's] youthful time was one Charles Chester, that often kept company with his acquaintance. He was a bold, impertinent fellow, and they would never be at quiet for him, a perpetual talker, and made a noise like a drum in a room. So one time at a tavern, Sir Walter Raleigh beats him and seals up his mouth, i.e. his upper and nether beard, with hard wax.'

Another version of a 'sealing up' is in *Merry Passages and Jests* by Sir Nicholas Lestrange (MS Harleian 6395, quoted in *Anecdotes and Traditions illustrative of Early English History and Literature*, ed. W. J. Thomas, 1839, p. 56):

'Charles Chester, a Court fool in Queen Elizabeth's time, used to be girding very often at my Lord Knollys and Sir Walter Raleigh. Says Sir Walter Raleigh: "My Lord, get but this fool to dinner one day, and you shall see what a trick we'll serve him." So he did; and when his paunch was well filled (for he was a notable trencher man), and he went out of the chamber, Sir Walter Raleigh followed him. "Come, sirrah," says he, "now we'll be revenged on you for all your roguery"; and having some servants by, tied him hand and foot, set him right up in a corner, called a mason or two, built him up presently to the chin, and so close as he could not move, and threatened to cover him in, but that he begged hard and swore he would abuse them no more; so they let him stand till night.'

From Chester's extant letters to Cecil it is quite clear that he was an adhesive bore, but Raleigh suffered him, introduced him to the Lord Admiral, brought him to Plymouth.

    6 Birch II 10, 11; *Commentaries of Sir Francis Vere*, Cambridge 1657, p. 48.

141   *1* Birch II 14.

page 144 1 Edward Reynolds to Essex 9.8.96, Birch II 95.

    2 MS Harleian 6845 fol 101.

145 1 Raleigh to Cecil 24.1.97, *Hatfield* VII 35, quoted Edwards II 161.

    2 Collins II 54.

    3 *Brief Lives*, MS Aubrey 6 fol 76v, 77.

147 1 Raleigh to Cecil 6.7.97: 'I acquainted the Lord General with your letter to me, and your kind acceptance of your entertainment; he was also wonderful merry at your conceit of "Richard the Second".' *SP. Dom* CCLXIV 10, quoted Edwards II 169.

148 1 *Relation of the Islands Voyage*, Purchas XX 81.

152 1 Hist. MS Comm. *Various Collections*, I 371.

    2 I have not included Sir Henry Wotton's story about Essex: '. . . and then his glorious feather-triumph, when he caused two thousand orange-tawny feathers, in despite of Sir Walter Raleigh, to be worn in the Tiltyard, even before her Majesty's own face . . .' (*Reliquiae Wottoniae*, 1651, p. 190). No further detail is known, and no date. It is sometimes attributed to Coronation Day, 17 November 1598, but Chamberlain in a letter to Carleton of 20.11.98 says: 'Her day passed without any extraordinary matter more than running and singing.'

    3 Collins II 83.

153 1 Gifts and gambling debts between Raleigh and Northumberland are noted from 1586 onwards in the accounts at Syon House, *Hist. MS Comm. Sixth Report*, 1877, App.

154 1 *Hatfield* X 459.

    2 *Hatfield* X 84, quoted Edwards II 202.

155 1 For evidence in trials of Essex and Blount, see *Complete State Trials*, ed. Cobbett, I col 1342–1344, 1346–1347, 1424; Gorges' apologia, MS Cotton, Julius F vii fol 428.

156 1 *Complete State Trials*, ed. Cobbett, I col 1414.

    2 SP *Dom* CCLXXVIII 23, quoted *Poetical Miscellanies*, ed. J. O. Halliwell, 1845.

157 1 *Gentleman's Magazine*, 1853 II 435–443, 1854 I 17–23.

    2 SP *Dom* CCLXXXI 64, quoted Edwards II 227.

    3 *Hatfield* X 273, quoted Edwards II 226.

    4 *Hatfield* XI 392, quoted Edwards II 235.

158 1 *Hatfield* XI 462, quoted Edwards II 244.

162 1 Lord Henry Howard to Earl of Marr 4.6.02, *The Secret Correspondence of Sir Robert Cecil with James VI, King of Scotland*, ed. D. Dalrymple, Edinburgh 1766, p. 133.

    2 Lord Henry Howard to E. Bruce 4.10.01; *ibid* p. 29.

    3 Cecil Papers CXXXV 65, quoted *Correspondence of James VI of Scotland with Sir Robert Cecil and others*, ed. J. Bruce, 1861, p. 18.

    4 Lord Henry Howard to Cecil, MS Cotton, Titus C vi 386–392.

page 163 *1* Raleigh to Cecil 21.8.02, *Hatfield* XII 311, quoted Edwards II 251.

   164 *1* Cecil to Carew 5.9.01, 25.3.02, 4.11.02, *Letters of Sir Robert Cecil to Sir George Carew*, ed. John Maclean, 1864, p. 92, 106, 147.

     2 *Hatfield* XII 239, quoted Edwards II 247.

     3 R. R. Lemprière, Messire Walter Raleigh, *Bulletin Société Jersiaise*, IX.

     4 Lord Henry Howard to E. Bruce 1.5.02, *The Secret Correspondence . . .,* ed. Dalrymple, 107.

     5 *Hatfield*, XIV 265, quoted *Correspondence of James VI . . .*, ed. J. Bruce, 66.

   165 *1* Ed. J. Bruce, 1868.

PART FIVE

   167 *1* Sir John Popham to Cecil 27.3.03, *Hatfield* XV 11; *Diary of John Manningham*, ed. Bruce, 7, 13 April 1603.

     2 *Brief Lives*, MS Aubrey 6 fol 76v.

     3 *Hatfield* XV 57.

   168 *1* *Brief Lives*, MS Aubrey 6 fol 76v.

   169 *1* *Egerton Papers*, ed. J. Payne Collier, 1840, p. 380.

   170 *1* Raleigh to Lords Commissioners for examination of conspirators of 1603, 14.10.03, *Works* VIII 644, reprinted Edwards II 273.

     2 *Hatfield* XV 208.

   171 *1* A letter from Raleigh to Bess, written before the suicide attempt, has been praised and abominated, thought genuine and thought forged or part-forged. A copy is at All Souls. The false notes in it do not seem to me the false notes of rhetoric into which despair sometimes thrust Raleigh, but the letter contains some convincing details. It mentions a daughter whom Raleigh feels he has neglected. A. M. C. Latham discusses it fully in 'Sir Walter Raleigh's Farewell Letter', *Essays and Letters*, English Ass. 1939.

   172 *1* *SP Dom* IV 76.

     2 *Poetical Miscellanies*, ed. J. O. Halliwell, 1845.

     3 ibid.

   173 *1* MS Harleian 39 fol 265 *et seq*; *SP Dom* IV 83; *The Arraignment and Conviction of Sir Walter Raleigh at the King's Bench Bar at Winchester on the 17 of Nov 1603*, by Sir Thomas Overbury, 1648; *Complete State Trials*, ed. Cobbett, II col 1 *et seq*.

   205 *1* She was 'showing *veteris vestigia flammae*', Carleton to Chamberlain 27.11.03.

   206 *1* *SP Dom* V 9, MS Sloane 3520 fol 14, quoted Edwards II 284.

page 211　1　*Hatfield* XVI 9, quoted Edwards II 296.

213　1　*Hatfield* XVII 624, quoted Edwards II 317.

214　1　*SP Dom* XIX 112.

2　Examination of Edward Cotterell 4.2.07, *SP Dom* XXVI 42.

3　MS at Syon House, *Hist. MS Comm. Sixth Report*, 1877, App.; J. W. Shirley, 'The Scientific Experiments of Sir Walter Raleigh, the Wizard Earl and the Three Magi in the Tower 1603–17', *Ambix*, Dec. 1947.

215　1　MS Sloane 359 fol 63.

2　Antony Weldon, *Court and Character of King James*, reprinted *Secret History of the Court of James the First*, 1811, I 349.

3　*Brief Lives*, MS Aubrey 6 fol 75.

4　Chamberlain to Carleton 11.8.12.

5　Examination of Lawrence Davies 3.10.15, *SP Dom* LXXXII.

216　1　*Othello* I iii 144–145.

2　MS Addl 6178 fol 827, quoted Edwards II 389.

217　1　MS Sloane 359 fol 52b.

218　1　*Remains of Sir Walter Raleigh*, 1656–1657, reprinted Edwards II 330.

219　1　Francis Osborne, *Historical Memoirs on the reigns of Queen Elizabeth and King James*, 1658, p. 142.

222　1　A Copernicus is in the booklist in Raleigh's handwriting described in W. F. Oakeshott, *The Queen and the Poet*, 1960, p. 119.

2　In 1606 Henry Garnett, the Jesuit, had been imprisoned below Raleigh, accused of complicity in the Gunpowder Plot. In the next room to Father Garnett was Father Thomas Oldcorne, and the two of them were supposed not to be able to communicate. A means of secretly talking together was put in their way, while Cecil's private secretary and a magistrate were concealed in order to hear them. Under examination Father Garnett denied at first that he had spoken with Father Oldcorne and he was revealed as an equivocator. Moreover he defended the use of equivocation. Protestant England was more shocked by his defence of equivocation than by his association with the plotters; Catholic England regarded him as a martyr.

224　1　*Brief Relation of Sir Walter Raleigh's Troubles*, by his son Carew Raleigh, reprinted *Works* VIII 786.

228　1　MS Harleian 39 fol 350–351, quoted Edwards II 337.

2　MS Rawlinson DXLVII 54, 56–57.

229　1　*Notes of Ben Jonson's Conversations with William Drummond of Hawthornden January 1619*, 1842, p. 21.

2　*SP Dom* LXXI 32.

231　1　*SP Dom* LXXX 1.

page 233　*1* *SP Dom* LXXXVI 111.

235　*1* *Brief Lives*, MS Aubrey 6 fol 74v.

236　*1* *Autobiography of Phineas Pett*, ed. W. G. Perrin, 1918.

237　*1* *SP Dom* XC 146.

　　　2 H.C.A. 1.48, summarised in C. L'Estrange Ewen, *Raleigh's Last Adventure*, 1938.

238　*1* MS Cotton, Titus B viii 153, quoted in Raleigh, *The Discovery of Guiana*, ed. R. H. Schomburgk, 1848, p. 197.

239　*1* *SP Dom* XCVI 9.

240　*1* *Remains of Sir Walter Raleigh*, 1656–1657, reprinted Edwards II 347.

241　*1* James Howell, *Epistolae Ho-Elianae*, 1645, p. 6, discounted by S. R. Gardiner, *History of England 1603–1642*, 1883 ed., III 131.

242　*1* MS Harleian 4761 fol 23–25, MS Sloane 3520 fol 2–4, MS Addl 34631 fol 47; quoted Edwards II 359.

246　*1* Rev. Thos. Lorkin to Sir Thos. Puckering 30.6.18, MS Harleian 7002 fol 410.

　　　2 *A Declaration of the Demeanour and Carriage of Sir Walter Raleigh . . .*, 1618, p. 47.

250　*1* Raleigh to James, date given as 5 Oct., from Spanish translation in Archivio General de Indias at Simancas, printed J. A. St John, *Life of Sir Walter Raleigh*, 1868, II 331–333.

　　　2 *SP Dom* XCIX 69, quoted Edwards II 368.

251　*1* *Works* VIII 772.

252　*1* *SP Dom* CIII 21A, quoted Edwards II 498.

　　　2 The correspondence between James and the Commissioners is printed in Vincent Harlow, *Raleigh's Last Voyage*, 295–296.

　　　3 *Complete State Trials*, ed. Cobbett, II col 33.

254　*1* Walterus de Hemingburgh, *Historia de rebus gestis Edward I, etc.*, ed. Thos. Hearne, Oxford 1731, p. clxxxiv, reprinted *Works* VIII 780.

255　*1* *SP Dom* CIII 73.

256　*1* *SP Dom* CIII 74.

257　*1* MS in Archbishop Sancroft's writing, 'The effect of Sir Walter Raleigh's speech, written in the hearing of him, before he was beheaded', MS Tanner 299 no. 9, quoted in *Works* VIII 775; Sir Thomas Overbury, *The Arraignment and Conviction . . . of Sir Walter Raleigh*, 1648; *SP Dom* CIII 51–53, 74; *Complete State Trials*, ed. Cobbett, II col 40; Chamberlain to Carleton 31.10.18, 7.11.18, *SP Dom* CIII 58, 73; John Pory to Carleton 31.10.18, 7.11.18, *SP Dom* CIII 61, 74.

264　*1* Owen Manning, *History of Surrey*, 1804–1814, II 527, reprinted Edwards II 413.

SELECTED BIBLIOGRAPHY

I CONVENIENT SOURCES OF TEXTS AND REFERENCES

WORKS: *The Works of Sir Walter Raleigh*, ed. W. Oldys, 8 vols, Oxford 1829. Vol I Life; vols II–VII The History of the World; vol VIII Miscellaneous.

POEMS: *The Poems of Sir Walter Raleigh*, ed. Agnes M. C. Latham, 1951.

The Queen and the Poet, by Walter Oakeshott, 1960.

LETTERS: *The Life of Sir Walter Raleigh*, by E. Edwards, 1868, vol II.

COURT: *The Progresses of Queen Elizabeth*, by John Nichols, 4 vols, 1828.

The Letters of John Chamberlain, ed. N. E. McClure, 2 vols, Philadelphia 1939.

Letters and Memorials of State, etc., ed. Arthur Collins, 2 vols, 1746.

IRELAND: *Calendar of State Papers, Ireland (SP Ireland)*.

Calendar of the Carew Manuscripts in Lambeth Palace.

Chronicles of England, Scotland and Ireland, by Raphael Holinshed, ed. John Hooker, 1587, vol II.

VOYAGES: *The Voyages and Colonising Expeditions of Sir Humphrey Gilbert*, by D. B. Quinn, 1940.

The Roanoke Voyages, by D. B. Quinn, 2 vols, 1955.

The Discovery of Guiana, by Vincent Harlow, 1928.

Raleigh's Last Voyage, by Vincent Harlow, 1932.

The Principal Navigations . . ., by Richard Hakluyt, Glasgow 1904, 12 vols.

Hakluytus Posthumus, or Purchas his Pilgrims, by Samuel Purchas, Glasgow 1907, 20 vols.

PARLIAMENT: *The Journals of all the Parliaments during the reign of Queen Elizabeth*, by Sir Simonds D'Ewes, 1682.

Historical Collections, or . . . the Four Last Parliaments of Queen Elizabeth, by Heywood Townshend, 1680.

GENERAL: *Calendar of State Papers Domestic (SP Dom)*.

Acts of the Privy Council (APC).

Calendar of the Salisbury Manuscripts at Hatfield (Hatfield).

Calendar of Letters and State Papers . . . in the Archives of Simancas. (*SP Spanish*).

2 BIOGRAPHIES

W. Oldys, Oxford 1829 (vol I of *Works*); E. Edwards, 1868, 2 vols; W. Stebbing, Oxford 1899; Edward Thompson, 1938; M. Waldman, 1950; Hugh Ross Williamson, 1951; P. W. Edwards, 1953.

3 BIBLIOGRAPHIES

The Bibliography of Sir Walter Raleigh, by T. N. Brushfield, 1908; there is a bibliography in Thompson's biography.

4 WORKS NOT INCLUDED IN THE ABOVE BIBLIOGRAPHIES

ANDREWS, K. R., *Economic Aspects of Elizabethan Privateering,* Univ. of London Ph.D. thesis, 1951.

BETTS, R. E., 'The Lost Colony', *Cornhill Mag.,* July 1938.

BRADBROOK, M. C., *School of Night,* 1936.

CARAMAN, P., *The Other Face,* 1960.

CHAMBERS, E. K., 'The Court', *Shakespeare's England,* Oxford 1916; *The Elizabethan Stage,* Oxford 1923.

CLARK, E. G., *Raleigh and Marlowe,* New York 1941.

EAGLESTON, A. J., *The Channel Islands under Tudor Government,* Cambridge 1949.

EMDEN, C. S., *Oriel Papers,* Oxford 1948.

EWEN, C. L'ESTRANGE, *Raleigh's Last Adventure,* 1938.

FALLS, CYRIL, *Elizabeth's Irish Wars,* 1950.

FIRTH, C. H., 'Sir Walter Raleigh's "History of the World"', *Essays Historical and Literary,* Oxford 1938.

FRENCH, J. M., 'The Capture of the Carrack', *Notes and Queries,* 7 May 1938.

Gentleman's Magazine, 1853 vol II, 1854 vol I, 'Sir Walter Raleigh at Sherborne'.

GILBERT, A. H., 'Belphoebe's Misdeeming of Timias', *Proc. Mod. Langs. Ass.,* vol LXII (1947).

GRIFFITHS, G. M., 'An Account Book of Raleigh's Voyage 1592', *Nat. Lib. of Wales Jl*, 1952.

HANDOVER, P. M., *The Second Cecil*, 1959.

HARRISON, G. B., *The Life and Death of Robert Devereux, Earl of Essex*, 1937; *A Jacobean Journal*, 1941.

HENNELL, R., *History of the King's Bodyguard of the Yeomen of the Guard*, 1904.

KOLLER, K., 'Spenser and Raleigh', *English Literary History*, 1934.

LATHAM, A. M. C., 'Sir Walter Raleigh's Farewell Letter', *Essays and Letters*, Eng. Ass. 1939; 'A Birth-date for Sir Walter Raleigh', *Etudes Anglaises*, July/Sept. 1956.

LEFRANC, PIERRE, 'Un Inédit de Raleigh sur le Conduite de la Guerre 1596–7', *Etudes Anglaises*, July/Sept. 1955; 'La Date du Mariage de Sir Walter Raleigh', *Etudes Anglaises*, July/Sept. 1956.

LEMPRIÈRE, R. R., 'Messire Walter Raleigh', *Bulletin Société Jersiaise*, vol IX (1918).

LEWIS, G. R., *The Stannaries*, Cambridge, Mass. 1906.

LONDON COUNTY COUNCIL, *Survey of London*, vols XIII, XIV, XVI, XVIII.

MATTINGLEY, G., *The Defeat of the Spanish Armada*, 1959.

NEALE, J. E., *The Elizabethan House of Commons*, 1949; *Elizabeth I and Her Parliaments*, 1953.

ROWSE, A. L., *Sir Richard Grenville of the 'Revenge'*, 1937; *The England of Elizabeth*, 1950; *The Elizabethans and America*, Cambridge 1958.

SALAMAN, R. N., *The History and Social Influence of the Potato*, Cambridge 1949.

SCOTT, W. R., *The Constitution and Finance of English, Scottish and Irish Joint Stock Companies to 1720*, Cambridge 1910–12.

SHIRLEY, J. W., 'Scientific Experiments of Sir Walter Raleigh, the Wizard Earl and the Three Magi in the Tower 1603–17', *Ambix*, 1949; 'Sir Walter Raleigh's Guiana Finances', *Huntingdon Library Qtly*, XIII.

SANDISON, H. E., 'Arthur Gorges, Spenser's Alcyon and Raleigh's Friend', *Proc. Mod. Langs. Ass.*, 1928; *Poems of Sir Arthur Gorges*, Oxford 1953.

SORENSEN, J. W., 'Sir Walter Raleigh's Marriage', *Studies in Philology*, 1936.

STRATHMANN, E. A., *Sir Walter Raleigh, a Study in Scepticism*, New York 1951; 'An Epitaph attributed to Sir Walter Raleigh', *Mod. Lang. Notes*, 1945.

TAYLOR, E. G. R., *Tudor Geography*, 1930; *The Haven-finding Art*, 1956; 'Hariot's Instructions for Sir Walter Raleigh's Voyage to Guiana 1595', *Jl of the Inst. of Navigation*, V.

The Times, 20–21 Jan. 1958, 'Ku-Klux-Klan routed by Indians'; 'Arrests after "Klan" Rout'.

VERE, SIR FRANCIS, 'The Commentaries', *Stuart Tracts* ed. C. H. Firth 1903.

WILSON, F. P., *Plague in Shakespeare's London*, Oxford 1927.

General Index

Hudson, Henry, 234
Humphreys, Dr Laurence, 9
Hungary, 5

Imokilly, Seneschal of, *see* John Fitz
    Edmund Fitzgerald
Inca, the, 125, 128, 133, 135, 137
India, 4, 7, 221, 234
Infanta of Spain, Maria, 161, 169, 234
Ireland, colonisation of Munster, 6;
    Fitzmaurice, 20; Desmond rebel-
    lion, 22–40; state of Ireland, 26;
    habits of Irish, 26, 28, 36; Spanish
    threat, 45; W. R. gives views to
    Council, 47; W. R.'s estates, 80,
    91–2, 115, 123, 156–7, 163; W. R.
    visits, 91–6, 238, 244, 261; Tyrone's
    rebellion, 151–3, 158, 163, 180
Ironside, Rev. Ralph, 119–21, 126
Isham, Sir John, 254, 256, 265
Islands Voyage, 146–50, 218
Isle of Wight, 25, 83–4, 86, 237
Islington, 16, 234
Israel, 185, 222–3, 225

James I, likely successor to Elizabeth,
    161–2, 164; accedes, 165–9; char-
    acteristics, 167; meets W. R.,
    167–8, 170; conspiracy against,
    170; coronation, 171; Coke, 173;
    W. R.'s trial, 173–204, reprieve
    205; enters London, 212; visited
    by Christian, 216; his tastes not
    Henry's, 218; backs Virginian ex-
    pedition, 224; Sherborne, 224;
    short of money, 224; marriages of
    children, 224, 234–5; *The History
    of the World*, 230–1; Parliament,
    231–2; Savoy-Milan war, 236;
    W. R. to Guiana, 236, 238, 241,
    245
    letters from W. R., 211–12, 250–1;
    from Northumberland, 164
Jamestown, 98, 216
Jansen, 239
Japan, 5
Jersey, 155, 164, 169, 171, 207, 270;
    W. R.'s trial, 176, 178–9, 183,
    189
Jesuits, 9, 40, 181, 241; plotting by,

45, 52, 59; persecution of, 61, 104,
127; *see* Campion, Drexelius, Gar-
nett, Oldcorne, Parsons, Roman
Catholics
Jonah, 147
Jonson, Ben, 56, 221, 228–9, 270
Joshua, 222–3
Judah, 223

Kepler, 215
Keymis, Lawrence, 57, 127, 171;
    Guiana, 138, 145, 147, 228, 237,
    242–3, 245, 261; W. R.'s trial, 177,
    191–2
King, Samuel, 237, 245–6, 248–9
Knollys, Elizabeth, 17, 18, 21, 267
Knollys, Sir Francis, 18, 267, 272
Knollys, Henry, 18
Knyvett, Thomas Lord, 228
Ku-Klux-Klan, 99
Kyd, Thomas, 118

La Chesnay, 248–50
Lake, Sir Thomas, James's reception of
    W. R., 167
Lancerota, 241
Lane, Sir Ralph, 17, 46, 65, 71, 75,
    82–3
Langharne, William, 77
Latimer, Hugh, 2, 212
Laurencie, 170, 176, 179, 182, 188, 196
Layton, Sir Thomas and Lady, 267–8
Leicester, Robert Dudley Earl of, 8, 46,
    56, 72, 88, 96; W. R., 31, 39, 46,
    71–2, 80, 84; Netherlands, 46, 71,
    79, 83; Elizabeth, 47, 61–2, 71–2,
    105
Leigh, Sir John, 243
Leighs, 216
Lennox, Lewis Stuart Duke of, 181
Leonard the Indian, 238
Levant Company, 60
Lisbon, 85, 195
Lismore, 38, 92, 94, 123
Lock, Major, 12
Loire, 267
London, 2, 23, 25, 117, 155–6, 165, 212;
    214; in 1575, 11–12; London
    Bridge, 12, 56; plague, 115, 123,
    127, 171–2, 213; in 1616, 233–4

[287]

Walsingham, Sir Francis, 33–6, 40,
52–3, 58, 61, 65, 72, 78
Walsingham, shrine, 92
Wanchese, 59–60, 63, 75; town, 60
Warbeck, Perkin, 175
Warburton, Sir Peter, 187
Warspite, the, 141–2, 147
Warwick, Anne Dudley Countess of, 81
Wat, the, 145, 147
Waterford, 26; County W., 80
Watson, Anthony, *see* Chichester
Watson, William, 170, 175, 188, 190–1,
205
West Indies, 4, 15, 59, 70–1, 74, 77, 98,
135, 143, 180, 193, 241, 244, 250–1;
see Granadas, Bermuda
Westminster, Abbey, 12, 153, 168, 234,
254; Dean of, *see* Tounson; Hall,
12, 171, 252; Palace, 12, 16, 21, 41–
3, 55–6, 165; School, 56
Westwood, 137
Weymouth, 86
Whelan, John, 38
Whiddon, Jacob, 57, 126–8, 133
White, John, 65, 75, 81–2, 85, 98–9
Whitehall Palace, *see* Westminster
Palace
Whitehall Stairs, 12, 41
Whitgift, John, *see* Canterbury
Whitney, 244

Whyte, Sir Rowland, W. R., Cecil,
Essex, 138; W. R. again Captain of
Guard, 145–6; W. R. at primero,
152
William I, 230
William of Orange, 45–7, 59
Williams, Sir Roger, 83, 90
Willoughby, Ambrose, 152
Willoughby, Sir Hugh, 5
Wilson, Sir Thomas, 250, 252
Wilton, 171
Winchester, 171–2; Dr Thomas Bilson,
Bishop of, 171, 205
Windsor, Thomas Lord, 257
Windsor Castle, 12, 49, 171, 179, 182
wine licences, W. R.'s, 51, 64–5, 90,
168, 203, 206–7, 213; Essex's, 155
Wingandacon, 59–60, 63
Winwood, Sir Ralph, 232, 235, 237,
240
Wollaston, 237, 244
Wotton, Sir Henry, 273
Wright, Nicholas, 37
Wyatt, Sir Thomas, 2

Yelverton, Henry, 252
York House, 56, 154, 234
Youghal, 32, 34, 36, 77, 91–2
Young, James, W. R. at Plasden's
execution, 103–4

Index of Poems